Investigative Reporting
for
Print and Broadcast

INVESTIGATIVE REPORTING

for
Print and Broadcast

WILLIAM GAINES

Nelson-Hall Publishers
Chicago

Cover Painting: *Solvents Dispatch Shadow's Spook* by Will Northerner

Library of Congress Cataloging-in-Publication Data

Gaines, William.
    Investigative reporting for print and broadcast / William Gaines.
      p. cm.
    Includes index.
    ISBN 0-8304-1283-2
    1. Investigative reporting. 2. Reporters and reporting.
  I. Title.
  PN4781.G27 1994
  070.4'3 – dc20
                                            92-2757
                                           CIP

Manufactured in the United States of America

10   9   8   7   6   5   4   3   2   1

Contents

CHAPTER ONE

The Who, What, Where, When, Why, and How of Investigative Reporting

Investigative reporting is a small yet powerful area of journalism that stands in the forefront.

- It produces the story that is gathered and published or broadcast that would not have been revealed without the enterprise of the reporter.
- It provides the reader with a story of public importance that had to be pieced together from diverse and often obscure sources.
- It reveals a story that may be contrary to the version announced by government or business officials who might have tried to conceal the truth.
- It results in a story that usually is displayed prominently in a newspaper or that leads the nightly TV newscast.

Investigative reporting is an exciting part of journalism that has experienced growth and enhanced prestige during the later part of the twentieth century. For this text, investigative stories are those (1) which are the original work product of the reporter, rather than a report on a public agency investigation; (2) in which there was some attempt to conceal the information, and (3) which are of importance to the public.

WHO Does Investigative Reporting?

An investigative reporter typically is one of the more experienced reporters on the staff of a newspaper, magazine, broadcast station, or network. He or she knows how government is supposed to work and can judge if it really is working as it should. This reporter has built a network of people who are sources of information and can be trusted to conceal their identities. He or she knows where public records are kept and understands the documents and is an adept interviewer and good judge of human behavior.

A good investigative reporter has such personal traits as skepticism, patience, and a low boiling-point of outrage when he or she believes something to be unfair or abusive.

WHAT Are the Subjects of Investigative Stories?

No subject has ever been considered off-limits to an investigative reporter. He or she has more range than a public prosecutor because subjects may include wrongs that are not illegal. The story may point out the need for a new law and may result in one being enacted.

Many investigative stories are related to government corruption or consumer abuse. But an investigative story may be the response to a private business that takes unfair advantage of the public. It also would examine the government failing that allowed the unfair practice to go unchecked.

The investigative subject will not be so large that it cannot be completely contained and thoroughly examined in a story that can be managed by the reader. An investigative reporter would not attempt to investigate everything that might be lacking in state government. On the other hand, the subject would not be so small that it affects only a few people. The story would not be about a neighborhood cat that tears up a flower garden. But such a minor incident might prompt a story about the lack of control or licensing of pets if they had become a general nuisance.

WHERE Is Investigative Reporting Done?

Investigative reporting knows no geographical limitations. Washington-based reporters and those working in small towns, suburbs, rural areas, and school districts may do much the same kind of investigative reporting and win major journalism awards. It would not matter where an investigative story about a medical process or an environmental issue was reported because it could have impact on every living creature.

It would be difficult to argue that reporting on the state or national level is more important than reporting on a small local governmental unit, because the amount of public tax money saved by the aggregate of vigilant reporting on the local level may be greater than the amount saved from any expose of some huge government program. The lowest level government officials are scrutinized by legions of reporters; stories exposing them will prevent the waste, fraud, and corruption that might have been committed by those who read the stories and fear such exposure of wrongdoing. Also, the first hint that a large national government program or a private venture is not working may come from stories reported about malfunctions at the local level.

Therefore, an investigative reporter need not be too concerned about where he or she starts. But, no matter where, the reporter will get results from spending long hours in the news room, public buildings, and "on the street."

WHEN Did Investigative Reporting Start?

The Watergate investigation of *The Washington Post* in 1972 began as a follow-up to a routine story and ended in the resignation of President Richard Nixon. It touched off a revival of investigative efforts. It showed the public and, more profoundly, reporters and editors how perseverance can reveal truth in the face of a formidable opponent who seeks to hide it.

But investigative reporting did not start with Watergate. It was recognized by any name as good reporting for hundreds of years before the Watergate burglary. One could offer an argument that the New Testament of the Bible was investigative reporting. It could be categorized as a team reporting effort that was not the official version of the Roman government but what they attempted to hide. Fiction writers such as Charles Dickens wrote stories that exposed social injustice. They sometimes thinly veiled their characters, but they never used real names. And like today's investigative stories, some of those stories appeared first as newspaper series.

Pulitzer prizes in journalism have usually been awarded to investigative stories. A milestone was reached in 1985 when an award was designated under the title, "Investigative Reporting."

WHY Are Investigative Stories Done?

Newspaper readers and radio and television audiences have grown to accept investigative reporting as a public service. They may see the investigative reporter as their champion against the powerful and as a recourse when other efforts for justice fail.

But investigative reporting is also a business. A revealing book may be written to thoroughly examine an issue or event, and the reward is sales of copies. A magazine article may be investigative reporting of such interest that sales of the particular issue will soar. A television station may broadcast an investigative series at the time it is being judged by audience rating services, and it will draw viewers and boost its commercial rates.

More indirectly, a newspaper may publish investigative stories so that its readers will gain confidence that the newspaper is an advocate of the taxpayer and consumer. It is the overall hope of the newspaper owners that the investigative stories will forge a closer bond between the reader and the newspaper and therefore foster a long-term relationship, loyalty, and a strong base for circulation. Television station owners might want to have investigative stories broadcast so that on-the-air news reporters will be thought of by viewers as doers, not merely talkers.

Other investigative reporting might be done with more specific and perhaps selfish purposes. A publication that espouses a certain cause may seek to expose those who dispute that cause. A publication might promote a certain political party and seek to investigate and discredit its opponents.

But a dedicated investigative reporter does the job because he or she believes in its importance. The work provides a constant challenge. The reporter is sure that he or she is on the side of truth and fairness and knows that a job well done will result in public approval.

HOW Is Investigative Reporting Done?

While journalism is considered an art, investigative reporting is more like a science within that art. An artist who stands before an empty canvas or a writer who faces a blank piece of paper will attempt to project his or her innermost feelings onto it. There are rules, but for the most part, rules are designed to facilitate projecting the artistic talents.

A science, like electronics or surgery, is taught differently. Capable electronics engineers and doctors have built their careers from the knowledge of others who came before them. There may be some latitude for experimentation, but right and wrong ways to proceed have been established. In practicing the science of investigative reporting, the reporter knows what to do when he or she gets a tip as easily as an electrician knows what to do when a fuse blows. If the reporter is investigating a government program or a social issue, there are certain steps to take. The laws and limitations in gathering information are known.

This book will concentrate on the "HOW"of investigative reporting: *How* to investigate and *how* to then report on the findings.

All characters, organizations and locations in Case Histories are fictional, but the cases are based on real investigations or composites of investigations by journalists. They employ realistic methods and true sources of information. However, in the examples, for the purpose of understanding how to write an investigative story, actual stories are reprinted with permission. These stories contain names of actual persons and places. An investigative reporter who puts together information that suggests improper conduct or illegal activity will not make that conclusion. In their writing of the stories we use for examples, the writers do not conclude wrongdoing by anyone mentioned—they don't write that a person has been defrauded or an official has broken the law—and the inclusion of those stories in this textbook should not indicate wrong-doing. When we label a person a "victim," in the text, we are using the term as a journalist because the person being interviewed believes himself or herself to be a victim. We do not conclude that the person has been victimized by anyone.

Case History: Gladys Tydings' Big Break

Gladys Tydings enjoys her job reporting government news in Eastchester, the suburb of a big city. She started as a part-time reporter covering night meetings while she was in journalism school, and now she works full time.

When she started covering town government in Eastchester, she was well received by the mayor, the town board, and the administrators. They seemed to be interested in what she thought about their performance, and she immediately felt that she was an important person in the community, one whose ideas and opinions were valued.

Now, after two years, she has developed not only a friendly relation-ship with the town officials but also a good knowledge of the history of the community and of its present problems. She has taken on another job of turning in stories from Eastchester to the metropolitan paper on a part-time basis. Her dream is to be the editor of the twice-weekly *Eastchester Reliable* or even to own it.

After one of the town board meetings, Dee Z. Dent, a long-time opponent of the mayor and the current board, took Gladys aside and told her that there was routine corruption in the town and that no one seemed interested in doing anything about it. He told her that the mayor secretly owned a construction company that got a contract to remodel the village hall. Over the years, the mayor had received similar contracts with the village through different companies he had set up and steered business to, because of his powerful position as mayor.

Although Gladys had no experience in pursuing an investigative story, she recognized a potential story that needed to be done. First of all, she knew Dent's allegations would have to be proved to be true. Then there would be more work to learn all the details of the transactions. She went to Roy O'Boy, editor and publisher of the *Reliable*, and told him what she had been told. She asked if she could set aside other assignments to make some time to work on the story.

Publisher O'Boy had never been a journalist. He once owned a hard-ware store and acquired the newspaper when the previous owner, who rented offices over the hardware store, had fallen behind in the rent. O'Boy knew little about publishing a newspaper but found that owning one elevated his social and business status around town.

Gladys was disappointed with his response: "I don't think that's much of a story. The mayor has done a whole lot for this town. It doesn't matter even if it is true. I'd rather have him doing the work than some outsiders," he said. "A story like that has a negative sound to it. We like the stories you've been doing. People want to read good things, and they have come to know that Gladys Tydings writes about good things. Besides, I know who's been talking to you. Dent. The guy's a joke around town. Always complaining about something."

Gladys could not forget what Dent had told her. Even if he were not a reliable source and even if the newspaper would not print the story, she still was determined to at least learn if Dent's allegations were true. She determined to pursue the subject on her own time.

In public records in the town hall, she found the minutes of the board meetings at the time the contract for the work was approved, a copy of the contract itself, the bill or vouchers for the work that was done, and the cancelled checks that were paid out by the town treasurer. These documents provided her with the cost of the contract, a description of the work to be done, the dates the work was completed and paid for, and the name of the company that got the contract and the payments.

Then she called the Secretary of State Corporations Division in the state capital and got the names of the officers of the corporation. The mayor and his wife were the only officers.

Gladys thought that she might be able to interest the metropolitan paper in the story. The editors there were more receptive than O'Boy, but they thought that the story was insignificant for their larger area readership. "Why don't you try to get more on it?" an editor suggested.

So Gladys quietly kept searching through public records and learned that during the twelve years the mayor had been in office, he had created companies that then got contracts from the town. The companies were merely on paper. Money passed through them, but they owned no equipment and had no workers. The actual work was done by other companies, or subcontractors, but the final cost was almost twice as much as the cost for similar work done in other towns.

During the twelve years of his administration, the mayor's involvement with town contracts had cost the local taxpayers millions of extra dollars. They paid not only for the cost of the contracts but also for later repair work caused by the poor quality of the initial work done. Subcontractors cheated on workmanship and materials to give the mayor's companies even more profit.

Gladys found a large crack in the foundation of the new city hall and got pictures of it. The park playground equipment that was installed by a company owned by the mayor was unsafe. She remembered that several children had been injured there during the previous summer, and she got more details about it from accident reports in the police department.

Gladys now knew that she had a much more important story and one that the metropolitan paper would want. But she was faced with a decision. She weighed the possibility that if she turned in such a story, she would be so unpopular with the town officials that they would never help her with a story again. She probably would lose her job at the *Reliable*. Should she go ahead and submit the story? Vote yes or no. Support your vote with an argument.

The Case for Yes

The right of the public to know is at issue. If the publisher of the *Reliable* thinks there is nothing wrong with what the mayor is doing, then why should he object to having the facts published either in his or in the metropolitan paper and then letting the public decide.

If the facts are known, it may be that the mayor's political allies will desert him, and the mayor instead of the newspaper or reporter will be disgraced. The newspaper would be elevated to a status where it would be recognized as having a much more influential role in community life.

It also is possible that the mayor has a conflict of interest in violation of state law. The newspaper story would be vindicated if the mayor were indicted.

It would establish Gladys as a serious reporter, ready to move on to a bigger newspaper.

The Case for No

The *Reliable* is a private business, controlled by one man. He has a right to print what he wants in his newspaper and to employ whomever he wants and control what they write. He is obviously going to be angered when he finds that one of his reporters has written a story critical of his town and his friends and sold it to another newspaper. Gladys is sure to be fired. She is paid by him rather than by the public, and she should be loyal to her employer.

The real mission of a newspaper is to inform, educate, and entertain. Investigative reporting is just a small part of what the newspaper produces, and many newspapers do none at all. There are government investigative agencies that could do a far better job of investigating official corruption in a town than Gladys could.

How dare she set herself up as the judge and jury of an experienced and accomplished elected official when she is merely a recent journalism school graduate? Who elected her?

Gladys belongs in a small town. If she really gets to go to a big city newspaper because of the story, she is going to find that it is too competitive for her. She will do small stories and get the least desirable assignments for years and probably will never become an accomplished reporter. Meanwhile, she is famous in her own town and is doing stories that she can handle. Let the big city newspapers send one of their top investigative reporters out to do the story if they want it.

The Decision

Gladys is faced with the same decision that has been faced by most reporters in the course of their careers. Those who become investigative reporters may have reached such a crossroads and launched their careers by choosing to do the story. But those who have decided otherwise may not have made a choice that was wrong for them.

If she chooses to pass over the investigative story and continue to do routine reporting, Gladys will have the satisfaction of being knowledgeable about all aspects of her community. The pressures on her will not be great. She will be invited to important gatherings and will be respected for her accurate reporting.

If she chooses to be an investigative reporter and succeeds, Gladys will also have a certain amount of respect as long as she does not abuse the power she will acquire. She will have few friends outside the newsroom and her family. Each story will take all of her concentration and energy, and there will be little time for hobbies or social life. But the satisfaction of accomplishment might compensate for the loss.

Gladys made the decision that will be made by most persons interested in learning investigative reporting—she stayed on the story and got it published in the *Daily Metro*, the metropolitan newspaper for which she had worked part-time.

Gladys was prepared to be an investigative reporter because she had taken all of the initial steps to complete a basic investigative story. Now she can continue and expand her investigation. She determined if the state requires a disclosure statement from elected officials. Although they vary in different states, counties, and cities, disclosure laws may require a public official to put in writing for public viewing the financial interests he or she has in addition to the government job. The mayor may list even more companies in which he is involved. For instance, Gladys might learn that the mayor had an interest in an insurance company or agency that sells the insurance to the town at high rates or to people who do business with the town. Such a conflict of interest could mean that they paid him higher rates and then added it to the price that the taxpayers must pay for their services.

She then researched the laws regarding ethics and conflicts of interest but did not try to make a conclusion of law on her own in the story . Her story would state what the mayor had done and would quote the wording of the law but would not conclude that the mayor had broken that law. The courts may make that determination later.

Whether a law has been broken will not make or break her story. Investigative stories are written to protect tax dollars from waste and to defend the rights of other people even if no law has been broken.

Vital to rounding out the story is the close-out interview. Gladys will confront the mayor with the allegations that she is prepared to write. Because all of the information is a matter of record, the mayor is likely to admit what he has done but may make an excuse, such as he did it for the benefit of the town.

With the mayor's comments in hand, Gladys wrote her story.

Documents Used in This Story

Minutes of town board meetings. Public meetings of all government voting bodies are just that, they are open to the public. State constitutions generally require that those public bodies admit anyone to the meetings; therefore, the official minutes taken by the clerk are just as open and should be on file and readily accessible to anyone. This rule would apply to the school board, the state assembly, and legislative bodies at all levels of government.

Secretary of State, corporation records. Each state has a department, usually called the Secretary of State Corporation Division, that requires corporations doing business in the state to file their incorporation papers and make annual reports of officers. The state agencies that have these records are set up to receive routine inquiries about any corporation.

Building permits. The application for a permit and the permit that is then issued by the government to construct a new building or make changes in a building are public records kept in the city, town, or village offices. However, blueprints or other details of the construction plan may be protected from public disclosure, because they are considered to be confidential business information that could be used by a competitor.

Financial disclosure statements. Some states or local government units require extensive personal financial information from elected officials and administrators. Others ask for little more than a declaration that the public official has no conflict of interest. Either way, reporters routinely check for any information these public forms may contain.

Expenditures by the town treasurer. These records are public but are more difficult to obtain because they are difficult to store and file. It requires persistance to work with clerks to dig them out but they are necessary to complete a story on a transaction because they show that a contract was completed and exactly how much tax money was paid for the job.

Police accident reports. Accident reports may be obtained in most localities as may other police incident reports. Usually the original report will be released to a reporter but the follow up or investigative reports will not. Local laws or an established working relationship with the police department will determine what is available.

MEMO

- Investigative reporting is a distinct area of journalism that is not always done by every reporter, either by choice or circumstance.

- Investigative reporters must make some sacrifices in return for unique rewards.

- A reporter can confirm otherwise hidden, complex business and government transactions by researching public records.

GLOSSARY

Conflict of interest.   Federal and state conflict of interest laws make it illegal for an elected official to take official action that would benefit the official personally. In a broader sense, the term is used in journalism if a person in any capacity cannot fairly function because personal interests or biases affect his or her decisions.

Subcontractor.   When a contract is given to a person or company by a government agency, portions of the work may be assigned to others at the discretion of the winner of the contract. These subcontractors may not be publicly known and could be persons in conflicts of interest who are being rewarded for their official actions.

CHAPTER TWO

Tools of the Investigative Reporter

Except for some scattered state shield laws that keep a reporter from being forced to reveal unidentified source of information, there are no special laws for reporters. The First Amendment to the Constitution provides for freedom of the press, but its rights extend to everyone, not just reporters and newspaper publishers.

An investigative reporter must live by the law. No employer would want otherwise. Stealing information and trespassing on private property are violations that are most tempting to an aggressive reporter, but the reporter must be prepared to face the consequences. They could include a prison sentence in the worst circumstances.

The unofficial ethics of the journalism profession apply to all reporters. They admonish against deliberate misrepresentation of facts, personal gain, and personal bias that might cloud the judgment of any journalist. Those possibilities exist with general assignment reporters as well as specialists, such as political and real estate writers, sports reporters, and even the garden editor.

The investigative reporter might have to restrain personal feelings when doing a story. But it is less likely that he or she will receive personal gain from an unfavorable story about someone than would the garden editor, who may be offered outside compensation for writing a favorable story.

A common complaint about investigative reporters is that they are too aggressive. They might ignore the rights of privacy or step over the line of legality in the rush to gather information for a story. Investigative reporters have no power to subpoena records. They must recognize that they have no more right to information than any other citizen.

But armed with the knowledge of what tools are at their disposal, investigative reporters can operate within the law and without being abusive or unfair and achieve a more solid story. They proceed with the job as anyone would in other professions. They rely mostly on instinct, upbringing, or schooling to decide what is right and wrong and doing what will be productive rather than harmful. Their methods are: interviews, documents, surveillance and surveys.

1. *Interviews.* Interviews will be spaced throughout an investigation. There will be introductory interviews to gather general knowledge from experts, then interviews with persons who have been victimized by a particular injustice that is the subject of the investigation. Finally, and of extreme importance, is the interview with subjects of the investigation to make sure that they have an opportunity to explain all facts or answers all complaints or allegations that may have been made against them.

2. *Documents.* A document is information that is written (doc.u.ment [dak'ye.ment] n. anything written, printed, etc., relied upon to record or prove something—*Webster's New World Dictionary.*) Documentation can be found in the strangest places, not just in an official file, so the "etc." in the dictionary definition gives an investigative reporter extra room to work. A document, unlike a human source, will not change its story. In reporting and investigative jargon, if the subject of an interview who has been quoted in a story reverses a statement later, the reporter says that the interviewee "flipped." A document has built-in security. It will not flip.

3. *Surveillance.* Few investigative stories are done without some first-person observation by the reporter, and some stories would not be achieved without it. If a reporter is doing a story on slum conditions, he or she will want to see the neighborhood and go inside some of the buildings, not just write what is in building inspection reports or what tenants and landlords say on the telephone. Not only will seeing the situation support the story, there also may be new leads to follow.

4. *Surveys.* A survey is a systematic examination of a group or a list of items within a subject of investigation. A survey might produce a story, for example, when a reporter looks at all of the tax assessments in a location to determine if property is being fairly assessed. A survey could be used to determine true equity in the criminal justice system by comparing the sentences ordered by different judges for similar crimes. If a reporter takes an automobile to several repair garages to report on what they charge, he or she is conducting a survey. A survey or examination is also used to test a product by taking it to outside authorities or laboratories.

Using Interviews

The investigative interview, whether or not the interviewee may be thought of as the target of the investigation, is conducted in an informal manner rather than as a harsh or belligerent interrogation. The reporter attempts to extract facts and the views of the interviewee by being a good listener as well as asking the right questions. Major interviews for an investigative project are usually thought out well in advance. The reporter will have a list of questions or will have committed them to memory.

Interviews are done both in person and on the telephone. Telephone interviews are usually done if the reporter is facing a deadline or if the subject of the interview is far enough away to make travel inconvenient. It is easier to take notes in a telephone interview because the notebook and pen are not visible and therefore do not make the interviewee self-conscious. If the person being interviewed is hostile, he or she has the option of hanging up the telephone and ending the interview.

If the interview is in person, the conversation might best be tape-recorded after getting the permission of the person being interviewed. If permission is not granted, one reporter may write while another asks questions. (Investigative reporters often travel in teams.) An interview conducted in person gives the reporter the advantage of being able to see the facial reactions of the subject. The reporter will often be able to tell if the question is understood or if the person appears nervous or defensive. The interviewee also may want to produce documents. If time permits, an investigative reporter will want to meet with a person who is the subject of an important story for an interview so that the person is given the opportunity to respond and express him- or herself. Unless the telephone interview is formal and scheduled in advance, the person-to-person interview is the fairest, because it gives both parties time to prepare.

It is also possible to interview a person in writing. If the person to be interviewed insists on having questions submitted in writing to answer in writing, it may be better than no contact at all. But reporters should avoid such an awkward situation. They know they will not get natural sounding quotations and will not be able to have an answer clarified or to ask additional questions that are suggested by the answers.

After doing the initial round of interviews and/or compiling the necessary documents, reporters will often have the advantage of knowing more about the information being discussed than the persons they interview. This is often used to advantage. If reporters find that subjects stray from the truth, they can be pulled back into line by being corrected with facts.

Using Documents

An investigative reporter needs proof of an allegation and seeks the best documentation to be found. It was stated earlier that a document is "something written," however, pictures and electronic impulses recorded on tape contain information and can also be called documents.

The "etc." in the definition of *document* might also be expanded to include etched or inscribed or impressed information. A credit card is information impressed on plastic. Information is etched in stone on a tombstone or a building cornerstone.

If all the possible clues at a murder scene are gathered and taken to the police station, a police officer lists them on an inventory and signs it. The items themselves are evidence, but the inventory is a document. A dental chart may be considered a document although it may contain no words, only marks on a drawing. Dental charts may be used to identify a body. The teeth are evidence; the dental chart is the documentation.

Investigative reporters know that their search for the truth will lead them to documents, but documents are not the end of the trail. The documents need to be understood and their meanings properly related to the story being researched.

Documents have their failings. Reporters can't ask questions of documents. They must find the persons who supplied the information in the documents so that they may address questions. A document standing alone without its human source must be correctly interpreted.

The primary documents used by reporters are those that make up public records; including court cases, minutes of public meetings, inspection reports, land transfers, public contracts, and professional licenses. But not all documents that can be used in a story are public. Private records can be obtained legally by permission of the owner or because of their inclusion in public files. Those private records could be telephone bills, letters, hotel registers, utility bills, medical records, and tax returns. Other documents include published reports, such as previously published news stories and directories that can be found in a library. Investigative reporters are not strangers to the library.

At one time, public documents were stored in vaults and indexed by hand in large books that resemble hotel registers. Then came microfiche, and those documents were photographed and stored on film to be viewed through electronic viewers. Computerization is the latest technology in document indexing and storage and has become increasingly important to investigative research. Now, in some public offices, investigators can type a name of a person or corporation into a computer terminal and pull out real estate transactions and court cases recorded in the system that involve the person or corporation named.

Using Surveillance

Surveillance may consist of following a vehicle, watching a place of business, or timing a parking meter to learn if it registers correctly. It could be taking down license numbers at a specific location to check ownership.

Information and documentation can be obtained from a street sign, the sign on the front of a bus, or the phone number on the side of a plumber's truck. A flag worn on a shirt is not writing, but it conveys information to an observer. So, in gathering information, the reporter gets documentation from surveillance.

Surveillance may require picture taking. That way the reporter turns surveillance into a document. A dead cat provides documentation, but a picture of a dead cat is considered a document and is easier for a reporter to put in a file!

An elaborate surveillance situation occurs when a reporter hides the fact that he or she is a reporter and poses as someone else. For example, one such tactic is to take the role of an unsuspecting consumer to expose a fraudulent sales pitch. Undercover white and black reporters approaching the same real estate salesperson might expose racial bias. Reporters have even hidden their identities and gotten jobs to get a story. Most newspapers will not allow reporters to do such undercover reporting because they consider it to be too deceitful. But investigative reporters have succeeded in getting sensational and productive stories from undercover reporting without breaking laws, and some of those stories have won major journalism awards. An undercover job might be as simple as hiring on as a taxi driver to report the problems that a driver routinely faces. A more complex project would be getting a job inside a nursing home to report on conditions dangerous to public care or safety that the home is trying to hide and which could not be learned about otherwise. On the downside, ethical questions arise when a reporter does not reveal his- or herself when gathering material for a story. Also, much time can be spent in going undercover, and the results may turn out to be of little value.

Using Surveys

Making a survey does not sound investigative on the surface, because it may seem that no one has attempted to hide information. But reporters often find information when they match up surveys. For example, comparing a list of campaign contributions from government employees in a department with a list of promotions within that department is a variation of a survey. It could reveal information that is hidden—that the public official is promoting those people who contribute to his or her campaign.

A survey will result in statistics in most instances. Studying all of the land purchases for the highway right-of-way to determine if the government paid too much would result in statistics that could then be applied to maps and graphics. An investigative reporter might want to compare the costs of street maintenance in different municipalities and then try to find out why some municipalities spent more than others. The result would be a story of numbers, and the numbers would raise questions that the story would answer.

When a survey is used in investigative reporting, not all of the subjects in the category need to be surveyed. A predetermined number or group can be isolated or an at-random sample can be taken. But once committed to a survey, the reporter cannot change the sample and must abide by the findings. He or she does not have the right to throw out the parts that do not prove the story idea.

Summary

Interviews, documents, surveillance, and surveys are the tools of the investigative reporter. The reporter learns which to use at a certain time, like a golfer who knows which club to use under different conditions as he or she progresses through a course. The best investigators during the course of their investigation may draw on all of the tools at one time or another.

GLOSSARY

Shield laws.   About half of the states have some laws that protect a reporter from being cited for contempt of court for not revealing sources. Such protection applies only under various circumstances and may exclude the protection of the reporter in a libel suit filed against him or her.

PROJECT

Find a published investigative news story. What tools of the investigative reporter were used?

Case History: Bud Munn Tries Investigative Reporting

O. M. "Bud" Munn had been a police reporter when he started at the *Daily Metro* years ago. That was when newspapers had a heavy emphasis on crime stories. There were reporters in every police station, and the most successful and admired reporters were those with good police contacts who got big breaking stories about a murder or a murder arrest.

Bud was the youngest of a generation of reporters who chomped on cigars, talked out of the side of their mouth, and had to appear to be as tough as the beat they covered. Bud wasn't very good at that, and when the newspaper started to deemphasize crime reporting, he was not unhappy.

In an effort to compete with increased news coverage by television, newspapers were putting a premium on stories that covered social issues and analyzed problems. Sports reporting was changing in the same manner. Sports reporters no longer went to the games only to report on the outcome. They looked for important stories about the game and the people involved in it. What used to be called a human interest feature—an occasional story about policemen finding a boy's dog—was changing. The newspaper began to staff a separate department that produced interesting feature stories about people, different cultures, and scientific advances that were published in a separate section. The newspaper that he first knew and which sought mostly breaking news had become more like the general circulation magazines. Many of those had gone out of business over the years, and the newspaper had moved in to fill the void.

Bud considered becoming a sports writer or a regular feature writer, but he recognized that investigative reporting was becoming an important part of what newspapers offered their readers, and he believed that that suited him the best. He began working on small investigative stories as he covered his police beat. It was not his assignment, but he had learned that the editors would appreciate some enterprise and would not turn down a good story, no matter who did it.

Bud found that a suburban mayor had put his entire family on the village payroll. His sons were the police chief and fire chief, and his wife was the clerk. It wasn't much of a story, because there had been no effort to hide it, but the story did question the conduct of the mayor and whether he was acting in the public interest or his own interest. He wrote the story in a light, almost humorous fashion.

That first story caused readers to call and give him tips about possible wrongdoing by other local officials, and so his first story caused him to follow up on a few more from different parts of the metropolitan area. Then, soon after the local elections, when he had run out of information to pursue for other short investigative stories, Bud got the idea to call the defeated candidates and ask them what they knew about their opponents. Once again, he produced a series of stories that revealed minor corruption within the metropolitan area.

Bud's stories grew in size, number, and importance. The story that might be called "big" came about when Bud was told that the metropolitan government had been granted federal money to hire people who were unemployed and whose unemployment compensation benefits had expired. But, instead of those people getting the jobs, the jobs were going to political workers. He remembered that the mayor had gone on television and announced that the new job program was available. The mayor had invited anyone who qualified and was interested in applying to call a phone number that he gave and said that the city would send them information and an application.

Bud's source was an employee of the city office that authorized the federal expenditure. She told him that as many as a thousand people had called the number, the forms had been sent to them, they had been filled out, and returned. But instead of the applicants being interviewed for the jobs, all of the applications were stuffed in three large mail bags which were then thrown into a back office in City Hall.

Bud had always been an advocate of the city administration. His parents and grandparents had lived in the city, and he had gone to school there. He had been taught to respect authority, and he considered the mayor and his top aides to be honorable. He had read of corruption in the city government, but he believed that it was only a small part of an otherwise well-run operation. His own association with public employees had been with policemen, firemen, and teachers, and he had seen how difficult their jobs were and how little thanks they got. The idea that the mayor would deliberately misrepresent something as important as jobs for the unemployed was disturbing. He wanted to find out for himself.

Bud called his source at home at night because she feared she would be fired if it were known that she had leaked the information. She told Bud the names of the new employees who had been hired under the job program and that they had to have a letter from a political sponsor to get the jobs. The letter was in a file somewhere in the city offices, but she did not have access to it.

Bud knew that if he filed a Freedom of Information Act (FOIA) request, people in the city administration would know that he was looking into the program and might try to hide the information. He considered the possibility that the city would just tell him that there were no letters there, or that they would refuse to release information from personnel files on the grounds that it was private. So he pursued his story quietly. He could look at the city payroll without anyone knowing exactly what he was looking for. He compared the names on the payroll with those he had been given by his informant. The names were on the payroll, all in a unit of workers who patched holes in the streets. But that did not document the allegation that they were political workers.

Bud believed that because of his lack of experience, he might not be able to document and deliver the story. He asked himself if he should enlist the help of an outside authority, such as a federal agency, or if he should proceed with demands for the information from the city and risk that the city would cover up what it had done.

The Argument for Taking the Information to a Government Agency

This story is too important for a reporter with little investigative experience to handle. One slip and documents could be destroyed or his source could get in trouble. Also, what if he goes ahead and thinks he got the story, but he's wrong? Bud would be in trouble instead of being commended for his work and would never again be trusted with an important investigative story. By working with a government official, he would be able to do more than he could otherwise. For sake of the public, Bud has to learn that the story is more important than his own personal career or ambition.

The Argument for Going Ahead on His Own

Bud has the time, the energy, and the intelligence to do an investigative story just as well as a professional government investigator could do it. After all, he is not looking for a criminal conviction, only a story. All he has to do is gather and display the facts. There may be no way that the city can cover up what it has done, so why should he worry? If the allegations are true, it can be proved one way or another, and Bud can prove it. If he does not do the work on his own, there is a risk of a cover-up on a higher level. He would risk the possibility that the federal official would conspire with the local officials to fill the jobs improperly or that the federal official would rather help the city cover up its violations. Major investigative stories of government malfeasance and cover-ups would not be exposed if all reporters worked with government officials. For the sake of the public, a reporter's work should not be compromised.

The Decision

To join with an investigator would put Bud in the middle ground of investigative reporting. He would not have a story that was entirely a newspaper investigation. But a reporter with little experience who is beginning to develop important stories may want to work with government investigators. There are other ways to get information, either through developing more inside sources or through the Freedom of Information Act.

Bud decided to enlist help. He talked to an investigator for the federal jobs program and told him what he knew. The investigator said that he did not know if giving the jobs to politically connected people had violated any laws but agreed to go to City Hall and look at the files and find out if there was a letter from a political sponsor. If he found such a letter, he would tell Bud in exchange for Bud's information. Bud and the federal investigator reached another agreement. The investigator would wait for the story to be published before he took any action against the city. Because Bud and the government investigator cooperated and worked out an arrangement that benefitted each, the outcome was successful.

The investigator not only found the letters but also examined the applications in the file and found that some of the same men who were hired under the program had worked on the regular city payroll before. They had merely been switched over to other jobs, creating new vacancies that were filled by other political appointments. Therefore, they were not qualified because they were not long-term unemployed, and the city was violating the federal law that provided the money for the jobs.

When Bud learned the full story of what the city had done, he was angry. He always became angry when he believed people were being treated unfairly, and he thought of all those unemployed people who had trusted the government and had taken the time to fill out applications and send them in. He wanted his readers to be just as angry. There would be no better way than to get a picture of those mail bags in the back room at City Hall. His source in City Hall told him exactly where the bags should be located and sketched a floor plan of the office. Then, waiting until most of the employees had gone to lunch, Bud and a photographer swept by a receptionist and headed straight for the back room. While Bud talked to the only employee in the room, asking for directions, the photographer took pictures of the bags. The pictures were in color and the bags were literally spilling over with bright yellow, official job applications.

Bud called on Jake Honcho, the city personnel director, and told him what he had found. He asked for his official comment.

"You're not going to print a story like that are you? Who cares about a few jobs," Honcho asked. "The other guys at the paper tell me you've always been a good, solid reporter. You report what's good for the city, and that's what a reporter should do. A story like you're talking about is not good for the city. People are going to think we did something wrong. We ought to have a right to hire the guys we want. We can't take some unemployed scum and put them on the payroll. If people like that get a toe-hold in this city, who knows what might happen!"

As Bud was writing the story, a reporter who covered the police station on another shift told him that he was making a mistake. "If you write a story like that, nobody around here is going to trust you anymore," he said. "You are burning your bridges behind you."

The story ran on the front page, and the color pictures of the mail bags were played above the fold. Bud never went back to his job at the police station. He became a full-time investigative reporter. The federal government took over the administration of the jobs program in the city and started hiring people who were eligible for it.

MEMO

- A beginning investigative reporter may want to work with a government enforcement agency rather than go it alone.

- A reporter may alienate routine news gathering contacts as he works on investigative stories.

- A picture can underscore the emotions of a story.

Documents Used in This Investigation

Payroll. This list of employees would have some identifying information such as Social Security numbers or addresses. It would always contain each employee's name, the amount of money he or she received, and a job classification. Some smaller governmental units might not have a formal payroll, but they would make disclosure of who receives their expenditures in some form, and the names of employees would be included.

GLOSSARY

Freedom of Information Act.   A federal act defines what information a federal government agency must provide on request. It requires a formal procedure (explained in chapter 5). State and local governments have similar laws. Reporters use the letters FOIA for Freedom of Information Act and refer to it as "foy-ya."

CHAPTER THREE

Following the Tip
and the Breaking Story

It may be an unknown voice on the telephone, a casual remark from a friend, or the whispered remark of another reporter that gives an investigative reporter a tip on a story. The immediate response by the reporter might be several quick phone calls or a perfunctory search of documents in the county building or city hall. The goal would be to substantiate at least part of what he or she has been told or to find out that the report of some wrongdoing might be impossible to document. Then the reporter or the editor to whom he reports must decide whether or not to keep working on the story.

Chasing the Tip

Following up a tip is the most basic of all investigations. The reporter is told that something has happened and may immediately decide that, if true, the tip is worthy of an investigative story. The reporter determines if it is true through documentation. The goal of the search has already been set. The reporter is in a much better position having a tip to work from than only suspecting that something is amiss. However, when working from a tip, the reporter is not in control of the story at the beginning. The circumstance of someone knowing something and telling a reporter has put the tipster temporarily in control. When the reporter finds documentation for the tip, he or she can take the initiative and start expanding on the story idea.

Gladys Tydings got her first story from a tip given to her by a source. The tipster may have had personal reasons for giving the information to her and wished to profit from it politically. The motives of a source are not a factor to be considered when deciding whether or not a story based on a tip should be published. If the story is about an important issue, vital to the public interest, and documented, it will stand on its own merits.

A source may not tell all he or she knows at first. During her investigation, Gladys may have talked with her source several times. But she did not answer to him by reporting her activities as if she were working for the source. The reporter's association with the source depends on how much more the source knows. Is he or she a whistle-blower inside a government agency being investigated? Or is the source an outside party with only a secondary knowledge of the agency? The outside party may have provided all he or she knows. The inside whistle-blower may not only have access to other information but also arrange for other inside sources to contact the reporter.

An investigative reporter learns to handle a source with care because often the source is emotionally attached to the events that prompted the investigation. The source may be impatient and fearful. He or she may not understand that the reporter must check the facts of the investigation. The reporter must assure the source that research and documentation will enhance the story and add to the protection of the identity of the source. If the information can be substantiated from other sources, there will be no indication of involvement of the original informant. In some circumstances, the investigative reporter may never learn the identity of the tipster, knowing the person only as a voice on the phone. Such an arrangement is the best protection for both the source and the reporter. Even if subpoenaed and asked to reveal the source, the reporter can honestly say he or she doesn't know.

Sometimes, a tip is in the form of documents that mysteriously end up on the desk of the reporter. There is no return address, so the reporter is unable to ask questions of the source. If the information has value as the basis of an investigative story, it is checked out carefully.

Then as the reporter employs the investigative tools, he or she may produce the story or may be convinced that the story is either not true or cannot be developed. Finding that something did not happen can be much more time consuming than documenting something that did happen. The reporter's work may show that whatever the allegation, it did not or could not have happened as the tipster claimed. But seldom does it turn out that there is no truth at all to the tip.

At some point the reporter concedes that the allegations cannot be substantiated and will move on to other work. But he or she will have learned a little more about the ins and outs of business and politics in the community from the documents and interviews generated by the tip. For that reason, successful investigative reporters don't mind chasing after a story from a tip even though it does not turn out to be a big story.

When a tip proves to be a good one and a story is done, it is very possible that the reporter will become involved in a running story. A competing newspaper may also pick up the story and add new information that the reporter who originally broke the story will have to confirm. Also, the investigative reporter may be in the position of re-covering the competition's investigative story. He or she may want to confirm the story through sources and try to top the competition with even more revelations.

But, more likely, the reporter who breaks an investigative story will develop new sources from it and have new leads to pursue. The story may run for weeks and die for a lack of interest or because it is eclipsed by another story. Or, the story may run in the media off and on for months or years until all aspects are revealed and the public or government enforcement agencies have taken action to remedy the problem.

Chasing the Breaking Story

If a fire breaks out in a nursing home, a general assignment or police reporter will respond. The reporter may go to the scene of the fire and ask the fire department commander for the cause, an estimate of the damage, the severity of injuries, and the number of men and amount of equipment used to fight the fire. He or she might then return to the newspaper office and write the story or phone the information to another reporter who would write it for the next edition of the newspaper. The story might be accurate and complete, but it is not investigative.

An investigative reporter comes upon the scene later in such circumstances, much like the police detective who follows up an officer's incident report. Using the tools of investigation, the reporter seeks documents and asks questions. Who is the owner of the nursing home? When was the last building or fire inspection? What did it show? Were the owners warned of a fire hazard or ordered to install safety equipment like smoke detectors? Then this information is pulled together. Let's say that the owner was a politician or political campaign contributor who was allowed to ignore fire safety violations because of political power. That is a story the investigative reporter will pursue and may be able to close out through use of public records.

News stories of the events of the day may call for some kind of a follow-up investigation and may bring surprising results. The Watergate investigation by the *Washington Post* grew out of developments brought to light by reporters after a burglary attempt. When a candidate for high office picks a running mate who is not widely known, reporters want to do an investigative profile. When the name of a U.S. Supreme Court nominee is announced, reporters swarm to the nominee's hometown for information. The breaking story of an airplane crash or an assassination may generate an investigation on how the disaster could have been prevented. A natural disaster, such as an earthquake or flood, may generate investigative follow-ups about lack of preparedness or poor response on the part of the responsible government agencies.

By leafing through a local newspaper, an investigative reporter can spot stories that leave questions unanswered.

Board OK's Work on Golf Course

The Eastchester Park and Recreation Board has approved improvements for Chicken Creek Golf Course. Work on the course, near 16th and Deep Canyon Road, will be contracted with Middle Chester Associates of Middle Chester. The board approved a contract agreement for architectural work Thursday, including expanding the clubhouse and parking, all engineering work and designing a rest area with restrooms in the ninth-hole area. The board originally approved Westchester Delux Contractors, Inc. for the contract after it provided the lowest bid. Bids had ranged from $9,300 to $77,000. Board attorney Loyal Barrister said Westchester Delux failed to sign the final contract, although he tried several times to reach an agreement. Although he wasn't sure why, Barrister told the board he thought Westchester Delux didn't understand the scope of the project. He recommended Middle Chester which bid $24,610 be accepted and the board unanimously approved awarding the contract to Middle Chester.

Who are the owners of the two companies that bid? Does either have personal or financial ties to Barrister or the board members? Were the bid specifications written in a misleading or restrictive manner that caused only Middle Chester to qualify? Is this work necessary, or is it a pet project of the board members so they can enjoy its use? Did the voters get an opportunity to choose whether they wanted the golf course upgraded or would rather have more picnic tables and playground equipment? Is Middle Chester qualified to do the work? What other work have they done?

Girl Killed While Leaning Out of School Bus Window.

A 12-year-old girl heading home from a racketball tournament was killed when she hit her head on a light pole while hanging out of a bus window, police said yesterday. Pepper Schuler, a sixth-grader at White Lark Junior High School died in White Lark Hospital, a sheriff's investigator said. She was hanging out the bus window talking to a friend when the accident occurred. No charges were filed against the driver of the bus.

What are the rules and regulations for school buses? Do they allow a window to be open? Why was the girl not seated when the bus was in motion? Does the driver have any record of past accidents or incidents? Has the bus company had a record of lawsuits filed against it? Why is a light pole so close to the street that a person who is leaning out the window of a vehicle would be struck? Are there other hazards like light poles and street signs that are located in dangerous spots in the town?

Urges County Buy Hospital

Dinero Krankenhaus, Snake County board president, recommended Monday that the county buy Community General Hospital to replace the deteriorating children's building at Snake County Hospital. Krankenhaus, who leaves office next month to become a state senator, recommended the County Board spend $4.9 million to buy the financially troubled, 212-bed hospital at 301 E. Snake Hollow Rd. Krankenhaus told the commissioners that acquiring Community General and spending an additional $5 million to convert it into a children's hospital would eliminate the need to spend $39 million in renovations at the County Hospital children's facility.

Is the hospital building worth the $4.9 million to buy it? Who came up with that price? Was there a detailed study of the cost of remodeling the buildings or is it an off-the-wall estimate? Who owns the hospital? If it is owned by a not-for-profit organization, does that organization own the land and the building or is there some private, hidden ownership? Did someone connected with the hospital contribute money to the board president's political campaign? Would some other site better serve the county? Even if there is a savings now, would the county be better off to construct a modern facility at the most appropriate location?

These stories are typical of local stories in daily and weekly newspapers across the country. Almost all stories leave questions unanswered. Some present obvious questions that will cry out to an investigative reporter for answers.

- There is an outbreak of food poisoning. Are restaurants being properly inspected?
- A sewer collapses. What is the condition of the sewers? Are they being properly maintained?
- Bus fares are increased. Is the government agency that operates public transportation wasting money? If a private company operates the buses, is it being correctly regulated?
- The fire department is late in responding to a fire. Where were the firemen when the call came in? Is the department properly manned

and equipped? How does the response time, on average, compare with that of other fire departments?

Why are investigative reporters so negative and suspicious? Why do they seem to look for all the worst possible angles? An investigative reporter seeks to reveal hidden information. People don't hide good things. Perhaps the reporter does look on the dark side, but the object of the investigative reporter is to throw some light on the event—and to turn it into something good. If utility poles and other obstacles bordering streets in the town are moved because of an investigative story, the town is safer, and that is good. If the remodeling of the clubhouse at the golf course is scrapped and the people got something they want, that is good. If it turns out that the idea that the county board president proposed about the hospital is a sound money-saver, that is good; and if it is not a sound idea and voters are alerted to its problems, that is good, too.

The reporter who chases after the story from a tip, follows up a breaking story with investigations, or picks up and runs with a competing investigation is an asset to a news operation. But he or she does not have much control over the work and the subjects of the stories. However, an investigative reporter also can choose topics and take time to do a thorough job of investigation of a particular subject, which is the topic of another chapter.

PROJECT

Find a breaking story in a daily newspaper that you believe could produce a follow-up for an investigative reporter. What questions would you ask? How would you go about the investigation?

GLOSSARY

Whistle-blower.   A recognized entity in law who is an employee of government who goes outside that agency to complain about its operation. Legislation has been passed to protect the jobs of government people who are whistle-blowers. (This term may also be used in relation to private concerns.)

Case History: Bud Munn Uses the Tools of the Investigative Reporter to Check Out a Story from a Tip

Consider this question while reading the following information: What obvious, important step in investigative reporting did Bud Munn omit before he proposed his first story?

O. M. "Bud" Munn was in the city room. He finished a story about city workers loafing on the job and did several reaction stories about some workers being suspended by the city and promises by city officials that they would do a better job of supervising workers. Bud had some long-standing ideas for important investigative stories he would like to do, one on school bus safety and another on the poor response by state government to complaints about medical doctors. But the managing editor called him into his office and showed him an unsigned letter. It stated that the mayor of the city has a hidden ownership with a developer and a county judge in a 2,600-unit apartment complex to be built in the city. The mayor was elected on his record as a proponent of open space and had fought new residential construction in the community because, he said, it would overburden the schools and taxpayers. The mayor was running for reelection in an emotional campaign that was expected to be close. Election day was less than three weeks away.

Bud knew a good story when he heard one, and this story qualified. However, he also knew that tips about political candidates are common at election time because they are usually planted by the opposing candidate or supporters. But the idea that a political candidate would take a stand on one side of an issue and then secretly do the opposite had all the makings of an important investigative story.

Bud checked land records and found that the land on which the housing project was to be built and the application for rezoning was held in the name of a corporation that was formed for the sole purpose of the project. The only officer of the corporation was a local attorney. The attorney agreed to an interview and talked freely about the plans for the housing development. When Bud asked him who owned the project, he said only that the officers of the corporation were himself and his wife. The owners were a group of private investors, he said.

Bud went to the site of the project which was then under construction and talked to workmen. He learned that the workers were feuding with the builder over wages. The builder who had been hired by the corporation to build the apartments was rumored to have organized crime connections.

A foreman on the job told Bud that a bookkeeper recently quit because she was upset over the way the builder operated his business, including his loose reporting of income for taxes. Bud found the bookkeeper at the bank where she was working and asked her for any information she might have about the ownership of the project. She told him that, to protect herself from blame if there were an IRS investigation, she had made copies of the business records when she left, but she would not reveal them because they were private records.

Bud continued to pursue other ideas, such as checking the building inspection reports for indications of the ownership and discretely asking city officials about what they knew without revealing to them why he was inquiring. He had no success in substantiating the anonymous tip.

Then, two days after he had spoken to the former bookkeeper, a bulging envelope addressed to Munn arrived at the front desk of the newspaper. There was no return address and no letter inside. Instead, it contained copies of cancelled checks and the ledgers and memos of the development corporation that proved the involvement of the mayor.

Bud now had documentation—the facts of the story. He and his editors now must decide if he should immediately write a story based on the information he has.

- Should this story be published? Is it important?
- What is the responsibility of an investigative reporter during a political campaign?
- Is it proper to accept information from a political candidate's opponent or from disgruntled employees?
- Should private documents be used in an investigative story?
- Would you have written a story with the information that Bud Munn had? Vote yes or no. Support your opinion with an argument.

The Case for Yes

Bud is faced with an important public issue. The city is nearing a crucial election. If the story is not written, voters will not have the necessary information to make their choice for mayor. Obviously, the truth is being withheld from them, and Bud believes that it is his duty to reveal the truth.

Bud knows his facts are correct, but he also knows that he may not reveal his source. How can he not report on an important matter that he knows to be true?

Bud realizes that he has been chosen by his editors to get the story because they trust him more than any other reporter on the staff. Now, because his original source is anonymous, Bud fears that his competition have been given the same leads. They may have been luckier than he was in proving the tip correct and are preparing to print it. They might have an inside source who has confirmed the truth or they may have just done a better job of confirming it. If he lets the competition beat him into print with the story, he will feel that he has failed himself and his employer. And, if his paper and the competition fail to print the story, Bud believes he will have failed his readers. If reporters spent their time thinking of reasons not to report a story, journalism would suffer. Readers who turn to the newspaper as they would to an ombudsman would be short changed.

The Case for No

The documents that Bud received that seem to prove that the mayor is involved in the project could have been forged. They could have come from the same source that supplied his original tip, a person who could be trying to trick him into writing a false story, rather than from the bookkeeper. There may be only a slim chance that Bud is the victim of such a hoax or forgery, but how can a reporter take such a chance? If he makes a practice of reporting on the *chance* that the information is true, sooner or later he will be wrong.

Even if the information Bud has in the bulging, unattributed envelope is legitimate and factual, if those documents are private and are sent without the permission of the person who owns them, they may be considered stolen. A piece of paper has little value. The value of a document is the information it contains. Possession and use of the information could constitute theft or invasion of privacy even if it is a copy.

It is more important for Bud to preserve the integrity of his profession than to reveal the information he has received improperly. If Bud writes the story he is inviting criminal or civil action against himself and his employer and will have failed the newspaper more than if he were to allow the competition to have the story first.

If the story appears and is denied by the mayor, Bud and his newspaper will not be able to respond to reinforce the truth of their story by revealing the source of the information, because it is anonymous and it might have been stolen. Readers will be skeptical of a printed report that cannot be substantiated and will lose faith in the journalistic integrity of the newspaper.

If Bud proceeds, he may be inviting more trouble than he can handle and could be accused of being irresponsible.

The Decision

Reporting and editorial decisions involving investigative stories are complex activities. Newspapers that regularly pursue investigative stories are continually faced with difficult decisions. To help resolve the problem, Bud Munn must make every effort to prove the information that is necessary for his story. He will check public records other than state corporation registration that could indicate ownership. Among these are court records, which will tell Bud if the company has been sued and the ownership revealed in testimony, liens and mortgages registered against the title, licenses, building permits, inspection reports, and minutes of zoning hearings.

Even if such efforts don't break the big story by confirming ownership, they will be important, because Bud will learn about the project from the time it was proposed, through getting zoning, to the current construction phase. He needs that kind of background for his story.

But before he writes a story, Bud must take one vital step. The answer to the question at the beginning of this exercise is: Bud has neglected to talk to the subjects, or targets, of the investigative story. It would be unfair to write a story of any kind that names an individual and accuses him of wrongdoing without making an extensive effort to contact him, disclose the information gathered, and allow him the opportunity to respond. A good reporter will make an aggressive effort to find and talk to the subject of a story short of harassment, when it is obvious that the person does not wish to be contacted. If the subject cannot be reached by the reporter or refuses to comment, that should be mentioned in the story. Reporters keep careful records of the times they attempt to contact the prime subjects of their stories so that they may respond accurately to any allegations that they did not try to verify their claims.

Interviews with subjects or targets of investigative stories often provide new insights into how and why they acted as they did. While a newspaper is not obligated to publish everything a subject might say in response to an allegation, it should clearly portray the subject's defenses. An interview also adds color, making a dull story about business transactions and public records come alive.

Because Bud already is convinced that he knows the truth, he has an advantage in interviews with the mayor, the county judge, and the developer. They do not know how he got the information, and because it is so exact, they are not likely to deny it and then be caught lying. The information from interviews of other persons involved in the story may be valuable. While the mayor may be eager to hide his ownership because of the election or the possibility that he has violated conflict of interest laws by secretly acting on matters concerning the property, others in the partnership, including the judge, may have no reason to hide their interest and may reveal the involvement of the others. The story might work just as well if the lead states that a county judge revealed to the newspaper that he was in a partnership with the mayor.

After Bud has checked out the tips, interviewed sources, made every effort to get a complete response from the subjects in the story and confirm the truth of the story aside from the anonymous sources, there is still a decision to be made about when to print the story. The impending election may rush that decision. But, as with other stories, the reporter must decide if he or she has the best possible story or if more research is needed.

At this point Bud falls back on his intuition and experience. If the mayor is involved in the land deal, did the mayor vote on vital matters that allowed the development? If he did not directly vote, did he use his political influence with others to get favors for the developer? Did the judge make any rulings that enabled the project to be built? Is the builder with alleged organized crime connections a campaign contributor?

Who was hurt? Did people in the neighborhood where the project is being built have an opportunity to be heard? Are the apartments to be built as high quality as others in the area or have city officials let the builder get by with inadequate and perhaps unsafe construction?

Some aspects of the tip that Bud Munn routinely checked out will not be included in the story. Reporters must fight the temptation to include everything that sounds negative in an investigative story if the information does not support the main theme. Bud envisions a story about an important public official who says one thing and then takes advantage of his office and does the opposite. It may not be important at all that the builder on the project has organized crime connections. Mere "connections" are difficult to define. Therefore, some of the information from the investigation may be stored in the reporter's memory and memos at the newspaper for some future story.

Documents Used in This Story

Court records. Civil lawsuits and records of criminal court cases are public records. Civil suits are those brought by one citizen against another or in certain circumstances by the government against a citizen. A criminal case is a charge brought by the government against a person for violation of criminal statutes, such as theft or violence, that would call for their immediate detainment. Clerks of the courts are mandated by law to provide information from civil complaints and criminal changes to the public.

Land records. When land is bought and sold, a mortgage is gotten or paid off, or a lien is placed on property, the documents may be recorded with the land records office of the county, often called the records of deeds. If it is recorded, it is available for public inspection.

Campaign disclosure. States have various degrees of disclosure requirements for candidates for public office, but most require that the candidate show who gave money for the campaign, how much each person or company gave, and how the money was spent.

PROJECT

Find an investigative story in a daily newspaper. Decide if it is truly investigative—did the reporter investigate and report on his or her findings or did the reporter only describe the investigations of a public agency? What documents are cited to prove allegations in the story? Are there other documents that might have been checked? Did the reporter make an effort to allow the target of the story to respond? Is the story written clearly and in a straightforward manner? Or does the writer try to hide the fact that there is missing information by "writing around it"?

GLOSSARY

Ombudsman.   An ombudsman is an impartial consumer advocate. The term originated in Sweden, where ombudsmen are appointed by the government to receive and investigate complaints by individuals against government officials. Investigative reporters often find themselves playing a similar role.

Mortgage.   Almost everyone who buys a home has a mortgage, a loan of money to purchase the home. Whoever loans the money has an interest in the property equivalent to the amount owed. The lender goes on public record to show such an interest by recording the loan with the county.

Lien.   If a property owner owes money to the government or to a private party, those owed may get a court judgment and have the debt recorded against the property. Like a mortgage, the lien shows that the lien holder has an interest in or owns a little piece of the property.

Zoning.   Laws enable governments to determine the best use of land. Zoning laws, for example, keep factories from being built in the middle of residential subdivisions and prohibit nightclubs from opening next to a church. Builders must have their plans approved by governments, and their applications and hearings are in the public record.

CHAPTER FOUR

Designing an Investigative Project

Not all investigative stories come from tips or from following up *breaking news stories*. In recent years, winners of investigative reporting awards have revealed major problems or injustices through planned stories.

To develop a planned investigative story, reporters gather a large amount of information about a topic, but they do not publish the information as soon as they confirm it as they would in a *developing story*. They stockpile it, organize it, and spend the time to present it in the most understandable manner. It may seem that the reporters working on a planned story do so at a more relaxed pace than when they are chasing a tip or following up a breaking story. But the investigative project requires a great deal of time and effort. A reporter may spend entire weeks gathering information, studying it for its significance, and then mentally categorizing or discarding it. He or she may assemble a large stack of documents and notes. A chronology—a list of all the events in the order they happened—may be compiled to better understand and follow the investigation. The project is all-consuming and is carried on in the reporter's mind even when he or she is away from the job.

Investigative projects may involve several reporters. Some major newspapers, television stations, and networks have standing teams of reporters who specialize in investigative series. Other news organizations may put together a team when the need for an investigative project arises. Newspapers and other media may produce one big investigative project each year, and while they might not readily admit it, they could have journalism prize entries in mind.

When a team is being put together, it is often beneficial to include reporters who have varied talents. An investigative group might have three members: one reporter who is an expert in the subject to be investigated and who has contacts in that field from his or her regular beat; another reporter who is experienced in investigative techniques such as gathering documents and interviewing; and a third who will be the designated writer and will assist throughout the investigation so that he or she understands the subject matter when the time to write arrives.

The media seldom buy an investigative story from a freelancer or hire an outside investigator for a project. Because the outcome of the story is the responsibility of the newspaper or television station, the editors want to have it done by persons with proven records of accuracy who can be supervised. They also believe the outsider, who may have his or her judgment clouded by conflicts or prejudices unknown to the editors, to be the much greater risk. But before a group can be put together the subject of the investigation must be firmly in place.

The investigative story starts with an idea. The idea usually stems from an unpleasant experience that someone shares with other people and learns that they have had similar experiences. For example:

- Their children don't eat the food at school now that the school has contracted with a company for frozen pre-plated meals. Is the food unappetizing? Does it have all the nutritional requirements of the U.S. Department of Agriculture school food program? How did this company get the contract? Did it go to the low bidder and in this case would the low bidder necessarily be the best provider?
- They were splashed by water from the street on the way to work. Why doesn't the sewer system carry off the water? Does it have enough capacity? Is it cleaned regularly or is debris allowed to collect and impede the flow of water? What is the budget for sewer cleaning? Is it being wasted on unnecessary jobs for friends of politicians?
- They were tailgated by a truck on the expressway. Are trucks speeding? Do the trucking companies bribe the police to keep from getting ticketed? Are truckers speeding because they have unreasonable schedules to make? Are these speeding and tailgating trucks safe? Who inspects them? Are the drivers trained and competent?

With the shared-experience method, choosing a subject becomes a game. It soon becomes obvious that every unpleasant experience in day-to-day life can become an investigative project, and a group can gather and ask questions that lead to other questions. The strength in planning an investigative story from personal experiences lies in the fact that it is known from the start that there is a problem that has impact on the individual.

Each idea leads to a search for blame, and the reporter often finds a government agency not doing its job. He or she finds that the administrators of the agency either do not enforce the laws which they have at their disposal or do not have the necessary laws to properly function. Some investigations even show that the government agency itself is operating contrary to the law. The investigative story points out which of these is the problem and, hopefully, leads to a remedy.

Investigative reporters like to apply the phrase, "a well-intentioned government program gone awry." Most government programs are grand in design and are put in place with the object of providing solutions to widespread social needs. Most government programs, however, never live up to those expectations, and some are disasterously disappointing. After all the oratory is over and the program is put in place, flaws begin to surface at the level where people are being served. As complaints grow and those flaws become more apparent, an investigative story idea emerges.

- A new computer system has been installed in the state unemployment benefits office, but people who should be getting checks are not getting them, and others are able to cheat the system.
- A government "outreach" program to educate the public about welfare benefits has been turned into an arm of the administration's political campaign.
- Doctors are billing public health agencies for more minor operations than there is time in the day for them to perform.

Other times, a government agency is routinely checked. In a major city, it could be the public transportation system or the public housing agency. In a smaller community, it might be the volunteer fire department, the water department, or the county court system. In such an investigation, the reporter looks at the entire operation of the department or agency.

Reporters may choose from a variety of subjects within the entire spectrum of society that involve public safety and government regulation. Some of the favorite subjects under constant scrutiny may be categorized:

1. Big things that move. Trucks, airplanes, school buses, taxis, trains, ambulances, and automobiles are important to our daily lives and our very survival if they are unsafe.
2. A home away from home. Nursing homes, prisons, and public housing are places people don't want to be, because they don't have complete freedom. No matter how good they are made to look they are usually undesirable.
3. A well-intentioned government program gone awry. Food stamps,

government loans, and expense accounts invite fraud. Abuse and laxity in control of agencies and programs allows some to benefit unfairly at the expense of others.

4. Under the gun from a salesman. Insurance and real estate sales, and auto and home repair are other realms rich in consumer fraud. The news media hope to send up enough warnings to unsuspecting consumers so that they may combat misrepresentation.

Each of these categories may be divided into two parts—performance and cost.

1. *Performance:* Is the school bus safe for the children? *Cost:* Are the schools being overcharged by the school bus companies?
2. *Performance:* Is the nursing home a healthy place for residents? *Cost:* Is the nursing home overbilling the Medicare program?
3. *Performance:* Is the individual being protected by the insurance? *Cost:* Is it unfairly priced?
4. *Performance:* Does the government housing program provide a proper place for residents? *Cost:* Is there money wasted in its operation?

Any of these subjects could be an investigative project for a reporter or a team of reporters. To produce the story, the same tools of the investigative reporter in following a tip or a breaking story are employed, but more planning is needed. In the planning stage, reporters promote their ideas with their editor in their best sales manner. Their enthusiasm will be important, but they must outline the story idea and explain how they plan to gather the story.

The outline or proposal is informal, but it can be broken down and analyzed. It describes the need for the project, what it will cover, the methods that will be used, the sources of information available, how the story will be presented to the reader or viewer, and what results it is expected to bring.

If the proposal were drafted in a formal manner, it might look like this:

Title: The Pill Pushers
Subject: Doctors who prescribe unnecessary, dangerous, and addictive drugs.
Need: Innocent people are becoming addicted to drugs because their doctors are too liberal with prescriptions. Others may deliberately seek prescription drugs for recreational purposes with the cooperation of the doctor. More than 10,000 people died last year from reactions to prescription drugs that they should not have taken. This is a growing

problem that is not given enough attention, because it is overshadowed by media coverage of illegal street drugs.

Scope: This project will investigate doctors who give people unnecessary prescriptions for profit. We will attempt to identify the doctors and learn why they are not disciplined. There will be no attempt to study the proliferation of street drugs.

Methods: The state drug enforcement administration keeps records that are public and lists the numbers of controlled drugs, such as amphetamines and sleeping pills, bought and prescribed by individual doctors. They don't show the doctors' names, but they do show the zip codes. We could determine who they are through interviews with local police or by sending in reporters who would request the drugs they are selling. The reporters would have to be briefed on exactly what to say so that they are not suggesting a crime.

Sources: In addition to the state lists, we would check for criminal arrests of any of the doctors to learn if they have been convicted of illegal drug sales and are still in business. We also would search the files of the state medical licensing agency to find if any have been brought up for disciplinary hearings.

Production: This would be a three-day newspaper series. We would try to get pictures of the doctors going into their offices. We could use the state statistics to make a chart or a graphic illustration such as a flow chart that would show how the government is supposed to control illegal prescriptions.

The scope section is most important. Each idea must be narrowed down and specific. In this example, the reporter states that he or she will investigate doctors in connection with numbers of prescriptions. The investigation is not "the problems caused by doctors who give people unnecessary prescriptions." If this were the scope, the team of reporters would have to delve into the social issues and document the long-range damage caused by such doctors. The investigation as stated is to identify certain doctors and show specifically what they are doing. The proposal is for a hard-hitting investigative piece that names names and reveals illegal activity. They will not investigate drug companies that manufacture and distribute the drugs to the doctor. They will not attempt to investigate the world of illegal drug use.

An outline with the proper scope not only helps sell the story, but allows reporters to start out knowing their goal and probing for the facts rather than groping about with uncertainty. Reporters know the goal of the story because they have done some preliminary investigation. They have talked to experts and gotten statistics. When they write of the need for this investigation, they may cite facts, such as a specific number of deaths from overdoses.

The reporter must show that he or she knows how to proceed with gathering the story. Posing as a patient in the doctor story would not be a difficult undercover assignment, but the reporter must demonstrate that it would be done with certain rules or controls. The availability of records and how they could be applied to the story are necessary to convince a supervisor that the project will work. Also, the reporter points out that the story will provide picture and graphics possibilities, and he or she will be looking for those possibilities as information is gathered.

The editor is now persuaded. Not only does this story idea have everything a successful investigative story needs, but it has a clear plan of execution. The next decision is how the findings will be presented.

It is obvious that the final decision on how to present the story will have to be made after all the facts are gathered and the interviews are completed, or "closed out." But going into the project, the newspaper reporter proposes the number of days that a series might run, and the television reporter suggests how the investigation might be programmed.

With a proper outline, the project is launched. The editor knows what to expect and the reporters know how to proceed.

PROJECT

Recall an incident you have experienced—like the examples here of being splashed with water or the poor quality of institutional food. Thoroughly discuss how the experience could be developed into an investigative project. Determine what questions could be asked.

Case History: Gladys Tydings Joins the Metropolitan Newspaper Staff

Gladys Tydings knows that she was lucky to get a job on the *Daily Metro*, and she has not regretted leaving Eastchester. But she has found that being a big city investigative reporter is more difficult than it had seemed from her view from the suburbs. Stories are more complicated because they involve larger dollar amounts, multiple transactions, and a much larger and diverse cast of characters.

Gladys gets more investigative tips to follow than she can possibly handle. Most of them, she finds, are insignificant complaints when put up against the daily stories that command space in the metropolitan newspaper. When a union official puts his son on the payroll, if a campaign contributor gets a public contract, or city workers are loafing on the job, urban readers are not likely to get excited.

Gladys has to look for a bigger story behind these simple leads. The tips themselves suggest larger stories: How open and democratic are the operations of local labor unions? How much money does the city lose by having an overstaffed department? Do public officials require contractors to make contributions which they then pass along to the taxpayer in inflated costs?

She has found that these more significant stories are seldom spelled out in the tips she gets. She must flesh out these simple suggestions. She must examine the accuracy of the information she gathers and weigh its importance to the public interest. She must learn how government should work so that she can compare that with how it is actually working.

At the metropolitan newspaper, reporters have a sarcastic comment about the degree of truth in facts gathered: "Is it the truth or what really happened?" But while she is a bit skeptical, Gladys may have an advantage over some of the more seasoned reporters by having retained what other reporters at the newspaper might consider an idyllic view of how things should be. As a newcomer, she does not accept what some of the more experienced reporters find to be commonplace and so fail to report. With that advantage, she considers some possible stories behind the tips she receives.

Should she look at the labor unions? Waste in government? Abuse of campaign solicitation?

By checking with the federal and state labor departments, she learns that these are tools at her disposal for a labor union story or other stories related to the welfare of the working force. For example, the U.S. Department of Labor requires union locals to file disclosure statements and companies to file reports of their benefit plans. Those records are public and usually can be had without a freedom of information request.

Disclosure statements (LM-2) are on file in the regional offices of the Labor Management Standards division. They contain the names and salaries of employees, receipts, expenditures, and loans. Another form (LM-1) contains by-laws and union election rules. The union pension and health plans are filed with the Pension and Welfare Benefits Administration, also in the regional U.S. Department offices in major cities throughout the country. Private company pension and welfare benefits plans can be ordered from the Washington offices.

State labor departments deal mostly with unemployment compensation payments and workers compensation. Unemployment compensation is the employer-paid unemployment insurance which is administered by the states and is not public record except when there is a hearing on a question of payment to a worker. Workers compensation is treated like any court which has, for public inspection, files of injury suits by employees against employers. From these sources Gladys could develop many stories:

- Who are the highest paid union leaders? Do some have jobs with more than one local?
- Are purchases or sales of property, hiring of consultants, and contracts with companies that provide health care benefits free of involvement by related persons that might cause a conflict of interest and consequently wasted benefits for members?
- Are the investments of union member pension funds safe?
- Are persons with criminal records on the union payroll?
- Are awards under workers compensation fair?
- Are certain lawyers soliciting clients?
- Are doctors conspiring with workers and lawyers to make fraudulent claims?
- How do state administrators interpret the rules for payment of unemployment compensation? Are they strict or lenient?

Although a real probe of the local labor unions is long overdue, Gladys thinks, such a story might have limited interest. Could the city worker story involving tax money be expanded into a more relevant story?

The Tools

Budgets. Every government agency has plans of operation with price tags so that it may levy taxes for those operations. For a reporter, budgets provide an estimate of the number of employees and their salaries and benefits, cost of supplies, outside consultants, and all other costs.

Annual financial reports. These reports have the same appearance as a budget, but instead of projecting what is to be spent in the year ahead, they show what was actually spent during the past year. They are audited by outside professional auditors.

Work sheets. In order to make out a payroll, the government agency must have some record of when and where the employees worked.

Observation. Because government workers are found in public buildings, public grounds, or public streets, they are readily available for observation. They often drive large marked vehicles.

The Possibilities

A number of questions can be asked:
- Are there unnecessary public payroll jobs?
- At what cost do other cities accomplish tasks such as painting a stripe down the center of the street, picking up a ton of garbage, or cleaning a mile of the same-sized sewer line?

- Are there "ghost" payrollers, public workers who are at home or at other jobs or doing political work when their names appear on the work sheets? Or perhaps they don't exist at all and their paychecks are cashed by the person who placed the fictitious names on the payrolls.
- Would contracting with private companies accomplish the same services that the workers are providing at a lower cost?
- What is the efficiency of public workers compared with those in the same jobs in the private sector?
- Do private utility company meter readers read more meters per hour than those on the public payroll? Or perhaps the private contracts for city services cost more than if the services were done by public employees.
- Would the quality of the food for inmates in the jail be better and the cost less if it were prepared there rather than being brought in from outside? The cost of food for the jail in the budget would be a starting point.
- Are friends and relatives of agency officials readily put on the payroll?
- Are political workers rewarded with jobs that may have been created just to accommodate them?
- Could a price tag in government waste be put on all these unnecessary jobs?

Could these questions ferret out the causes of high government costs? This would drive the story home to taxpayers, Gladys considered, but would probably get little response in the way of reform from the city. To crack down on government waste and corruption, should she turn to the story about the possibility of contracts going to campaign contributors?

More Tools

Campaign disclosure forms. These forms are checked for the names of persons who give money to the political campaign of the elected official who controls the contracts.

Vendor lists. These are the lists of persons or companies that do business with the local government. They are kept by the purchasing department, clerk, controller, or otherwise titled financial officer.

Contracts. A contract is a document used in public and private business that describes what services will be provided in exchange for a specified sum of money.

Bid specifications. Before entering into a contract, the government agency states exactly what it wants to buy and invites anyone to declare for what price they will provide those goods or services. The qualified low bidder *should* get the job—except in unusual circumstances. If the government is selling property, it goes to the high bidder at a public auction.

More Possibilities

- Are the vendors the same people who gave money to the elected official's political campaign?
- If they got contracts, were those contracts awarded through a fair bidding process?
- Were the bid specifications rigged? Rigged specifications are constructed so that only one provider can meet them and get the contract. That could be the person who contributed to the campaign and is being rewarded.
- Did the taxpayers get their money's worth from the contract? Or would a simple comparison of costs indicate that the cost of funding political campaigns is added to the cost of the government contract given to a contributor and then passed along to the taxpayer?

In approaching a story that matches campaign contributions with public contracts, Gladys observed that the same formula could be applied to any governmental unit, including Congress, all state agencies, and the smallest rural school district with elected officials.

The Decision

Before making a final decision, Gladys not only weighs the importance of the story to the public but also equates the amount of time she will spend against the projected outcome. It is a serious waste of time to go on a "fishing expedition" with little chance of success. Some of the ideas may seem to lead to a sure thing. But if Gladys has no concrete evidence of wrongdoing when she starts the project, her efforts may net her nothing. Shouldn't she, a person who is criticizing government for being inefficient and wasteful, guard against her own inefficiency and wastefulness?

So Gladys went back to her original tips. With a few days of concerted effort she was able to verify each lead. This gave her confidence to choose one of the subjects for an expanded investigation. Which would you choose?

Gladys' decision about what story to pursue came to her easily. Her mind was made up while she was driving near a downtown park. She noticed that four men were gathered around a decorative light pole, and a city truck was parked nearby. She stopped and observed that they were changing a light bulb—a simple bulb under a glass globe. One man stood near the top of a ladder and took off the globe, handed it to a second man who was half way up the ladder, and then screwed in the bulb. A third man was holding the ladder and the fourth was standing on the sidewalk watching. After the globe was replaced, they got into a truck and drove away. She noticed that there was a fifth man, the driver, who stayed in the truck all of the time.

When she got to the *Daily Metro* newsroom, Gladys called the head of the street department. She asked why it took so many men to change a light bulb. "It is important to their safety. Someone has to assist the man at the top or he might loose his balance. Of course, someone has to hold the ladder. The man you saw standing on the sidewalk was the supervisor."

"But what about the driver," she asked, "all he did was sit in the truck."

"Our men are specialists. Street light engineers change light bulbs and drivers drive trucks," he replied.

Gladys looked into the budget of the street department and was surprised to learn that all of the functions were broken down on a single line. The number of bulbs changed, the miles of white line put down the center of street, and the number of street signs erected were listed in addition to the amount of money each of those operations cost, because there were special crews for each function. She also noticed that a separate crew washed street signs, at a cost of $325,000.

Her next step was to call street departments in other cities of comparable size around the country. She asked how much each of these functions cost them. She immediately found that the cost for the local street department was far ahead of the others, sometimes twice as much or more. During the interviews with administrators in other street departments, she learned interesting facts about how a city provides basic services. In most cities, a two-man crew changed light bulbs.

But her greatest surprise came when she tried to get a comparison of the costs of washing street signs. "Nobody washes street signs," one department head told her. "They're laminated. We just let the good old wind and rain take care of them." She checked other cities and found that this was true; only her city washed street signs on a regular basis.

Early in the morning of the next day, she went to the city garage and followed street crews. It took several days before she found a sign-washing crew. They would go to a street and take short ladders out of the truck. They would put the ladders up to one-way, speed-limit, and stop signs, climb up, squirt the signs with a squeeze bottle of window spray, and wipe them with a cloth. She asked one of the workers why they were washing street signs. He said that it was for the public good, that people might not see them if they were not clean.

It was time for Gladys to propose a story to her editors. Here is how such a proposal would look using the outline method:

Title: City Waste

Subject: The waste of taxpayer money caused by overstaffing of city departments with people who provide unnecessary functions.

Need: There are so many unnecessary city jobs that residents are often paying twice as much for the same services as other cities the same size. The workers believe that they are serving a purpose when actually they are not needed. These jobs may be provided as favors to relatives of elected officials, their contributors, or political workers.

Scope: This will not be one of the routine newspaper stories about city workers loafing on the job. I will try to put an actual dollar amount on the waste and determine the motive behind putting so many people on the payroll. It would be difficult to make comparisons in operations of the police and fire departments, so I will limit the project to the street department, which has one of the largest budgets within the city.

Methods: I will make comparisons of the operating costs for the same functions with cities around the country. I will take into consideration any geographical differences that might make the comparisons invalid. It would be obvious that snow removal costs in Dallas would be different from that cost in Minneapolis. I will also observe city workers to report on exactly what they are doing.

Sources: I will get a copy of the budget and the payroll. I will interview department heads and administrators in other cities and talk to experts, such as associations of municipal officers and private consultants. I will interview city workers to learn how they got their jobs.

Production: This investigation would result in a series of stories that could be as extensive as five parts, depending on the amount of information I find. City workers doing the various jobs would provide many picture opportunities because they are in the open on public property. I think we could get a shot that would include all five men changing a light bulb. There could be graphics such as bar charts comparing the cost of each task in different cities.

The editors said they liked the idea, but they had some reservations. "We can't just take the word of people in other cities. We have to get their budgets and payrolls, too, to make a fair comparison," a senior editor said. "Also, we have to look at every aspect of each city's operation before we know we have a comparison. I mean, if we compare tree trimming costs, how do we know which city has the most or the biggest trees?"

Gladys suggested that the investigation be limited to only those functions that were standard in each city. "We could compare those things like cleaning one mile of sewer," she said.

"Just be sure the sewers aren't wider or deeper or something else that is going to give the city an opportunity to come back and make up excuses," the editor said. "I'm glad this isn't one of those city-worker-loafing stories," he added. "I'm always afraid they're going to come back at us by coming in the city room and getting pictures of reporters with their feet up on the desks."

As she gathered the story, Gladys found that waste in the city operations was much worse that she had thought. For instance, she learned that other cities didn't wait until a street light bulb was reported burned out before they sent out a truck-load of workers to replace it. Elsewhere, two men, one driving a truck and the other standing in a metal bucket on a crane, would go down the street and change all of the bulbs in a neighborhood as soon as the estimated life expectancy of those bulbs indicated that they were about to fail. The cost of any extra usage they would have gotten from the bulbs was small compared to the cost of city workers responding to complaints as bulbs failed in different areas of the city. Concerning the safety aspect, cities with fewer workers did not show a higher rate of injuries on the job.

The story worked out much as it had been planned. The waste comparisons ran side-by-side with a story about how city workers had to have a letter from a political boss to get a city job. Also, it showed that some jobs had been created to accommodate friends of the administration. The stories were the talk of the town, and the city administration was embarrassed, but defensive. A year later when the story was forgotten, Gladys got a copy of the new city budget. The city had quietly cut back the work crews, and the job of sign washing had been completely eliminated.

MEMO

- There are more investigative stories than there are investigative reporters to do them.

- A reporter must make a deliberate and wise choice about the importance, impact, and feasibility of an investigative project before committing an excessive amount of time to it.

- A reporter must assess the availability of information when starting on a larger investigation.

PROJECT

Find a routine story in a daily newspaper. Can this story be developed into an investigative project by looking at the broader problems it suggests?

Exercise: Student Investigative Outlines: How to Visualize and Explain an Investigative Idea

Step 1. Choose a project for an investigative outline. First select a subject, and then write a preliminary outline, adhering to the following form: (1) title, then state the (2) subject, argue the (3) need, describe the (4) scope, explain your proposed (5) methods, list your (6) sources, and finally establish your (7) production.

Here are some investigative ideas, shown in the form of the brief outline:

I. 1. *Title:* Highway

   2. *Subject:* Land purchase by the state for the new highway

   3. *Need:* The state highway department is buying land to build a stretch of highway north of the city. In the past, there have been scandals involving the purchase of land from persons who had inside information about where roads would be located and there is evidence that the state paid an inflated price for the land it acquired. Usually, these stories reveal problems after the money is spent. If we do a story now we can anticipate problems, head off any waste or corruption, and save taxpayers' money.

   4. *Scope:* This investigation will be limited to the land acquisition program and its cost. We will not attempt at this time to examine the contracts for construction work. We will avoid a story about the displacement of persons by the highway or the damage to the environment, since we have conceded that the highway is necessary. We will also look at the land that the state is not acquiring but that will increase in value because it is at an interchange. If insiders speculate on this land, does it mean that the decisions about locating the road and interchange were made to accommodate them? Even if we don't find insider dealings, we may find that the cost of the land acquisition is much more than the state has admitted to the public.

   5. *Methods:* Most of the information for this story will come from land records in the county recorder's office, from condemnation suits, and from interviews of landowners. We will compare the cost of land acquisition for other similar highways. We will tabulate the full cost of the land that has been bought so far to see if it already exceeds the estimated cost.

   6. *Sources:* We can get a list from the highway department of all properties to be acquired. If we run into any delays, we can immediately go to the land records office and find condemnation proceedings recorded against the properties. We will make a list of all of the properties and do a thorough research of each. By looking at land records and condemnation suits, we will establish past and present ownership. We will note especially the date the current owners bought the land and how much

they paid for it in the chance that there has been inside information and speculation that has driven up the price. If there were recent buyers who now are selling to the state, we will look into their backgrounds to see if they might have business or family connections to state officials. We will locate the previous owners and ask them with whom they negotiated in case the owner of record is not the only person involved. We will look for any recent changes in zoning from the county or towns that may have been sought for the sole purpose of increasing the market value of the land. We will look for any speculation involving the land that is adjacent to the highway to see if the speculators have connections with state officials. We will check on the business backgrounds of all persons and corporations involved in the ownership of the land or who might get broker fees. We will look for obvious overpricing, such as the state paying the rate for commercial property for land that is not suited to such use.

7. *Production:* We will tell this story in a series of newspaper articles. Maps will be extremely important, and we could get an aerial shot to best show the terrain we are writing about. We will plan on a sidebar showing the chronology of the highway project, how it was conceived, approved by the legislature, and funded, and all important happenings and dates up to the present. If we find that this highway project is extremely wasteful or corrupt, we could do an additional story on how a similar project was accomplished more efficiently elsewhere.

II. 1. *Title:* Convict

2. *Subject:* An investigation of whether a convicted murderer got a fair trial

3. *Need:* The public defender's office believes that Mark Kane, convicted of murder three years ago, did not get a fair trial and may be innocent. Although they don't have hard evidence of his innocence, their belief is so strong that I think it deserves investigating. Kane is a down-and-out itinerant who may have been in the wrong place at the wrong time. He has no friends to help him, the justice system may have failed him, and the newspaper is his only hope. Our readers will be interested in his story because I believe that everyone has a fear that they, too, could be victims of injustice.

4. *Scope:* We will attempt to determine if Kane got a fair trial and if, in fact, he is innocent. We already know that the evidence against him is circumstantial, and the public defender admits he did not have the time or staff to give him the best legal representation. If we can't find evidence that Kane could not have committed the murder, we might at least show how little evidence sent him to prison and hope that his case is reinvestigated or that he gets a new trial. We will concentrate on this case and not attempt a sweeping assessment of the court system or the competence of the police department.

5. *Methods:* This story can be produced with a series of interviews of trial witnesses, jury members, police investigators, prosecutors, and defense attorneys. We will try to get transcripts of the trial and police investigative reports.

6. *Sources:*

a. Interviews. witnesses in the trial, jury members, police investigators, witnesses the police may not have contacted, defense attorneys, prosecution attorneys, staff members of the prosecutor's office. We will arrange through the office of the prison warden to talk to Kane. We will talk to Kane's family and to the family and friends of the murder victim to learn if they are satisfied that Kane is the murderer.

b. Documents. the public defender would cooperate with us and may be able to provide us with a free transcript of the trial and also the police investigative materials that they got in discovery. Because this case is closed and there is a conviction, police reports should be available to us. We will ask his family and friends to look for documents that might prove his innocence, like a parking ticket in another town the day he was supposed to have committed the murder, or a sales slip or credit card purchase, or a check written, or a visit to a doctor.

7. *Production:* If this investigation is successful, we will tell it in a series of newspaper articles. We also would write a more detailed version in a 40,000 word nonfiction book. I think that the documentation in addition to the personal interviews will provide interesting reading, as in a mystery novel. It also will contain characterization of the most important participants and atmosphere about the time and place of the murder and trial.

III. 1. *Title:* Beggars

2. *Subject:* A look at the activities of beggars on the streets

3. *Need:* There have always been beggars, but it seems that they are appearing on the city streets in increasing numbers. Beggars are embarrassing to the city, and there needs to be some control. They range from passive beggars who sit with cups to panhandlers who approach people and demand money. Some of the latter's tactics border on robbery. People are becoming irritated by such tactics and will be interested in an investigative story on the subject. The story will be remembered because it is unusual; we don't know of any newspaper or television station having done such a story.

4. *Scope:* We won't attempt to examine the broad social aspects of why there are beggars, but will try instead to define the laws or lack of laws involving begging and efforts of enforcement. We will attempt to discover if beggars are really in need and also if there could be organized begging in which locations are assigned or agreed upon and a tax is paid to some street lord, as often is the situation with prostitution.

5. *Methods:* We will do legal research, but the bulk of our documenta-

tion will come from surveillance, because we don't believe there is much on the record about beggars. We will also survey the public to determine the level of irritation caused by beggars.

6. *Sources:* Because we don't know the names of beggars, we will go to law enforcement officials and ask if they recall any arrests and try to locate those cases in court files. If we find from those files that there are some infamous beggars and we can determine their mode of operation, we will try to find them and watch them. That way, it won't be our judgment alone about what they are doing.

If there have been arrests, there must be complainants who may talk to us. They will probably be businessmen who don't like beggars hanging around their stores.

7. *Production:* This story will be done as a television series. As soon as we establish patterns of individual beggars who may be especially malicious, we will film them by concealing cameras in a truck on the street. We will do on-camera interviews with government officials and any complainants or victims of beggars. We will also try to interview beggars themselves on camera.

Step 2. The completed student idea outlines are judged by the class as a whole. One way to do this is class members read them all and then vote on what they believe to be the best. A three-point value is given to the best, two points to the second best, and one point to the third. Outlines are judged on the interest and importance of the subject matter and whether the proposed approach is the best, all the possible resources have been considered, and the effort expended would be productive, instead of a fishing expedition.

Step 3. Discuss why some ideas were popular and others got few votes. Were those rated the best especially timely? Did they reveal problems that otherwise would not be addressed? Were the least favored ideas just someone's pet peeve that nobody else cared about? Or were they good ideas that were not explained well enough?

Discuss how these project outlines could be improved. Obviously, the outlines that got the lowest scores either need major revision to make them more workable or understandable or may need to be scrapped. Students would be better off if they chose another subject. Even the more popular outlines could be improved or at least that possibility should be discussed. For instance, let's discuss how the three examples could be improved.

I. *Highway.* How can we both anticipate the fraud and "get the goods on these guys?" We can't accuse someone of doing something until its done, such as an inside land deal, when we have solid evidence after the fact. Perhaps we should look at a past highway project instead. Or we could look only at the way the land acquisition program is being conducted. Isn't land acquisition for a highway a boring topic no matter what we find?

II. *Convict.* This man would have to be a saint if we are going to go that far out on a limb for him. Can we take a chance that he will be released from prison because of our reporting and then commit a crime? Will the readers be satisfied with a story that asks questions only about the man's guilt but provides no proof of his innocence? It could be that the public defenders are trying to redeem themselves because they lost the case, not because they have a real sense of his innocence. Would anyone want to buy a book about the murder conviction of a poor itinerant?

III. *Beggars.* Is this a large enough problem to command so much attention? Will our viewers feel that we are being unfair to beggars, who are already down and out? Would it be more meaningful to investigate the neglect by the public agencies that should be caring for them? Or wouldn't it? Should all beggars be chastised because of a few aggressive, criminal types? Will such a story bring solutions to an age-old problem?

The discussion need not be endless, but it should be thorough. All of these arguments could be rebutted, because we don't know what we will find until we try. The highway story might be boring, but it can be argued that the paper has a duty to the public and its readers to probe possible criminal conduct in government. And in the story of the convict, it is snobbery to think that people will not show compassion for a down-and-out person who has been treated unfairly. The story of the beggars may not be world-shaking, but it touches a familiar problem and if run on the TV news over several days, could help the ratings.

Step 4. When you have decided on a solid outline, it is time to move ahead and develop it into a final project. The sources section of the outline can be expanded as you find out about documents that can be obtained that would apply to the particular subject.

Some of those documents can be obtained at public offices or by writing for information under the Freedom of Information Act. Offices such as the court clerk, land records, municipal building inspection services, and the election board are accustomed to routine inquiries and to providing copies of records. There may not be a need to identify yourself or the purpose of the request. There is usually a small charge for copies, but there should be no fee for viewing public records.

It is impossible to complete an entire investigation as it would be published because of the expense and limited time. But a report can be produced from your experiences in getting some of the records and doing the research.

If a person is taught a particular skill, like fishing, he or she learns what tools are needed, how to care for them, and how to use them. Success is measured by his or her mastery of those skills. A thorough investigation and final report can be accomplished even if nothing turns up— just as accomplished as one that turns up evidence that promises to "blow the lid off the town."

PROJECT

Get one or more public documents that relate to the investigative project you've chosen. Discuss the meaning of your document in class, how it could relate to the proposed investigation, and what new leads it offers. The experiences you had in locating the right public office, encountering clerks or public officials, and requesting and getting the information can be shared and discussed.

CHAPTER FIVE

Investigating Government

One of the secrets of success of the United States is the structure of its local governments. The states, counties, cities, towns, villages, school districts, fire protection districts, airport authorities, and other small government entities stand separately. They are not divisions of the federal government. They have to tax separately and answer to the local voters. The Census Bureau of the U.S. Department of Commerce has counted more than 83,000 separate government units.

A variety of governments, each with its own laws and procedures, allows ideas to be tested in one place before being adopted in another. It also allows more people to participate in government. But for an investigative reporter, this variety presents an ongoing challenge. The reporter reveals when government is not working well and so has to know its inner workings. The reporter has to be familiar with each of the governments and must do research each time he or she gathers a story that involves a unit of government.

In addition, the federal government is a complex organization of agencies that interact with local governments. The investigative reporter must accept the challenge and learn to unravel the system. This is done in three steps. The reporter (1) suspects there is a wrong and identifies it; (2) learns *all* of the rules that are supposed to be followed in regard to that aspect of government; and (3) proves that there is a wrong by using the tools of the investigative reporter: interviews, documents, surveillance, and surveys.

Looking for Governmental Wrongdoing

Government can be examined through a system of organized questions and ideas that cut across individual government lines. This system can be used to identify a wrong in any governmental entity. The questions can be developed by looking at the functions common to governments:

1. *Elections.* The investigative reporter in his or her professional capacity doesn't care who wins—only that the election is fair.

- In the rush to get a candidate on the ballot, did political workers make up names or sign the names of others on petitions?
- Are fictitious names on the voter registration list?
- Are people who give campaign money promised favors in return?
- Are employees of a public agency required to make campaign contributions to keep their jobs or get promotions?
- Are public employees campaigning when they should be working at their government jobs?
- Are public funds used in a political campaign?
- Are dirty tricks, like anonymous letters, being used?
- Are workers for one political party being intimidated by the police powers of the party in office?
- Does campaign money openly buy votes?

2. *Revenue.* The investigative reporter swallows the fact that taxes are high but wants to make sure that people are fairly assessed and that the money, when collected, is handled properly.

- Are breaks being given to some favored people or neighborhoods in the assessment of personal property or real estate taxes?
- Does the government vigorously pursue tax cheats such as merchants who don't turn in sales taxes or motorists who don't pay parking tickets?
- Are taxes that are earmarked for certain uses, like motor fuel, being used in the best way for the purpose promised?
- Do towns have roadway speed traps only to raise money from fines?
- When tax money is collected, is it put in bank accounts that return no interest in return for personal favors to public officials from the bank?

3. *Employment.* An intimate knowledge of human failings will help the investigative reporter look at public employees.

- If a government job requires a test, is it fairly administered, scored, and rated?
- Is favoritism shown to relatives and political friends of officials?

- Are departments overstaffed or understaffed?
- Are there too many supervisors and too few workers?
- Are employees actually performing the same duties that their job descriptions show?
- Have the resumes submitted by employees been checked for accuracy or fraud?
- Would it be better to contract with an outside agency for some of the services that public employees now do?

4. *Enforcement Regulation.* Knowing that there is more to investigate than one person possibly can, the investigative reporter knows public enforcement also may be lacking.

- Are building inspectors and food inspectors so overworked that they are not able to make as thorough an inspection or complete all the inspections that the law directs? Are they lazy or incompetent?
- Are the people who sit on professional licensing boards so closely tied to the profession that they neglect the welfare of the public?
- Do the police use excessive force?
- Do the police coddle local residents but pounce on outsiders for drunken driving?
- Do the courts allow dangerous criminals to be freed on small bail bonds?
- Are the judges, prosecutors, and defense attorneys inclined to make deals rather than seek justice?

5. *Purchasing.* When someone is buying something with someone else's money, investigative reporters will want to take a close look.

- Does the government buy unnecessary items?
- How do the prices of items and services compare with what private business pays on the open market?
- Is the government entering into contracts for services that could be done by government employees?
- Are the specifications advertised in the bidding process designed to be favorable to certain suppliers?
- Are companies entertaining government employees, giving them gifts, or even bribing them either with cash payments or indirectly with business opportunities to influence their decisions?

6. *Services.* Services like picking up garbage and distributing government benefits bring people and government close together.

- Is the councilman's street paved first?
- Are the parks in the richest neighborhoods the best equipped and cleanest?
- Is the street department slow in response to a need for repairs?
- Is a bridge near collapse?
- Do the local public schools spend more than comparable schools elsewhere for administration, buildings, and sports, but less than the others for books or the school lunch program?
- What is the response time to emergencies by the police and fire departments?

7. *Ethics.* Lawmakers and public employees are also people.

- Do state assembly members have a personal interest in the legislation they pass?
- Do their official actions follow a pattern suggested by the people who give them campaign money?
- Is there a "good old boy" relationship between judges and the lawyers who appear before them?

Reporters may not know that something is wrong and worthy of investigation when they start asking such questions. They may have been asked to investigate the operation of a government unit and have no advanced knowledge of its workings or failings. Such an assignment might occur if the airport authority sells a $100 million bond issue for expansion or the water district wants to increase the area it serves. But more likely, when reporters set out to investigate a government agency, there has been a hint of specific wrongdoing. The hint might have come as a tip from inside the operation or complaints from the public about the performance of the agency.

It may seem that the reporter should know all about how a government unit operates before questioning the operations of that unit. But the reporter must identify the investigation to know what rules apply. He or she then moves to step two and becomes an expert in one slice of the administration of government.

While the public and even experienced reporters may think they know how government works, they often lack knowledge of details. Most people are exposed to the workings of government in school. Later, they become enamored with politics and political personalities of the day, following the elections and conflicts, but neglecting to try to understand the day-to-day operation of government.

To learn how a particular area of government works, the investigative reporter asks questions. The answers will differ from one governmental body to another, because the only limits to the various laws, rules, and regulations of the local governmental units are interpretations of the U.S. and state constitutions. They may even change from year to year. Reporters contact officials of the governmental entity to get information and research the laws that created it. Some of the information can be found in public libraries, and some cities and universities have law libraries that have more specialized information. But friendly, on-the-record interviews with knowledgeable public officials usually serve reporters best.

Asking questions to research the rules of the game may invite more story ideas.

1. *Elections:* What are the rules for gathering names on petitions to have a candidate or proposition placed on the ballot? What are the rules about posting campaign signs or campaigning in or near the polling place? What are the rules for collecting campaign contributions? May a candidate take the campaign money that is left in his or her fund for personal use? Who is qualified to run? Who is qualified to vote?

2. *Revenue:* What are the rules for apportioning property taxes? What is the procedure for appealing taxes? Under what authority does the government deposit tax money in bank accounts? What is the process for selling government property? How can the government borrow money?

3. *Employment:* Who is qualified to work for the government agency? Must job openings be advertised? Which jobs require tests? How are employees supervised?

4. *Enforcement/Regulation:* What kind of building requires inspection and how often? Which professions are regulated by the state? How are the members of the discipline board for the state medical licensing agency chosen? What is the step-by-step legal procedure that the police and courts must follow to make an arrest, hold a trial, and incarcerate or parole a person?

5. *Purchasing:* What is the procedure for advertising and letting bids? What is the law for accepting bids? What can be purchased without a bid? What proof of delivery of goods or services must be made before a check can be issued? What are the rules for government employee expense accounts?

6. *Services:* Who is empowered to decide where money for street repair is to be spent? What are the rules for distributing public assistance

money? Who qualifies for a student grant or a student loan? Who qualifies for subsidized housing?

7. *Ethics:* What business or personal ties are improper for a judge, law-maker, or public administrator? Is there a written list of unethical situations? Which government employees must file a public statement to show conflicts of interest?

Looking at the Records

Researching the laws regulating government units may reveal information that will lead to important stories. An investigative reporter may gain such insights as, "I didn't know policemen were not allowed to hold liquor licenses," or "I didn't know the prosecutor could reduce criminal charges of the police," or "I didn't know the town board couldn't get together and talk in a restaurant without declaring an official meeting."

With an idea identified and a knowledge of the law in mind, the investigative reporter mentally splices them together and asks questions of a different nature. The goal now will be to determine (1) if regulatory or enforcement administrators are lax in making people adhere to the laws, (2) if the laws are being followed by government administrators in the operation of their own offices, or (3) if, while the letter of a law is being adhered to, a law is not achieving the goal that legislators and the public intended when it was enacted. To find, expose and correct these faults, the investigative reporter needs to know what government records are available. Government records may be thought of in two categories— *operation* records and *disclosure* records.

Operation records include minutes of meetings, budgets, financial reports, payrolls, contracts, and bid specifications. These sources are common to government agencies and are usually available for public inspection. Other, more restricted information involving the operation of government includes expense account vouchers of public employees, telephone records of public agencies, and official correspondence.

Disclosure records relate to private operations outside of government. In these, otherwise private information is revealed for the public good: applications for licenses, inspection reports, court files, birth and death certificates, corporate registration, police reports, and land sale records. Some of these require action by the government, but others are kept on file only for the purpose of maintaining an orderly society. In the disclosure area, some more obscure records are public health inspections, corporate pension information, cemetery records, and fire department investigative files.

Freedom of Information Act

A reporter may need to make a formal request to gain access to information. A major tool for investigating government is the Freedom of Information Act (FOIA), a federal act that requires federal agencies to provide certain information. State and local governments have adopted similar laws. The FOIA requires that a letter be written to the agency from the person requesting access. Disclosure laws are not discriminatory, so it does not matter who requests the information. Whether the material is released is determined by its content and if the law then requires its release.

A public agency has a certain amount of time to respond to a request for information. The federal FOIA allows ten days. During that time the agency must determine whether it will release the information. If it decides that the request needs an interpretation of law, the agency may extend the deadline another ten days. If the information requested is similar to previous requests which resulted in release of information, the agency may quickly rule in favor of releasing it. But if it is a unique request, the full ten days may be taken.

A request can be turned down. Here are some reasons a request generally is refused:

1. It is for classified information that must be kept secret because it is vital to the national defense or foreign policy. Obviously, the blueprints of a new military weapon would not be released.
2. It is for informaton that was required of a corporation in an application for a public contract but which involves a trade secret or financial information. If the government wants to know the chicken soup recipe of the food supplier before entering into a contract for Veteran Administrations hospitals, it would have to agree to keep it secret.
3. It is for information that is considered to invade the privacy of an individual. Even if the government paid for the emergency medical care of a U.S. senator, it would probably consider his medical records private.
4. It is for material that would reveal details of an ongoing investigation. Investigators want to put in writing all that they are told, but to name suspects before an investigation is complete gives criminals an advantage.

Exemptions in the law call for interpretations. Who decides how long an investigation can be conducted before it is complete? Who is to say what invades the privacy of a person? What constitutes national defense? An administrator is likely to make those decisions to further his or her own political advantage. But the laws provide for appeals. On the administrative level, a person requesting information can appeal to the office of the chief administrator of an agency, who may also reject the request. The appeal process can be lengthy on the administrative level. A lawsuit can be filed in a local court and be appealed to the state courts or U.S. Supreme Courts.

Such a large amount of time is involved in a FOIA request, even to a cooperating agency, that an investigative reporter tends to avoid it. If there is another way to legally get the information, he or she will try that first. Perhaps the same or similar information can be provided by another agency that is more cooperative or a direct, personal appeal can be made to the head of an agency.

Freedom of Information laws do not require private citizens or corporations to provide information. But they may be used to help you get information about individuals or companies that are regulated by government or have public contracts.

MEMO

- An investigative reporter doesn't just study government; he or she *lives* it.

- All governments—local, county, state, and federal—have similar internal operations. The U.S. Defense Department and the county jail use brooms and soap. The White House and a small schoolhouse have electric bills.

- The public has a legal right—granted by legislation—to view certain documents and may exercise that right through the federal or local Freedom of Information Acts.

PROJECTS

1. What questions about ethics in government or the functions of government (elections, revenue, employment, purchasing, services, or enforcement/regulation) other than those asked in this chapter can you think of that present the possibility of investigative stories? Could those questions be applied to the government units or agencies most familiar to you?

2. How many questions can you ask about operation of your local police department that could lead to investigative stories?

3. Write a FOIA request letter to get information on the subject of an individual project or class investigative project. Research local FOIA laws to comply with local requirements. Requests should be specific. Here is a sample:

Mr. Fred O. Acht
Freedom Of Information Officer
Department of General Services Center
City of Metropolitan
Metropolitan, N.Y. 00000

Dear Mr. Acht,
This is a request under the state Freedom of Information Act.
I would like a list of all vacant land sold by the city between the dates October
1, 1998, and October 1, 1999, including the date of the sale, the property
index number, and the street address.

I am also requesting a list of all appraisers employed by the city to appraise
vacant land.

I am a reporter for *The Metropolitan Reliable* and feel that release of this
information will benefit the public. Accordingly, I request a waiver of any copying charges. Under the state law, you have seven days to comply with this
request. Since this request is of a timely nature, I would appreciate hearing
from you by a telephone call as soon as that information is available.
If you have questions, or if I can be of any assistance, please contact me at 555–
5555. Thank you in advance for your assistance.

Sincerely yours,
O. M. "Bud" Munn
Reporter

GLOSSARY

Public assistance money.   Government disburses welfare money either on an
emergency basis or for long-term subsistence. In some programs, the federal government pays part of the money, but the states differ in their rules
about who qualifies to receive it.

Good-old-boy relationship.   It would be contrary to the public interest if
judges and the lawyers who appear before them are socially involved to the
degree that they are club members, had business or family relationships,
or regularly did favors for each other. If someone says, "He's a good old
boy," it sounds like that person is one who is willing to go along with the
crowd to gain social acceptance.

Case History: Gladys and Bud Check on a
Government Program

About five years after the state passed legislation to legalize bingo, one of
the senior editors thought that it would be interesting to investigate the
bingo operations. The law was passed because churches were having small
games to raise funds, and although it was illegal, no law enforcement

official who wanted to be reelected dared to shut them down. The law allowed bingo to benefit the charities and be taxed by the state. It carried with it provisions designed to keep professional gamblers away.

The *Daily Metro* editor asked Bud Munn and Gladys Tydings to team up and investigate bingo. The public needed to know if the games really benefited charities, if they were being run fairly, and if professional gamblers had muscled in. Bud suggested that he and Gladys start by learning some of the history of the games and the legislation that governed them. They contacted the state gaming commission, which was supervising a lottery and dog races in addition to bingo. A public relations official for the gaming commission was amused at their interest. He said there wasn't much news from bingo. It was easy to regulate because the stakes were small and only a small segment of the population played the games. He described the players as "typical little old ladies."

Only not-for-profit charitable organizations qualified for a bingo license. A limit was placed on prizes, and the games could operate only one night each week for two hours. A card cost only one dollar, and it could be used for all the games. Anyone with a gambling conviction was not allowed to be involved in running the games and could not even be on the premises.

The reporters believed they were faced with an assignment that was easy to understand but difficult to find significant. They got a list of all the bingo licenses in the state and studied it. And they requested and got the official applications for those licenses.

Bud told Gladys that lists had never failed him in the past—a list of people who got Small Business Administration loans, a list of contracts for the sanitary district, the sheriff's payroll. Each time, he would find something amiss. People's names were there that should not have been, or someone was cheating in some way. "The good thing about a list is that someone always has to be the best and someone the worst when you get behind what they are doing, so there's at least something to write about," Bud said.

Gladys suggested that they would be able to best judge if bingo were beneficial by determining where the money went. They could rate the charities on which was spending the money in the best way or how efficient they were in their operations. They could determine efficiency by finding which charitable cause ended up with a larger portion of the money that had come in from the games. They would order IRS 990 forms of all of the not-for-profit organizations on the list. This would show how much of the money went to charity. Gladys filed a request with the Freedom of Information Act officer at the U.S. Internal Revenue Service.

Gladys also knew that people who solicited money for charitable purposes had to file similar information with the state. She found that the files of the Charitable Trust Division of the state Attorney General's office were open to anyone—no FOIA request was needed.

Bud and Gladys checked the newspaper clip files for stories about the organizations on the state list and got corporate registration information about the not-for-profit organizations from the state Secretary of State Corporations Division. Not-for-profits must file with the state just as for-profit companies. Almost immediately, the two reporters made a discovery. Many of the organizations had the same address for the location of their games. In fact, there were groups of ten or twelve organizations at six different places around the metropolitan area. That situation was easy enough to investigate. They jumped into a car that evening and drove to the addresses.

They found that the bingo game locations were big halls, some were converted supermarket buildings. Several had neon signs that advertised the bingo games. The parking lots were full, and people milled around outside. Few were "little old ladies."

The reporters went inside a hall and found a casino atmosphere. There was a bar, and uniformed employees were selling cards in the aisles. While players were supposed to have one card for $1.00, some had as many as sixty bingo cards taped in front of them on the table. A man called out the numbers from a platform, and they were also displayed on a board.

Bud and Gladys saw from the program that the law was being circumvented rather than broken. Each charity had a game for two hours and each had one game a week. But by having many games in one hall, the action could go all evening as one game ended and a new one started. The same callers and card sellers worked for all the games. Midnight bingo took place when busloads of players arrived from a nearby state.

The next day, the reporters began a records check of the halls where the games were being played. They checked the county building for land records to determine ownership, but when they contacted the owners they found they had rented the buildings and did not want to cooperate with the reporters for fear of bad publicity. However, Gladys remembered that liquor was sold at the games—there would be state and local liquor licenses. The applications not only would show the corporations that leased the halls but also would give the reporters some leads to the backgrounds of the liquor license holders.

They got the names of the corporations, checked for the names of their officers in the office of the secretary of state, and then started to do personal profile research on the officers. Consulting their newspaper clip files and criminal court records, they found that several officers were long-time gamblers with petty arrests and convictions. It was beginning to look like the halls, which were not licensed, made the big money rather than the licensed charitable games.

As they pursued the court records, they found that all the members of one family that owned a corporation that operated one of the big halls had changed their names. A check of the court record revealed the previous name, and when that name was researched, it turned out to be the name of an infamous, long-time, organized-crime family.

Then they studied the financial reports of the charities that were listed and were amazed to find that some had taken in as much as $400,000 a year in bingo card sales in their weekly two-hour sessions but ended the year with as little as $167 for charity. The money was eaten away by inflated hall rental, fees for the parking lot, and purchase of bingo cards and other supplies from the corporation that controlled the hall.

Several of the charities had the same officers—who turned out to be workers at the bingo hall. Bud and Gladys were able to identify the workers by taking down their auto license numbers in the parking lot. Some charities on the list were more like clubs. All the benefits went to the members for social outings and scholarships for their children.

Now that they believed themselves to be experts in what was going on in the bingo halls, the reporters went back to the state bingo licensing agency and interviewed the director. They were able to ask more educated questions. What are the questions you would ask?

Perhaps you would be tempted to ask, "Do you know what's going on out there?" But the purpose of the interview is to learn more about the operation of the government agency that's being investigated as well as the bingo operations. The interview might go like this:

Q: How is the agency insuring that only legitimate charities are licensed to run bingo games?
A: We require that all license applicants register with the Charitable Trust Division of the Attorney General's office.
Q: How are the rules of the game enforced?
A: We have a full-time employee who takes complaints and follows up on them.
Q: How many complaints have you had in the last five years?
A: We have had numerous complaints, but they all proved unfounded.

The reporters discussed their story. It appeared that the licensing agency allowed the Charitable Trust Division to decide whether or not a charity is legitimate. There was one inspector for the licensing agency and, rather than make the rounds, he sat at a desk in the state capitol and took complaints. But who complained? The charities and the hall operators were co-conspirators. The only persons who might have complained were players who thought they were being cheated because they were losers in a game; but the bingo operators would not have to cheat the players because the odds for bingo are already greatly in their favor. Then the reporters talked to the Charitable Trust Division and were told that they conducted investigations of persons who filed as a charity only if there was a complaint.

Then the reporters learned from other players that there was one game going on with higher prizes because it was not licensed.

Bud and Gladys became regular players of all the games, making the rounds of the bingo halls as they gathered and organized their story. They saw that large amounts of money were being spent and that at the end of the games in one hall, the money was counted in a back room. Although they could not actually see what happened in the counting room, they noticed that, throughout the evening, the card sellers took their money in there. They realized that there was no way that the state could know how much money was brought in because it was all in cash. The hall operators could underreport the gross receipts. Even those figures that they had seen on the charities' financial statements were probably only a portion of the money actually brought in.

They discussed whether they should pursue that additional avenue of investigation or use what they already had. Should they forget the new idea, do their close-out interviews, and write about what they had?

The Argument for Yes

A newspaper has a limited amount of space. Reporters should not try to expand their story beyond the limits of what a series can contain. Why bark up new trees when there is already an important story to tell. The new lead may not go anywhere. If it does, it could be a follow-up story. But there is no way to tell.

The Argument for No

If there is a bigger investigation to be pursued, readers would be cheated if reporters settled for the easy, superficial story. It wouldn't take much time to give it a try.

The Decision

Bud and Gladys, knowing they did not want to go into print with a story while they believed there might be a bigger story to be found, decided to chase the new lead. "Too many times I have found out after I wrote a story that I only scratched the surface—that the situation was much worse than I had ever dreamed," Bud said.

The two reporters learned that the bingo halls used thin paper bingo cards that were perforated with the date so that a player could not take them home, bring them back, and reuse them the next day. The colors also changed from day to day. They knew how much each bingo card cost, so all they had to do was count one session's cards to learn how much money was taken in. Each night a janitor cleared all the paper off the tables and hauled it out to the trash dumpster in the alley. One night, after the janitor had cleaned the hall and locked up, Bud and Gladys arrived with a rented truck. They emptied the dumpster, hauled the trash away, and spent three days sorting it and counting the cards.

They found that the evening's games had taken in twice as much money as had ever been reported to the state and twice as much as the average game reported by the charities on annual reports. The attendance that night was no more than it had been on other nights.

With evidence in hand, Bud and Gladys asked the gaming commissioner for his comments and confronted the charity operators and the hall owners. They got comments from federal officials about the danger of organized crime subverting local charities. And there was one other interesting development from the closing interviews. The gaming commissioner promised he would tighten up control by making regular inspections of the games, but he said there was nothing he could do about the unlicensed game. All he could do was take away a license, but if there was no license to take away, there was nothing he could do. He said that the local police would have to act. The reporters alerted the police, who placed the game under surveillance and made arrests the week before their series of stories appeared. The newspaper ran the arrest story as a regular news story.

When they wrote their four-part series, Bud and Gladys included a sidebar about a church that ran a legitimate bingo game and told how all of the players had been lured away by the more glamorous halls.

One of the results of the story was that the state legislature passed a law that removed control of the games from the hall operators. The charities could have their games in the halls, but they had to run their own games and count the money themselves.

MEMO

- Government agencies can smugly wear blinders and give a rosy picture of the job they are doing.

- There are large gaps in law enforcement, and there are people seeking to take advantage of them.

• If a seemingly insignificant operation of government fails, the consequences can be significant.

• An investigative reporter should not necessarily wrap up a story as soon as he or she finds something to write about.

Documents Used in This Investigation

License applications. There may be little information on a government license, but the application for the license, which is filed with the agency that issues the license, may require information about the officers, the purpose of the licensed operation, and disclaimers such as are prescribed by law. A disclaimer might be a statement on a liquor license application that the applicant has not been convicted of a felony. License applications are almost always public record.

Liquor licenses. Government has separate licensing for establishments that sell alcoholic beverages. Laws are strict about who may hold a liquor license, more so than with other business licenses. A violation of local liquor laws could mean a loss of the license.

IRS 990. This is a federal government Internal Revenue Service form that must be filed by every not-for-profit organization. It is public record. It is similar to the forms that a for-profit business or an individual files, but its purpose is to confirm that no one is taking profits out of the organization. It lists the officers, their salaries, how much money the organization made, and how much and how it was spent.

Charitable trust disclosure. States have offices that check on possible abuses by charities. They want to make sure that those people who collect money with the promise that it is going to benefit particular charitable causes are really using the money in that way. They are required to make financial disclosures.

Name change court record. A person must go to court to legally change his name, so such cases are indexed in court files. They will show the new name suing the old name.

GLOSSARY

Public relations official.   It surprises the public to learn that tax money pays the salaries of people whose job it is to publicize government. The official job description usually says they provide information to the public. In reality, they try to make their bosses, the elected officials, look good. Like the corporate public relations executive, they want positive publicity. When an investigative reporter wants information, he or she will usually be sent to the public relations official even though the reporter would rather talk directly to those government employees who are the most familiar with the subject.

Gaming Commission.   States have a separate agency or division of a department that regulates gambling. In Nevada, it may be the busiest job in the state government, but elsewhere there may be no licensed gambling provided or only horse or dog races, bingo, or lotteries. The state either runs the games or allows others to run them under strict rules.

Case History: From Food to Fraud

When an editor suggested to Gladys Tydings that she do an investigation of the quality of school food, she thought it sounded like a bad idea. Gladys considered herself the most promising investigative reporter on the newspaper and preferred to investigate police brutality, payoffs in the court system, or conditions at the county jail—anything that sounded more important than school food.

She imagined herself trying to squeeze into a chair built for a fifth grader and eating lunch with school kids. She thought bitterly that because she was a woman, she was being assigned soft stories.

She was somewhat relieved when she was told by her editor that he was looking for a more scientific approach. He wanted her to find out if the new frozen pre-plated meals that were being served to the elementary school children were nutritious and to take a complete look at the local school food program.

First, she gathered some comments from nutrition experts at the state university. She learned that there were minimum nutritional requirements for the food before a federal subsidy would be provided. She was able to get the rules and regulations for the school food program and some nutrition studies they had done from the U.S. Department of Agriculture, which administers the federally funded program. The question, then, was whether the meals being served local school children met those standards.

The story called for an outside expert, so she lined up a commercial laboratory where she could have the food chemically analyzed. They told her to get twelve meals from the food line as they were being served and bring them to the laboratory. There the food would be placed in a giant blender, thoroughly mixed and samples tested.

But Gladys had other ideas. She had already heard stories about how poorly the food was received by the children. They hated it, and they dumped large amounts in the garbage cans. What good were nutrients if the children would not eat the food? Her plan was to pick up the meals at various locations and on different days according to plan, but then she would gather the garbage bags and have the garbage put in the blender to be analyzed, too. They could count the number of discarded trays and divide by that number to get the average amount of nutrients per student that were thrown out. It could then be determined what the school children actually consumed. This would show which of the different meals in different schools were the most successful.

Because she had no authority to go into the schools, Gladys had to sell the idea to principals at several schools. "You've really got me on this one," one of them said. "I don't want the bother, but if I don't agree, parents are going to think there's something wrong with the food."

In carrying out the story, Gladys and another reporter ate the meals themselves at the time they were served so they could add their comments to the story. This also gave them an opportunity to overhear remarks about the food from pupils and teachers.

While she was working on the school food story, Gladys worked on other stories and routinely handled investigative tips for smaller stories or to file away for future use. One day an anonymous tipster called. "I was out at La Casa Chateau House last night and there was a sign out in the lobby pointing to one of the rooms," the caller said. "The sign said 'Board of Education Party,' and I looked in there and saw a wild party going on. They were drinking and really living it up. I don't think they ought to be spending taxpayers' money like that."

Gladys wasn't sure that the school board would spend taxpayers' money for a party, but it was her habit to check out any leads. She called the public relations spokesman for the schools and asked if he knew of the party. He said it probably was some private group of school people who pooled their money to have a party. The schools would not spend official money like that, he assured her. Gladys asked if he would check the school controller's office to see if there had been any expenditures to La Casa Chateau House.

She had an idea that while she was doing a story about the poor quality of the food in the school lunch program, she could contrast it with the blatant spending of money by school board members for their own food. She mentioned her idea to the editor who assigned the story, and he didn't think much of it. "I think it would detract from the main idea of the school food story. You are trying to mix apples and oranges," he said. And the public relations spokesman at the schools called back and said he could find no record of any school money going to La Casa Chateau House.

So Gladys continued her visits to the schools, hauling the food and garbage to the laboratory. The burgers and pizzas and orange sherbet and apple sauce all went into the big mixer and come out a sickly pudding. This was analyzed to reveal the nutrients in the meals.

Gladys produced her story as a three-part series. It could as well have been a TV investigation, and the next year, a local station did a similar study. The newspaper series was innovative, and it was well received by nutrition advocates because it showed what was consumed, not just what was served. Also, the series examined the reasons that the food was not being eaten and showed some of the steps other schools took to improve their food.

This story was the type that could best be told with pictures and graphics. The newspaper had been looking for an opportunity to use more color photography, so pictures of the meals as they were served were printed and then statistics about the nutrients consumed were superimposed.

As Gladys was writing the story and double-checking the facts of the study, she fielded another telephone tip. This time it was not anonymous—it was from a local contractor who had lost a bid to replace the furnaces in all the schools. He complained that the company that got the bid had cheated the schools by not constructing the walls around the furnaces as required in the bid specifications. Two layers of brick were supposed to be put around a concrete center to create a wall to insulate a furnace. The contractor had put two walls of brick up but left the inside empty, the caller said.

The work was completed, so at first she thought the only way the allegation could be proven was to tear down the walls. Doubting that she could get the schools to tear down walls, Gladys had another idea. She arranged to borrow a thermograph, a machine that measures the amount of heat escaping from an object. She would test the walls for the degree of heat escaping and then get expert opinion on whether or not the inner wall was missing. But first, she went to the controller's office at the school administration building to get the specifications for furnace installation.

Gladys told the school controller that she would like to see all of the bids for furnace replacement contracts as well as the vouchers and the payments. He could have required that she write a formal request under the Freedom of Information Act, but because he knew those records to be public, he did not delay the request. He called a clerk into his office and said, "Take her back to the files and help her look up whatever she wants."

As she walked through the office with the clerk, she told him about the furnace bids, and then she said, "Oh, and while we're at it, let's see if there are any payments to La Casa Chateau House." She was thrilled when the clerk dug out a stack of vouchers, bills, and checks from the restaurant that totalled more than $60,000. She got copies. Although she was excited, she did not forget to get copies of the specifications, bids, vouchers, and payments for the furnace work, too. Although she was happy she found the vouchers, she also felt sheepish about having allowed the public spokesman for the schools to fool her earlier. Maybe he didn't look very hard, or maybe he was trying to cover up the expenditures. Either way, Gladys was ashamed that she had been lazy and allowed someone else do her work for her.

The furnace story fell through. The thermography test did not indicate that the concrete center was missing. The losing bidder may have assumed too much. So Gladys pursued the restaurant voucher story. She noticed that the payments to the restaurant, about $4,000 each, came each month for more than a year. They were all charged to a federally funded school program for the economically disadvantaged and were signed by the administrator for the local schools who ran the program. She suggested to her editors that the newspaper examine all of the expenditures of the program to determine the amount of wasted tax dollars, because she knew already about the obvious waste of school money at La Casa Chateau House.

Gladys checked the index of stories in the newspaper library to see if anything had been written about the special school program, the administrator, or La Casa Chateau House. Nothing showed up in the clips on the first two, and there was only one story about the restaurant. The story was about the grand opening, and it turned out to be another break. She noticed that the date on one of the vouchers was before the restaurant had opened. Could it be that the restaurant started up its business and then had a grand opening? She called the manager of the restaurant who said his grand opening was his first night of business. "If somebody had a party out here that night, they had it in the parking lot," he said.

It was obvious that something was amiss. Her investigation now would be of a possible fraud, not just waste of taxpayer money.

When Gladys began asking questions about the special education program, she noticed that the people she questioned were nervous even when they discussed the rules governing the program. It seemed to her that they either didn't know much about it or were afraid to go on the record. The local school superintendent said that the state controlled the program; state officials said that although they examined the expenditures, the rules came from the federal government. A spokesman for the U.S. Department of Education said they had rules, but decisions about the actual expenditures came from the local level. Gladys had been given "the run around." She realized that she had waded into a complex government program. Not only were agencies passing the buck but when it came to getting approval for their expenditures from the school board, the administrators would tell them, "Don't worry about it; it's all federal money."

As she researched the workings of the program, she got all of the information she could find from each level of government. The most valuable source was the application for federal funds required by the U.S. Department of Education. In it, the local school district explained how it intended to use the money. There was no mention of dinner parties. She could now show what the money was intended for and where it was really spent.

Finding out how the money was being used required many trips to the controller's office. Gladys learned from the vouchers that administrators would travel to other cities to examine the operations of special education programs in those cities. Gladys noticed that they would go to southern resort cities in the winter, never northern industrial cities. Then she found that a group of school administrators traveled with their families for ten days, and were reimbursed for a visit to Disneyland at a cost of more than $20,000. Any voucher that was turned in was paid, apparently with no questions asked.

Gladys believed she had learned of enough abuses to start writing her story. She needed to plug in the facts and interviews. And there was still the question of the apparent fraudulent voucher. She started a series of interviews, first with the superintendent. She told him of her findings and learned that he allowed his chief administrators to sign his name on vouchers. (She held back her knowledge of one voucher—for the dinner meeting that could not have been held—for later.)

She checked back with the restaurant owner who opened his files. Many of the dinners had not been scheduled, some had been cancelled, and some had taken place. His contact was one man at the schools, a middle-level administrator.

Gladys confronted the administrator, asking him why he had so many dinner meetings at government expense. He told her they were for the parents of children in the special education program to keep them informed of their children's progress. It was part of his "community outreach" program, he said. Then she asked specifically what the purpose of the dinner meeting was that she knew could not have been held, who was there, and what was accomplished. He related a glowing story and described a meeting on that date, claiming he appeared and welcomed the parents. She told him that she could not understand why the voucher showed a dinner when the restaurant was not open. "I don't remember anything else about it. I have no more comment," he said. Gladys started working the telephone and driving throughout the city, locating and talking to parents of the children in the special education program. None had ever been invited to a dinner.

The story was complete with graphics that showed exactly how much money intended for the special education program went into direct education costs and how much went into other costs. By using the same facts from the annual financial report of the local school and those of other cities, a comparison was made in a chart that alerted readers to the gross misuse of money in the local program. In the story, the mystery of the dinner meetings was presented but still could not be fully explained.

The story resulted in a federal investigation of the program and the indictment and conviction of the administrator who held the dinner parties. Gladys did not cover the trial because her editors thought that she might be partial, having been part of the investigation. She didn't mind; by that time, she was deeply involved in another investigation.

In the trial, the full story of the expenses was revealed. The administrator had arranged a large private dinner for an organization to which he belonged and collected the money from members. He then got the idea to submit the bill to the schools, saying it was for a dinner for parents of special education children. The schools paid the restaurant, and he kept the money from the members. That worked well, so the next time, he put down a deposit of school money for a dinner and then cancelled it and had the refund from the restaurant sent to himself. While in the business office of the restaurant, he stole a pad of the blank forms they use for bills and filled them out, back dating them to show that he held and paid for a dinner meeting every month for the past twelve months. He made the mistake of extending the phony billing back to a date on which the construction of the restaurant had not been completed. The party that the telephone tipster saw was a party he held for himself to celebrate his birthday. He invited people who worked for him, and they brought gifts.

This was the only story Gladys ever worked on that resulted in a criminal conviction. She always believed that a much more important result than the conviction was the tightening of control of the school money. She knew, too, that the story may have stopped others who were improperly or fraudulently spending tax money.

Would the fact that some of the dinners were not held have been detected if Gladys had not found the newspaper clipping about the grand opening? Would it have been appropriate to include the story about the restaurant dinners in the school food story? Should Gladys have been assigned to cover the trial?

Documents and Sources Used in This Investigation

U.S. Department of Agriculture records. This federal department administers farm programs, but it comes into direct contact with city people because it also administers the food stamp program and the school lunch program. Each of those programs involves a government subsidy in which benefits are issued to the most needy.

U.S. Department of Education records. Education is a duty of local government, but when federal money is applied to the education system, this federal agency will administer it and require detailed disclosure from government agencies that apply for the money.

Controller (or comptroller) office. This is the office in government on the local and state level where the bills are paid and records of the payments are kept. It may be a part of the clerk's office or treasurer's office or have another name, like financial office. In some areas a controller is elected, in others he or she is appointed by an elected official.

Vouchers. Before any payment is made, someone has to vouch for the authenticity of the expenditure. An individual in government who has spent money will have to provide a voucher to get reimbursed and one who contracts for purchases will submit a voucher to have a check issued for payment.

Payments. The final step in the purchase process is for the government to issue a check. After the check is cashed it is returned by the bank to the controller and placed in a file, usually attached to the voucher. It provides final proof to a reporter that the work was done and paid with the signature of the recipient on the back of the check.

MEMO

- An investigative reporter works on many story ideas simultaneously and not all of them end up as stories.

- An investigative story can be a scientific study.

- It is poor strategy to allow a government employee to do the reporter's work.

- An investigative reporter may take a story to the point of indicating an impropriety and then let government enforcement officials follow through with proof of a crime.

- An investigative reporter may be excused from follow-up news stories about something he or she investigated.

PROJECT

Outline an investigative project that uses a scientific examination of a service or product.

CHAPTER SIX

Personal Profiles of Public and Private Persons

The most important investigative stories are written about political issues and social problems rather than individuals. However, as a story develops, the roles of individuals become apparent. Although a person may be less important that an issue, readers often remember a character and his or her role in relation to an issue better than the issue itself. The personal profile, then, becomes an important area of investigative journalism.

- Who played the most important role in your story?
- What is his or her background?
- Who are the person's associates?
- What motivates this person?

Personal profiles are often done when a new character comes upon the scene. If a police chief or school superintendent is hired from another city, an investigative profile might be in order. Also, if someone's suspicions are aroused about an individual, or rumors are circulating, the answers may be found while doing an investigative story.

Authorized biographers talk to their subjects and to his or her friends. Investigative reporters talk to a person's enemies and friends and gather all the documents they can find. They talk to their subject *after* they know as much or more about that person than anyone else does.

Some profiles are important enough to stand as separate stories, for example, profiles of political candidates or influential private citizens. Investigative reporters also do small profiles of persons important to their stories as they progress through an investigation, or they may do a larger profile of one person as a sidebar to a main story.

The information learned in an interview will steer the reporter toward documents. He or she learns that the subject of the investigation was divorced, was born in another state, or is licensed in a certain profession. The next step is to search for divorce court files, a birth certificate, and licenses. These may lead to other documents or to interviews which lead to other documents or interviews until the search is exhausted.

Another way to approach the personal profile is to first scan for documents. A reporter can search indexes for court cases, property transfers, and licenses. A short official biography of a notable person that might be found in campaign literature or in a biographical directory like *Who's Who* gives some clues about where to start looking. The reporter also looks for stories published about the subject.

But a reporter might want to investigate a person whose name has never appeared in a newspaper. Everyone generates public records. As we are born, educated, married, and employed, we leave a trail of public and private records. The paper accumulates. A newborn baby has a birth certificate and medical records. Adults have a driver's license, social security card, voter registration, school and employment records, and maybe a criminal arrest record for a traffic violation. An older business person or public official accumulates the most paper: divorce proceedings, real estate purchases, mortgages, liens, incorporation documents, and civil and criminal court cases.

When a person dies his or her life story is wrapped up in even more paper. There is a death certificate showing how, when, and where the person died. If it is a violent death, there will be an autopsy and a police report. And if the distribution of an estate is to be determined in probate court, all of the assets will be displayed in the public file.

An investigation of a person can start at the beginning, end, or anywhere in the middle of the documented life and, with little information, move in either direction. An investigation of a person could start with no more than an automobile license number or the dates on a tombstone.

Let's start with a name. It could be the name of another student about whom you know nothing. (We hope that the name is not too common!) If you have seen this person, you can guess his or her age.

1. Ask for driver information about everyone with this name from the state department that licenses automobiles and drivers. This may require a written request. The date of birth should be included in the information you get. Even in the case of a common name you may determine which of these persons is your subject from the date of birth or address. (If driver's information is not public in your state, you may have to start with voter registration information.)

2. Take the date of birth to the county clerk and get information from the person's birth certificate. If you don't have the date of birth, ask

the county clerk if you may scan the birth records and look for the name during the years you believe the person was born. Some counties have birth records indexed by name. Success depends on the size of the county and if the subject was born in the county where he or she now resides.

3. Driver information and birth information give you an address. Birth information shows parents' names, which can be checked in a phone book or city directory for an address. With an address in hand, you could get voter registration information from the authority that oversees local elections. This shows the dates of birth of everyone who votes from that address, which gives a clue to family relationships.

4. The investigation may branch out in several directions. Property records show when the residence was bought and the size of the mortgage. If it is an apartment building, there may be building inspection reports that describe its condition.

5. Once the person's age and address are known, it may be possible to get a high school yearbook with a picture, names of classmates, and even some information about the subject's school activities.

Background interviews of friends and neighbors move the investigation along. Their information can be checked against documents to make sure that each document refers to the right person and not someone with the same name.

But the final assurance that the information is valid comes when the person is interviewed and either confirms, denies, or corrects the information. Chances are, the person will be surprised at the thoroughness of the preparation of the reporter and will not try to mislead. One of the results of investigating a person who is an average citizen rather than a public figure is the realization that everyone is interesting.

Investigating the Elected Official

An investigation of a public figure, especially one with private business interests who holds elected office, yields a great deal of information from documents. The amount of paperwork may be so great that it will be necessary to set aside a period of time to organize and interpret the information before moving on to interviews. From the moment a person enters politics as a candidate, he or she is involved in a swirl of paper that is public information:

- The nominating petition reveals who worked to get signatures so that the person could appear on the ballot.

- The campaign disclosure form shows who paid what money and how it was spent on the campaign.
- The financial disclosure statement requires disclosure of private business affairs in varying degree according to the requirements of different states.

After the person is elected, even more goes into the record:

- Minutes of the public meetings attended, voting record, and even the words spoken in public discussions.
- Salary and expense vouchers.
- Names and salaries of employees and expenditures for an office.

Investigating Other Public Figures

It is generally accepted that a person does not have to be an elected official or public employee to be considered a public figure. Entertainment and sports personalities are written about more than others, but heads of giant corporations and experts in certain fields are often considered public figures, although their business transactions may all be private.

These private citizens also have public records that are available to the reporter, and the reporter must keep in mind also that the public official has a dual life as a private citizen, with the same possibilities of available information:

- Records of civil or criminal lawsuits, divorce cases, probate information.
- Bids and contacts for government work and applications for grants or government loans.
- Records of real estate transactions, mortgages, and liens recorded against property.

And then it is time for the close-out interview. Because the public figure is successful, he or she is usually attractive to the public. This person has learned to be quick with answers and to be pleasant and friendly. He or she may appear to be warm and open—and very convincing. Often the reporter must resist falling under the spell of the successful person. A good reporter absorbs all the information from the interview and then takes time to judge it for its worth.

The reporter has to keep the interview on the right track. He or she will usually find it counterproductive to let the subject go off the record, to ramble, and to avoid direct answers to the questions asked. There are circumstances when the subject may not have the specific answers, and the reporter will have to arrange to call back for that information. For example, if a reporter finds that there is a record of a tax lien on the property of the subject, and this person says it was paid but the tax lien was not released, the reporter would want to give the subject time to show evidence of the payment. Usually a deadline is set. The reporter says, "I'll call you on Friday to see if you have found it." Lacking the information on Friday, the reporter could write that a lien appeared, the subject said it was paid but could supply no evidence, and no release appeared in the record.

A Danger Zone

Stories about private persons and privately held businesses require the greatest degree of care. It is more likely that a libel or slander suit will result from a negative story about a private person or business than from favorable stories, or from a negative story about a political figure because of the emotional impact it has on the subject.

Investigative reporters believe that they are more likely to be a target of lawsuits than other reporters, because they wade into sensitive areas. A reporter who specializes in reporting on real estate development and always reports what the developers say is not as prone to attack as the reporter who reveals information that someone is trying to hide. Investigative reporters usually write negative stories. Even in a more balanced profile, negative information that has not been previously revealed will be included. However, being prone to attack does not mean that the investigative reporter is vulnerable if caution is taken and the law is understood.

Libel law covers the written word and slander law covers the spoken word, but they are similar in their purpose. To win a libel or slander suit, the aggrieved party will try to show (1) damage, (2) malice, and (3) untruth. Anyone can file a libel or slander suit, and the ruling of a jury can be unpredictable. So it is impossible to say that there is a sure defense against being sued or losing a suit.

But a reporter can be all but safe if he or she guards against two of the three elements. Those are untruth and malicious intent.

Untruth

An investigative reporter will do everything possible to make sure that what he or she writes is true. Not only will each fact be true, but the information will not be conveyed in a way that gives it a false meaning.

The hazards of libel and slander should not be compared with the hazard of malpractice that a medical doctor faces. A slip of the knife or an infection cannot be easily corrected. A wrong statement in the newspaper or a broadcast can be corrected. If, despite care, a reporter has reported an untruth, it may be possible to print a retraction.

Malicious Intent

Intent is difficult to prove in any legal circumstances. But if it can be shown that a reporter had a private reason for writing an untrue statement or knew something to be untrue when he or she wrote it, that reporter is open to an accusation of malicious intent.

An investigative reporter will not launch into an investigation to get even with someone and will stay away from stories about persons or companies with which he or she has had personal dealings. For example, malicious intent could be shown if the reporter had trouble with an insurance claim and then investigated and wrote an untruth about that company's claim practices.

While gathering information from interviews of associates of the subject of a profile, the reporter takes care to not make derogatory remarks about the subject (even if the reporter believes maligning the person would help gain information from the interview).

Damage

Because investigative stories reveal negative information that persons try to hide, this information may cause damage to the subject. A reporter will not always be able to control or be concerned with the extent of this damage if a true and unbiased story is to be written. However, if the investigation of a person or business is limited to a certain area, a good reporter would mention that the problem that is exposed does not extend to other operations. For instance, if the investigation is of improper financial manipulations by the head of a hospital, the reporter could state that this investigation is not critical of or did not examine the quality of care at the hospital. This would limit damage from a misunderstanding that everything about the hospital was improper, which would be an unfair and counterproductive conclusion.

In producing an investigative story, reporters must take care to not harm an innocent bystander. If a story exposes a wrongdoing, reporters will be careful to set out the case factually so that subjects will have no recourse for correction or lawsuit. Let's say the subject of an investigative story is violent bill collectors. A victim might be quoted as saying he was beaten by a man who was trying to collect a debt that was actually one incurred by his ex-wife. The bill collector was arrested and convicted. Unintentionally, the man's ex-wife, not the bill collector, could be harmed if it turns out that the debt really was the victim's and not his ex-wife's, an element that the reporter neglected to check. Although the ex-wife was not named, she could argue that all her friends know she was married to the man who was quoted, and it was implied in the story that she is a deadbeat. A correction and apology would be in order.

Civil suits charging invasion of privacy under separate provisions of the law may also result from a story. These laws protect a person from unreasonable disclosure of private, personal information without public or newsworthy purpose. If the subject of the investigation is truly newsworthy and the reporter has not stolen private information, he or she would have a strong defense against invasion of privacy.

Even without the specter of lawsuits, the investigative reporter should be a slave to truth and accuracy. A slight inaccuracy can call for an embarrassing correction which can be used as a weapon to counterattack by the target of the investigation and destroy the story's goal of reform. A reporter could write a five-part series that exposes millions of dollars of waste and corruption in city government. But if one small, statistical error was made, the city administration could blow that inaccuracy far out of proportion in public statements and use it to soften the impact of the entire project.

Because they are seeking the truth, investigative reporters are able to live with libel and slander laws without being constrained by them. Perhaps they even appreciate them. Libel and slander laws prevent a person from making up and distributing a lie about someone they want to hurt. For a society to allow such behavior would be similar to sanctioning physical attack on a person. Knowing there are such laws, readers have confidence in the news they read and hear, and reporters are therefore more influential.

MEMO

- Everyone leaves a trail of documents.

- An investigative reporter must have respect for, but not fear of, libel laws.

GLOSSARY

Sidebar.   A small, related story, usually of a feature nature, that accompanies a large, more general story in a newspaper.

Off the record.   In journalism, reporters may accept a condition where the subject of an interview goes "off the record" to explain something that he or she does not wish to make public, sometimes because of legal constraints. The reporter and subject agree that this information will not be attributed to the subject. "Off the record" is like time-out in sports. The reporter must remember to get the subject back "on the record" as soon as possible. In gathering information, the reporter grants off-the-record rights more freely than in a close-out interview of a subject. Then he or she wants answers to specific allegations.

Case History: The Hazards of Gathering a Personal Profile

Both Bud Munn and Gladys Tydings started their investigative reporting careers by checking out information that was provided to them by others, substantiating it with records and interviews, and writing the story.

Both reporters have found that they are seldom lucky enough to have the most important investigative stories brought in by an informant and laid at their feet to be checked out. They have learned that larger investigative stories have to be worked from the outside to the inside.

With his years of experience in following the paper trail, Bud Munn can approach a subject with scant prior knowledge and determine if there is an investigative story that needs to be produced. His editors have often ordered up an investigative story by telling him to "take a look" at a certain government agency or person.

The high style of living of Councilman Gray had been noticed by a few people, who commented about it to reporters and editors. "Take a look," Bud's editor's told him.

After checking newspaper clips for background material already published about Gray, a young councilman in his first term, Bud and another reporter arranged an interview with him. They told him that they might want to do a profile of him and indicated that they would take a "hard look" at him. He agreed, saying, "I've got nothing to hide." A meeting was set for the next week.

Meanwhile, Bud checked the indexes of court cases and land records looking for the councilman's name as a plaintiff or defendant or a purchaser or seller. He also checked with the Uniform Commercial Code section in the Secretary of State's office to learn if Gray had been listed as having borrowed money on equipment. He got Gray's ethics statement and campaign disclosure records. And he got driver's license information and voter registration forms, available to him as matters of public record.

Bud began asking other councilmen, both Gray's friends and his political opponents, about anything they knew about him. Because Gray was a lawyer, Bud got a helpful biography from an attorneys' association directory he found in the public library. He then checked with the county court clerk to see if attorneys were indexed according to cases they represent to get an idea of who Gray's clients were. When he found the clerk did not index cases by attorney name, he took an hour and browsed through court docket sheets, looking for Gray's name as the attorney on cases, noting and pulling the court case files.

The interview with Gray was cordial. While one reporter asked questions, the other wrote the answers. Bud's questions were more specific than those of the other reporter, whose specialty was political reporting.

"I decided at an early age to devote myself to a life of public service and have given it my full effort since my election," Gray said.

Bud asked Gray how he was able to find time for the many businesses he operated on the side, including a consulting firm. Gray could barely disguise his surprise that Bud knew of those activities, but he managed to say that his accountant handled most of his other business affairs, and he had little knowledge of them.

Bud then asked Gray if he was still active in his old law firm, having made thirty-six appearances in court for clients in the past year. Gray said that he did this as a favor to his former clients.

Gray then gave more specific information about those cases and his relationship with his clients. It had been Bud's experience from other interviews that once the interviewee knew that Bud had factual information about his or her background and current activities, the interviewee would be reluctant to misrepresent anything because of fear of being exposed as a liar.

When Bud asked how the councilman was able to live in such affluence on a city council salary, Gray became irritated. "I'm sure my political enemies put you up to this. My private finances are personal. I've been fortunate in my investments, and my family left me very comfortable. Also, I suppose I'm just one of those people who don't mind spending their money instead of stashing it away. In my public life, I've also given away my time and money to many charitable causes."

After the interview, the other reporter told Bud, "I guess he cleared himself. We don't have a thing to go on."

- Was it unfair to approach the subject of an investigation without telling him that an investigation was underway?
- Our legal system guarantees that a person be faced by his accusers. Why are those persons who are suspicious of the councilman hiding their identities behind the reporters? Is there a story?

"He's stealing something; I just don't know yet what it is," Bud said after the interview. One of the reasons Bud was so adamant was because of the information he had from his earlier records check, information that he had withheld from the interview.

Divorce court and other court records are public unless sealed by a court order. They often show the assets of a couple. Gray had been divorced for ten years, and the only assets he showed were a seven-year-old car and $315 in the bank. The probate court file of his father's estate, also a public record, showed total assets of $22,000 divided among four children, hardly enough for Gray to pay for the expensive home and cars that he now owned. Gray was hardly living from paycheck to paycheck, Bud learned, because eighteen months earlier he had paid off the $110,000 mortgage on his home, according to records filed with the county. So Bud went back to work with the public records and interviews.

Bud had learned by reading through the dockets of court cases in the circuit court, where lawyers write in their names when they file a case, that Gray continued his law practice after he was elected and appeared thirty-six times in court. He checked the names of the parties in the cases who were represented by Gray and set out to learn what he could about those people and corporations through interviews and public records.

The trail led Bud to the city council minutes. He found that each of Gray's clients had gone to the city council for favors. Most of them had asked for zoning variances, and Gray had supported their requests according to minutes of the council meetings and zoning committee hearings. He got on the phone and asked some of the private individuals whom Gray had represented why they chose Gray as their lawyer. They said that Gray sent them to his law firm when they came to Gray's city council office for advice on problems they were having.

At first, few of Gray's clients would talk to Bud about their dealings with Gray, but Bud showed them that he had public records of their zoning requests and legal connections. After that, some told him that they had hired Gray to do consulting work. The consulting work was to advise them on how to get their requests for zoning variances through the city council.

As Bud was organizing his information to interview Gray again before writing a story that would accuse Gray of profiting from his position on the city council, Gray held a news conference, which Bud and reporters from other media attended.

"My political enemies have been attempting to discredit me by having reporters contact my legal clients to harrass them into saying that they bought influence in the city council by retaining me," he read from a prepared statement. Then two prominent businessmen spoke in behalf of the councilman. They said they had used Gray's services because he was a good lawyer, he had not solicited business from them, and he never suggested that employing him would influence his vote.

The reporters (except for Bud) were puzzled about why Gray would make a denial before any accusation was made. Bud realized that some of the people he had contacted had gone to Gray and told him what type of information Bud was gathering about him.

- Should Bud stand up in the news conference and accuse Gray of having a pattern of clients who got favors?
- Should he attempt to write a story, and, if so, should he include the denial?
- Should he investigate those businessmen who sided with Gray to see if they had a history of questionable business practices?

Gray would be discredited if Bud stood up at the news conference and stated what he knew. But Bud knew that he must suppress such a desire so that he could remain impartial and not become a part of the story himself.

Bud knew that his exclusive story had been damaged, because Gray had aired much of it to his competitors. But if Bud confronted Gray with all of the facts at this time, any advantage he had over his competitors would be lost. Bud had a choice. He could immediately publish his story and include the denial or continue to gather information for a fuller, more important story.

Bud planned not only to include Gray's full denial in his story but also to call him and ask about some of the other details so that he could include those explanations and denials in the story. Bud knew that if he did not give Gray a chance for a full rebuttal, Gray could hold another news conference and claim again that he had been attacked unfairly. Slightly wounded and greatly skeptical of Gray's motives, Bud took refuge in the skills he had as an investigator and continued his investigation.

The substance of Bud's story was that Gray had become wealthy by using his public office indirectly. This brought up the question of a possible conflict of interest in zoning matters. The state law prohibited any state legislator from "accepting any business opportunity that could influence his vote," and the legislator could be removed from office if such a conflict were proved. But as a local official, Gray did not fall under this ruling. The local government had some rules, including one that prohibited an elected official from bidding on a contract with the government body, but Gray had violated no specific rules.

The newspaper realized that any misconduct by Gray was a gray area.

It could choose to run the story or drop it completely. What would you decide to do?

The Case for Yes

As long as the story is fair and it states the facts in a straightforward manner, whether or not a law has been broken should not be considered. The city council should institute better ethics rules for its members, and this story could initiate such action.

Gray is a public figure who may seek higher office. If there are significant untold facts about him, it is the duty of the newspaper to publish them.

The Case for No

Gray's personal business is of no concern to the public. The reporter is trying to make something out of nothing, because he has a grudge against Gray. The people who came to the editors with the idea of the story are jealous of Gray's success.

The public should be concerned about major local issues like running a good school system, holding down taxes, and providing for the safety of the residents, not some personal information about an individual public official.

The newspaper may be inviting libel action by delving into private matters without the consent of the subject of the story.

The Decision

Because no one sets rules for subject matter in the media, the choice rests with the editor. He or she will have to make the decision of whether or not to publish based on the weight of the material in the story—its interest and importance. The editor may say, "We don't have it," or, "We need more stories like this."

Bud got his story in the paper and set an example of how public records could be used. The story was acclaimed by readers. Because of Bud's success with the story, all reporters at the newspaper now check some public records even when doing a feature article about an important person or subject.

After the story ran, Bud was invited to debate with Gray, but he declined, pointing out that he was a reporter of, rather than a participant in, the political process. However, Gray's political enemies did use the information against him in his reelection campaign.

Bud was irritated by the businessmen who supported Gray, believing them to be insincere; but he made no special effort to do critical stories about them. He had a personal rule that he would decide whether or not to investigate on the merits of the story, not on any personal feelings he had.

MEMO

- An investigative story can explore questions of ethics that might not be clear-cut violations of law.

- An investigative reporter should make every effort to remove him- or herself from participation in the events reported.

Documents Used in This Story

Court docket sheets. To keep track of the progress of a court case, a clerk keeps a running list of each development in a case alongside the date it occurred, starting with the day it was filed. A reporter can find the names of parties to the suit and of attorneys and judges, and a brief summary of what happened each time the case came up for a hearing.

Divorce records. To get a divorce, one of the marriage partners sues the other in divorce court. As in other courts, the file is public. There may be charges and countercharges of mental and physical abuse, but a reporter does not accept these as fact. He or she usually seeks to learn the assets of the couple which are stated and divided.

Probate records. If the estate of a deceased person is to be divided by the court, the file will be public. It shows not only the total amount of the estate and the taxes paid on it, but also the names of the heirs and real estate and stocks inventoried and divided.

UCC filings. The Uniform Commercial Code establishes a system in each state whereby a lender can record a loan made on movable equipment against the name of the person or corporation that put up the equipment as security for the loan. That way, the same equipment can't be used again and again for loans. This is similar to recording a mortgage loan on fixed property. A reporter can contact the Uniform Commercial Code office in state government, submit a name, and be told if there is a loan outstanding. The value to the reporter is that he or she may learn that the subject of the investigation has taken out a loan on property that no one knew he or she owned.

CHAPTER SEVEN

Producing the Investigative Story

News people say that the best news stories inform, educate, and entertain, an axiom that investigative reporters are likely to forget when they sit down to write. Because of the importance they perceive in the information they have gathered, reporters tend to write long columns of gray type that read like a grand jury indictment. And those in broadcasting write copy that would suit the foreman of a jury.

Reporters are tempted to write every detail of a convoluted financial transaction, reporting on each document assembled and every dollar spent, weaving names and titles in a web of interrelationships. What does it all mean? Impressed but baffled by the complex story a newspaper has offered, the reader skips to the sports section, and the TV viewer switches off.

How to Write Investigative Features and Breaking Stories

Investigative reporters are faced with one of the most difficult of writing assignments. They must make an understandable story out of the mountain of information that they have gathered and have become emotionally attached to. They must judge the story material in a detached manner and then organize and write a story for persons who have no prior knowledge of the subject. They also must somehow preserve its importance, accuracy, and excitement.

Knowing the difficulty of such a job, some editors have turned to team efforts in investigative reporting. One reporter gathers and another writes. Or, a reporter/writer's material is heavily edited. But it is also possible for one investigative reporter to get an idea, pursue the investigation, and write a complete story. To accomplish that, broadcast reporters will tell their story with fewer words than the print reporter. But each will have the same organizational problems, and the goals of each will be to educate, inform, and entertain.

What the reporter/writer will do can be shown as a step-by-step process: (1) determining the thrust; (2) making the sacrifice; (3) lining up the ducks; (4) deciding on the format; (5) setting the tone; and (6) conveying documentation.

The Thrust

The reporter ponders exactly what he or she is going to tell the reader or viewer. Looking over the massive information gathered, let's say about the waterworks, the reporter questions if there should be a personal profile of the man who runs the city waterworks, telling all that's known of a corrupt past. Or should the story tell how inefficiently the waterworks is run? Or should the story deal with the dual facts that the waterworks is being inefficiently run by a man with a corrupt past?

The reporter/writer usually finds the thrust long before all the information has been gathered and it is time to write. The discovery is most likely to come while the information is being collected. With the thrust in mind as he or she closes out the investigation, the reporter gathers what is needed to make the point of the story clear.

The Sacrifice

Let's say that, in this story, the reporter has decided that the thrust is the inefficient operation of the waterworks, because the cost to the taxpayers and the potential hazards are more important to the readers than the person who heads the waterworks. That means the reporter has accepted the reality that "all that good stuff" about the waterworks superintendent from his bitterly contested divorce case is going to be thrown out despite how hard it was to get and how much fun it was to read. It is a sacrifice that must be made. It was important to research the divorce because the case listed the marital assets and could have shown a business interest in a company that might have done work with the city. But it did not. And to drag incidentals of the divorce into the story would cause readers to be confused.

The sacrificial step is not easy, but it can be done through self-discipline. Disagreements may occur among reporting team members about what should be tossed out, but a proper decision is important to the success or even survival of a project.

The *"Line of Ducks"*

With the thrust in mind and the superfluous information stored away, the reporter/writer can "line up the ducks." At this point the reporter knows what he or she has but may not know what is missing. By laying out all the facts, the absence of a few "ducks" can be spotted. This must be done at the time of writing. And it has been the investigator's responsibility all along to gather facts that are meaningful and contribute to the story. The reporter may have been writing the story in his or her mind as the investigation progressed. The lead and the supporting paragraphs may be formed, and the reporter has been looking for the bits and pieces needed to support that lead. But even at the time of writing, most investigative stories will need more research.

When a first version of an investigative story goes to an editor, questions are generated that call for more research. When a reporter works alone, he or she must function as an editor and refrain from writing around the missing information in the rush to get a story done. The missing facts must be plugged in. Most of the time, the last minute questions can be dealt with quickly because they are probably clarifications of information that is not specific enough. But this stage of the gathering and writing could also mean the life or death of the story. Has the reporter reached an erroneous conclusion? Suppose the thrust has been that the cost of water is high because of inefficiency in the waterworks administration, and this conclusion is based on a comparison of water rates with another city. But the reporter has not considered that the major reason the other city has low rates is that it is situated on one of the Great Lakes so has abundant water reserves. The reporter's city is far inland and must maintain an expensive reservoir system. The reporter hopes to catch such a flaw, but should not bemoan the fact that an editor or an associate finds it. The reporter's immediate embarrassment is small compared to the later public embarrassment that he or she would have experienced.

"Lining up ducks" may call for writing an outline. If the story is long or has more than one part, it is obvious that an organizational outline is needed. Even a short investigative story may benefit from an outline to determine the progression of the material.

At this stage, imbalance can also be spotted. Reporters try to achieve balance in their reporting and writing by giving equal attention to the many sides of a controversy. In investigative reporting, there can be balance of a sort, but the purpose of the investigative story is to drive home a point that has been concluded from facts that have been gathered. Therefore, the story is weighted heavily to one side. To achieve some balance in the investigative story it is necessary to give the person about whom any allegation is made an opportunity for response. When any opinion is expressed, the reporter must seek contrary opinions.

The thrust is known, the usable material lined up, and all of the questions are answered. Is it time for a lead paragraph? Not yet.

The Format

Before a writer can decide on the lead, he or she must decide if this story is to be written as a straight news story, a serious feature, or a lighter vignette approach.

The straight news story.   An investigative story is a news story even though it did not originate from an outside agency. It can be treated as if it did, but instead of attributing it to an outside source, the writer can say "a Daily News investigation has revealed." After that, individual documents or persons may be cited as attribution for specific details. The tone of the writing is not unique. It is no different from the news story in the column adjacent to it.

The news feature.   A logo or information box may be inserted into the copy of a feature-style story. This will alert the reader to the fact that the story is an investigation, the scope of the subject investigated, if it is part of a series of stories, and the names of the reporters who worked on it. This frees the writer to use an anecdotal lead or any of the other skills of creative writing that aid in telling the story. The tone of the writing is heavily narrative as in story telling, and there may be some light editorial expression that is not found in the straight news story.

The vignette feature.   A small feature about one incident or character can run as a sidebar to a series of feature articles or stand alone. A vignette usually is centered on an individual or an incident, and gives the writer room for creativity. Not all investigative stories portend the end of the world, although a good investigative reporter believes that the story in the works at that moment is the most important story of his or her career. Even if the story is important, the approach can be light-hearted: "When city hall people dine out, taxpayers pick up the tab." Stories that lend themselves to a light touch are those which deal with small amounts of money and common issues with which the reader is familiar, such as the public transportation system, driver's license examinations, or auto repairs. The writing can be fun, and the story will be appreciated and remembered.

But even after the format for the story is established, the story can't be written until the reporter/writer's mind is in sync with the tone of the story.

The Tone

The tone is set by the choice of words and a formal or informal style. Writers seldom think about the tone because they instinctively adapt their writing style to the message of the story, just as a speaker changes the tone of his or her voice when changing from talk of the commonplace to the bizarre. The tone of the writing must be established. Mistakes can be made in the tone. All investigative stories need not be shrill and accusatory, tinged with sarcasm, or loaded with reporting jargon. The reporter/writer tries to make a point with facts and must not allow opinion to creep into the story, as in an angry letter to the editor.

Could the story be told better if the writer calmly presented the facts? Reporting jargon can be spotted easily. It is a combination of police jargon picked up by reporters a generation or two ago in police press rooms and salted with the headline writers' favorite words. Is a city worker routinely called a "payroller"? Does the reporter write that one man was "an agent," "representative," or "nominee" of another? Or that one man "fronted" for the other? When the writer has a question about the tone, he or she may read the story aloud. Hearing the words helps a writer decide if those words and the tone of voice that results from speaking them are appropriate for the story.

Conveying Documentation

When the facts of an investigative story are organized, the goal of the reporter is to convey them fairly, without editorial comment. As the reporter organizes various items of documentation, he or she must recognize different levels of reliability. For example, students write information on paper when they take notes in class; the notes provide documentation. The notes do not provide proof of what was said in class—only some indication of what the student understood to be said. The documentation is just as reliable as the person who wrote it. The reporter must have some sense of the accuracy of the documentation used in the story.

A student wears a shirt with the name of a university printed on it. Does this prove that the student went to that university? No, it only shows that the student has a shirt with the name of a university printed on it. But the shirt might provide a clue, leading the reporter to check to learn if the student went to the university.

At the other end of the spectrum of documentation is a sworn official statement, such as voting registration, recorded court testimony, or birth and death certificates. A reporter would be lucky if all documentation were sworn official documents. But perhaps some of the least reliable documentation is often necessary for an investigative story. How can a reporter judge which is the most reliable of the documents? How does one know whether the town clerk was sober or intoxicated when he wrote the minutes of the meeting? How can one state as a fact that a political candidate got a certain amount of dollars for a campaign unless one knows the candidate was truthful when he or she filled out the forms?

The answer is that the reporter doesn't know and may never know. But the resolution of the problem is simple. Just as a reporter does not insert editorial comment into stories, he or she does not state that the documentation is true. Instead, the reporter states the facts and tells readers where they came from so the reader may decide. This simple device is called "attribution." Through attribution, the reporter is off the hook; the burden of truth is placed on the document itself.

The reporter attributes all documentation. If it can't be attributed, it is not documentation. The reporter writes that the candidate raised a certain number of dollars, *according to his campaign disclosure forms.* He got a $200,000 loan on his home *records in the county recorder's files indicate.* A business had certain assets and liabilities *it was reported to bankruptcy court.* Such attribution not only passes the buck but also assures the reader that the story is well researched.

When format, tone, and relevant material are properly lined up, the writing can flow. Several drafts will be made before a final version is approved. The reporter and editor will scan the story to check and recheck any questionable statements. As a matter of routine, an experienced reporter will make last-minute reconfirmations of facts, reworking statistics and going back to original notes and documents, to feel absolutely sure of the story, so that when it is locked up, he or she will sleep well.

MEMO

- Investigative stories don't have to be written solemnly or dryly.

- All styles of writing can be used for investigative stories.

- Investigative reporters often write their stories in their heads as they gather information.

- Investigative reporters can't hope to get all their information into a story, no matter how much it hurts to trim.

PROJECT

Write a straight investigative story by using the information that Gladys gathered about the mayor of Eastchester in the first case history in this book. Here is some more information you may or may not want to use in your story:

In this fictitious setting, the name of the mayor is Ward Healy. He is fifty-five and has two children—Ward, Jr. and Chester. He is a member of the East-chester Better Citizens party. His third four-year term as mayor expires next year. Last year, the mayor received an award—Distinguished Knight of the Perplexed Order.

On March 13 of last year, the town advertised for bids on a remodelling job on the town hall. On May 1, bids were opened by the town board in its regular meeting. Perfectly Pure Construction Company had the lowest bid of $1.1 million. But Travis Fellows, a town board member and political crony from the same political party as Mayor Healy, moved that the board accept a higher bid of $1.3 million from Flo-thru Construction Corporation because, he said, "They've got a good reputation, and besides, I'm not sure Perfectly Pure can really do it that cheaply." Fellows owns a dairy and has been divorced twice. A vote to accept Flo-thru was held, and the members voted 2 to 2. The mayor cast a tie-breaking vote in favor of Flo-thru.

The work was done November 1, and vouchers for $1.8 million were submitted to the town treasurer, who paid out that amount the next week. There was no record of any inspection of the work before it was paid for.

Corporate records filed with the state showed that Flo-thru was incorporated January 15 the same year. Ward Healy was the president, and his wife, Flo, was the secretary. When questioned, Mayor Healy did not deny ownership. "I did it because I wanted the work to be done right. I don't want some outside people coming in here and messing up everything." Asked if he believed he was in violation of the state conflict of interest law, Healy said, "I'm not familiar with that law. I'll have the town attorney take a look at it." Asked why there was no inspection, Healy said, "Oh, I knew the work was done okay."

Here is part of the wording of the state law: "No elected official may have a financial interest in any contract in which he votes in his official capacity and no administrator of a governmental unit may have a financial interest in any contract granted by his governmental unit." The penalty is removal from office.

Exercise: Writing the Investigative Feature

The following story was written in 1978 as a single, stand-alone feature in a group of investigative stories by the *Chicago Tribune* about problems of the elderly. It was reported by John Gorman and written by Ray Moseley.

> Navajo, Ariz. John Plummer, 60, remembers the idyllic promises made in the brochures for Big Valley Ranches: abundant water, recreation, a town nearby for convenient shopping, swimming pools, and "just wonderful living."

In one short paragraph, the writer of this consumer-oriented investigative story has told the reader that this is a story about people, their experiences and their feelings. Already, an ominous note has been sounded. Something "idyllic" has been promised. Could it be delivered?

> Life in Big Valley hasn't exactly been like that for Plummer, a retired engineer from Fort Wayne, Indiana, and his wife, Opal, since they bought land here five years ago.

The writer has immediately questioned whether the promises were kept and has supplied the reader with more background information to identify the people involved and what happened to them.

> The Plummers live in a mobile home on scrub land that is scorched by blistering heat in summer and raked by freezing winds in winter. There is no town nearby, "and there probably never will be," Plummer said. Their nearest neighbor is five miles away, and they travel 150 miles to Gallup, N.M., to shop because it is less expensive than anywhere closer.

The idyllic promises in the lead paragraph have been questioned, and the reader is made to feel sympathy for people who have now emerged as victims.

> Lots of water, the brochure said. Plummer said he drilled two wells and spent $19,091 before he found water.
> The brochure mentioned electric power and other utilities. "After we moved in and there was still no power, we went to the power company, and the man said he didn't know anything about it," Plummer said. "He figured it would cost about $850 a month to get electricity out here."
> Plummer has his own generator, powered by a gas engine. He runs it intermittently because running it 24 hours a day would cost $9,000 a year.
> The brochure spoke of "rich, fertile alluvial soil" that would grow almost anything "when touched with the magic of water." Plummer said he planted a garden and watered it from April to August but nothing came up. He believes the soil is too sandy.

The writer has now used a device of comparing the official version, as stated in the brochure, side-by-side with what was alleged by buyers.

> Plummer, who had not seen the land when he bought it, paid $14,400 for his 80-acre retirement retreat in the back of nowhere, and he can hardly believe what happened to him.
> "It knocked the socks right off me. I saved all my life and now

we're down to nothing. If I had it to do over again, I'd have stayed in Fort Wayne."

The writer uses realistic quotes. Many others in the same circumstances were interviewed, and the writer had the luxury of using as a lead a quote from the victim who expressed himself best.

A lot of other landowners—mostly elderly people who came to this area to retire and to escape the hard Northern winters—also wish they had it to do over again.

The writer has used the quote as a transition to a statement that shows concern about the widespread problem, not just one victim.

There are 250 families on 65,000 acres in Big Valley, and thousands more in other land developments across the Sun Belt who have found that reality falls short of the glowing brochures, the fascinating sales spiels, and the bright dreams nurtured in their pre-retirement years.

This may be the "nut graph" of the story, that paragraph that explains the overall problem to be examined. If it were written as a straight news story, the "nut graph" might stand as the lead to the story.

The 11-million member American Association of Retired Persons and the National Retired Teachers Association have said that "fraud and deception in the land sales industry are two of the more serious consumer problems facing our members."

The "nut graph" has been backed up by statements by authorities who present statistics.

The land developments in question are concentrated in New Mexico, Arizona, Colorado, Florida, Texas, and California.

The writer has now established the scope of the investigative story. He will now proceed with a story about how elderly people are lured to some retirement developments.

Many people buy such land as an investment, often taking it sight unseen. When they try to sell it several years later, they find in many cases that the land is worth less than they paid for it. Typically, the developers show them brochures with pictures of happy people having drinks beside a swimming pool, lovely homes with expansive lawns, and handsome tennis courts and golf courses.

The writer has qualified what would otherwise be a sweeping condemnation of all land sales in certain states. He has used qualifying words: *many, often, in many cases,* and *typically.*

What the buyers do not realize is that the amenities pictured are usually confined to a small core area. Beyond that there may be only barren, windblown range land, miles from paved roads, utility lines, and shopping.

It's tough to get sympathy for someone who buys land without seeing it, so the writer goes into detail about how it could happen.

Testimony before the House Banking, Finance, and Urban Affairs subcommittees in 1977 indicated that much of the land sold so far is subject to earthquakes, landslides, or floods.

The federal and state governments have begun cracking down on developers using fraudulent promises to peddle such land at wildly inflated prices, and some of the elderly victims have banded together to bring lawsuits. But many of them may be unable to recover their money.

The Arizona attorney general's office is trying to close down the Big Valley Land Company and obtain restitution for victims like the Plummers. The company's assets have been frozen, and it has been prohibited from selling land pending the outcome of the state's suit.

It is shown that governmental agencies are aware of the problem and can take action. There is some hope, but no guarantee that anyone will get money back.

According to Thomas McClory, an assistant attorney general, Big Valley bought 60,000 acres from two ranchers for $200 an acre and sold most of it for about $400 an acre before further sales were blocked.

Some statistics are given to show the amount of money involved.

Royden Brown, a small, sun-wrinkled man, is the board chairman of Big Valley. He denied in an interview in his Scottsdale office that he had promised water, electricity, and other amenities to buyers. Those who say he did are liars, Brown said.

As for the promised town, he said it "went to hell" because an investor withdrew his money.

"We said there was going to be a future town built there," he said. "We didn't say we were going to build it. You know these people shape the truth to their situations, and soon they begin to believe it."

The other side is graphically introduced, a flat-out denial is summarized, and the official is allowed to pass the blame.

> In 1973, Pasquale Mategrano, a retired Chicago baker, was visited by a nephew who was accompanied by a salesman for Big Valley. After a short sales presentation, Mategrano bought a 40-acre plot for $9,000.
> A year later, a second salesman called on Mategrano to describe the glories of Big Valley.
> Mategrano bought a second plot, for $26,000. He said that Ron Kaghan, the second salesman, told him the land would be worth a lot more in a few years.

A second victim is introduced, and the reader is now familiar with Big Valley. The sales pitch reinforces the premise of the story and rebuts the comments of the company board chairman.

> "He gave us the big pitch," said Mategrano, now 71. "He said this was a prime piece of property. He said it was up in the mountains, where the air would be cool."
> There are no mountains in the Big Valley development. Mategrano is still paying for his land in monthly installments, but he has no plans to live there.
> "I have one son, and I thought maybe this could be for him to go to Arizona some day," he said.
> Kaghan is now district sales manager in suburban Park Ridge for Palm Coast, Inc., a subsidiary of the International Telephone and Telegraph Corp. that sells land in Florida. When questioned by a *Tribune* reporter, he said he could not remember selling the land to the Mategranos, though he received a $2,000-plus commission on the deal.

The writer proceeds to develop the story, using examples of sales pitches, other victims, and land sales in other states. Finally, after telling of another land development, the reporter closes out the story.

> Rio Rancho officials declined to answer questions from the *Tribune* about the land sales.
> Joseph Canepa, an Arizona assistant attorney general, said some people paid $15,000 an acre for land that the firm had bought for $12 an acre.
> "They were told the area was mushrooming and it was a good investment," he said. "But they will be long gone before that land ever increases in value. We have an expert who is going to testify in one suit that that land won't be developed until the year 3000 if it continues at the same rate."

The story is concluded on a strong note, rather than tapering off. This feature was presented with pictures of the land buyers which were taken at their property or in their city homes. It also used a map to show location of properties.

Investigating the Investigators

It is difficult to get investigative reporters to tell exactly how they got certain stories. They may tell of their adventures; but when it comes to details, somewhat like the magician, they will want to wrap their moves in the mystery of their profession and say little. They may offer the excuse that they must protect a secret source. But also, they do not want their competitors to know their methods.

However, with knowledge of how investigative reporters work, one can analyze a story that appears in print or on TV for its sources. One can investigate how investigative stories were investigated.

Let's take a look again at the retirement-land story.

1. Where did the reporter get the idea for the story and a general idea of where to look? A suggestion could have come from anywhere. But one paragraph mentions the American Association of Retired Persons and the National Retired Teachers Association; this gives us the clue that the reporter talked to them. We can imagine that the tip or assignment came to the reporter, and then he or she looked for organizations that might be concerned with the problem. The reporter would find the names of such organizations in a directory of associations in a library.

2. Where did the reporter find the people willing to talk about their experiences? Let's eliminate the possibility that the reporters went to the Southwest, drove to the most remote places in several states, and asked people how they got there. If that is what the reporters did, they certainly did it at a great expenditure of time and money, and left themselves open to the risk of not finding a story. Besides, some of the victims don't live out on their land. They are investors who live in cities. This story has ideal victim accounts. The victims are all people from the Midwest, the general circulation area of the *Chicago Tribune*. They are elderly and have middle-class or working-class backgrounds. Because they got such appropriate victim stories, the reporters apparently had a large group from which to choose.

   Reading on, we learn that several class action suits have been filed and that the attorney general of the state is acting in behalf of people who claim they were defrauded. The attorney general would have the names—the names would be included in the list of those who are suing. Let's guess that that is where the reporters got the names and that the people were contacted and were willing to talk.

But how would the reporters have gone from step one to step two to learn of the lawsuits? The retirement associations could have mentioned the lawsuits, or there may have been stories found in newspaper clips or magazine articles that mentioned the lawsuits. Or the reporter may have called government enforcement agencies in those states believed to have the greatest incidence of this problem and asked them what action was being taken.

3. How did the reporters know where the salesman was now? They knew that the salesman was selling land in Florida, where real estate salesmen are licensed and especially closely regulated. It is possible that the reporters checked with the real estate licensing department in Florida or Illinois and found an address or the name of the company that currently employs him.

By dissecting a story to try to determine how other reporters get their information, the investigative reporter reinforces his or her knowledge of the business. In some circumstances, a reporter will pick up the story and further develop it. In this situation, however, the reporter wants to know how someone else did it for future reference. The same approach could be used for a story about sales of franchises or business opportunities, for instance.

This kind of story is the least difficult for an investigative reporter. Although it reveals information that someone attempted to hide, most of the reporting is secondary. The information is taken from lawsuits and investigators' files after the damage has been done rather than originating from the reporters and revealing a previously unknown practice. For instance, the reporters could have made their own surveys of how much the land that was sold had cost the companies that marketed it rather than quote an official. Such information could have been a major undertaking that would result in statistics for graphics. Also, instead of investigating companies that were already being sued by government officials, reporters could have found and exposed land sales for which sales pitches were still being made at the time of publication. Such an investigation would require that the reporters hear the sales pitch, then travel to the land and compare the claims against reality. Also, they would check on the background of the salesmen and of the organizer of the project to find out if they had been in trouble in previous ventures. But that is a decision to be made by the media editors and depends on the time that can be allocated weighed against the importance of the subject.

PROJECTS

1. Design a television presentation for this investigation.

2. Study any investigative story. How did the reporter get the information? Write a report on how you think he or she got the idea, obtained the documentation, and accomplished the investigation.

GLOSSARY

Class action suit.   A group of people get together and sue to collect for damages suffered not only by them but by everyone under similar circumstances. A private attorney can put together a group in a class action suit or it can be done by a public attorney in behalf of the people.

Exercise: Writing an Investigative Series

This investigative story is the third of a series of six daily reports for which Bissinger and Biddle gathered information for two years. It was written by Bissinger.

> Connections Between Lawyers and Judges They Help Elect by H. G. Bissinger and Daniel R. Biddle of the *Philadelphia Inquirer,* January 28, 1986.
>
> When Municipal Court Judge Mitchell S. Lipschutz decided to run for Common Pleas Court in 1983, he did what nearly every candidate does: He formed a campaign committee to help him.
>
> As it turned out, Lipschutz's bid to join the Common Pleas bench that year failed, and he remained a Municipal Court judge. But for seven lawyers who had joined his committee, it hardly meant the end of their contact with him.
>
> Within months of being named to the campaign committee, these lawyers defended 18 clients in front of Lipschutz, according to court records. Fourteen of the defendants won their cases.
>
> At no time in the courtroom did the lawyers of the judge publicly disclose their recent political relationship, according to interviews and court records. One lawyer served as Lipschutz's campaign treasurer and helped organize a fund-raising event, but even that connection was not disclosed in the court case.

In four paragraphs, a complicated story of judicial ethics is explained, with an example that summarizes what happened in one judge's relationship with the lawyers who appeared before him. It describes what some might consider to be improper judicial conduct, but it is written calmly, with easily understood words and simple sentence structure. Yet, it maintains a tone of importance and urgency.

The example used in the lead is not a teaser that asks but does not answer questions. It is so complete a summary of the facts that it would stand alone as a story. Of course, no story of this type would ever be written to stand alone in four paragraphs, because the reader demands to know much more.

> A comparison of criminal-case records and state campaign finance reports shows that Lipschutz was far from alone in hearing cases from lawyers who had helped his campaign.

In this type of story structure, the lead cannot be cluttered with supporting facts such as the source of information or it becomes too complicated. The source is only briefly alluded to in the lead—"according to court records." This paragraph also serves as a transition by telling the reader that Lipschutz' conduct is an example of a greater question which is to be examined in the story.

> The records show that candidates for judgeships in Philadelphia routinely accept donations from lawyers—and then allow those lawyers to try cases in front of them a short time later.

This is the "nut graph" (that paragraph in every story that might be the lead if the story were written as a straight news story rather than a news feature). The news feature approach—using an example or a vignette—works best here because the reader understands what the "nut graph" means. He or she has read the easy-to-understand account in the lead and is ready to learn how bad the situation may be.

> From 1979 to 1984, 15 judges placed lawyers on their campaign committees or accepted sizable contributions—$300 or more—from lawyers and then presided over cases involving the same lawyers.
> According to an Inquirer study, lawyers appeared before these 15 judges in 63 cases within a year after their campaigns. Fifty-five were Municipal Court cases, and eight were heard in Common Pleas Court.

This is a story of public records and statistics, and the writer will offer them in digestable doses. Notice that the writer refers to a "study" rather than an "investigation." "Investigation" has a harsher ring to it and a connotation that it is conducted by an official agency. Some newspapers decline to use this word in their writing but will refer to the reporters as "investigative" and not "study" reporters.

> From a statistical viewpoint, these defense lawyers were highly successful.

Newspaper readers are accustomed to short paragraphs, and a complicated story is more easily digested in sentences or paragraphs that deliver one idea at a time. This paragraph introduces the documentation of a second alleged wrong. Not only do records show that the lawyers appeared before the judges, they also question if the association may have influenced the outcome of the court case.

> In Municipal Court from 1979 to 1984, 35 percent of all the cases entering the system did not result in convictions. In the 55 Municipal Court cases, where there was a campaign connection between the lawyer and the judge, 71 percent [39 of the cases] did not result in convictions.
>
> Some of these cases resulted in not-guilty verdicts or were discharged by judges. Others were withdrawn by the prosecution, in some cases because witnesses failed to appear and in other cases because judges granted motions suppressing key evidence.

Consider how involved and confusing this story might have been if the writer had tried to explain it all in one paragraph, ticking off how many of the 71 percent were disposed of in different ways. By stating that the cases "did not result in convictions," the writer could use the next paragraph to explain the alternatives. One reader-baffling paragraph at this point could have caused the reader to give up.

> Lawyers say that contributing to judicial candidates and rallying to their political support are time-honored traditions in Philadelphia. It is a game, they say, and it is hard to find an active courtroom lawyer who isn't asked to play it.
>
> Some attorneys say there is an accepted belief that what a lawyer does for a judicial candidate outside the courtroom may one day make a difference inside the courtroom. At the very least, lawyers don't want to take the risk of what will happen if they don't participate.

These paragraphs summarize the opinions of lawyers and are based on numerous interviews, some of which may have been off the record. However, the writer will have to produce real people to relate these feelings if he is to convince the reader.

> "Given the system we have to work with, if a judge asks you to buy tickets or be on a committee, you have a definite problem if you reject them," said lawyer Michael A. DeFino. "You better start practicing in front of another judge."
>
> Adam O. Renfroe Jr., another Philadelphia lawyer, said he has served on several judges' campaign committees. Campaign records show he donated $1,225 to 11 judges between 1981 and 1984.
>
> "Anybody who doesn't is crazy," Renfroe said. "It may not necessarily help me, but I don't want to be hurt. We're the only thing that separates a defendant from jail. We need every club in our armor we possibly can. We have to do everything that is legal and aboveboard to prevent him from going to jail."

These are strong quotations. (Weak quotations result when the speaker dances around the subject instead of speaking his or her mind.) The writer has selected the strongest quotes and has chosen to not alter the natural speech patterns in favor of more concise wording.

> Many lawyers and judges believe that it is difficult to forget these relationships when a lawyer brings a case before a judge.
> "If you're going to be really independent as a judge, I think they should pass a law that no lawyer can contribute to a judge," said Common Pleas Court Judge Albert F. Sabo. "Even subconsciously, you're going to feel you owe him [the lawyer who gives campaign money] a favor."

The judges have also been interviewed, and the writer sets out a pattern by first summarizing opinions that include those of judges and then backing it up with the words of a judge.

> In lengthy interviews, lawyers and judges said that the low number of convictions in cases handled by judges and lawyers with campaign ties did not necessarily point to anything improper. Nor is there anything illegal about the campaign donations; no law prohibits lawyers from contributing to judicial campaigns.

For the first time, the writer offers a rebuttal by the group of people who are the target of the story. It is pointed out that no law has been broken and perhaps nothing improper has occurred.

Later, more thorough rebuttals will be written, including specific comments by Judge Lipschultz and attorneys who made campaign contributions and appeared before him.

> However, many lawyers say the very existence of the political and financial relationship between lawyers and judges taints the integrity of the justice system, offering at least the appearance of a conflict of interest.

The writer has countered the rebuttal with an argument that shows he doesn't have to write only about law breaking or specific improper conduct. He reports a failing in the system. But he doesn't editorialize in this format of writing, so he attributes the opinion to "many lawyers." Once again, he produces a lawyer to make such a statement.

> "It astonishes me that the [state] Supreme Court has not imposed some type of regulation over that very type of thing," said Bruce A. Franzel, a criminal lawyer who was 1985 chairman of the Philadelphia Bar Association Commission on Judicial Selection and Retention.
> "The appearance of impropriety is there, whether there is a $5,000

contribution or a $50 contribution," Franzel said. "It has the appearance that one or the other [the lawyer or the judge] is expecting a quid pro quo."

The writer and reporter have staked the validity of their story premise on this expert opinion and reach some kind of conclusion, stating it at this point of the story. Space is taken to establish the expert's credentials as an authority.

Such relationships show up in the court system in cases ranging from theft to drunken driving to aggravated assault.

Having sold the story to the reader, the writer takes a quick breath and starts detailing what he has learned.

The *Inquirer* did a computer analysis of the campaign finance reports of the 55 Municipal and Common Pleas judges who ran for elections and formed fund-raising committees from 1979 through 1984. The study included candidates running for Municipal and Common Pleas Court, incumbent judges seeking to be retained, and Philadelphia judges who ran for statewide appellate courts.
    Among the findings:

- In 63 criminal cases, defense lawyers appeared in front of judges within a year after serving on those judges' campaign committees or contributing at least $300 to their campaigns. Only two judges, Common Pleas Court Judge Charles P. Mirarchi, Jr. and Municipal Court Judge Matthew F. Coppolino, said they remembered ever disclosing their prior political ties with defense lawyers during a case.
- Six judges named lawyers to the post of treasurer or chairman of their campaign committees and then heard cases from these lawyers without any disclosure during the case. In one instance, Municipal Court Judge Kenneth S. Harris, then running for Common Pleas Court, appointed attorney Ronald White as his campaign chairman and then tried three of White's clients just 21 days later. Harris found all three defendants not guilty of gambling charges.
- Two judges running for seats on higher courts accepted campaign donations of $450 or more from lawyers and then heard those lawyers' cases in court less than five weeks afterward without disclosure.

The writer has used "bullets," black dots that look like bullet holes that emphasize points and create a list of paragraphs. Space is saved because the writer can tell the source of the information in the introduction to the list and needs no transitions between paragraphs. A longer investigative story may use more than one set of bullets.

The organization of this investigative story is similar to that of the land retirement story, but on a grander scale. There are no individual victim stories because the victim is society. Instead, the writer uses the story of an individual judge for a lead. Then, much in the same manner as the retirement land story, this story proceeds with other examples, statistics, opinions of experts, and an examination of the law or lack of laws. The first part of the series winds down with more said in defense and ends with a surprise:

> In an interview, Renfroe said he did not even know he had been on Lipschutz's election committee. He said he could not explain how his name was included on the printed stationery listing Lipschutz's campaign members.
>
> Renfroe did acknowledge that his sister, Patty-Michele, is Lipschutz's law clerk. Because of that relationship, Lipschutz said, he was told at one point by the Judicial Inquiry and Review board that Renfroe could not try cases before him. However, Lipschutz said, the review board revised its decision and allowed him to hear cases involving Renfroe as long as the judge disclosed to the prosecution that Patty-Michele Renfroe was his law clerk.
>
> Renfroe described Lipschutz as "one of the most fair and impartial judges I've had to encounter" and said he thought there was no reason he should not try cases in front of him.
>
> On the evening of Jan. 3, 1986, after Lipschutz was sworn in as a Common Pleas Court judge, his supporters held a reception in the city council's high-ceiling caucus room. Many of the guests—judges, lawyers, politicians—had departed by the time Renfroe arrived.
>
> Renfroe walked across the room, hugged Lipschutz and kissed him on the cheek.

This story about judicial conduct is written with a tone of immediacy. It tells of specific conduct that is happening up to the time of publication, and the information it reveals had been hidden inasmuch as the lawyers and judges did not report their association. The thrust of the story has to be proved with statistics and examples.

How the Story Was Gathered

This is the lead story of a five-part series that is obviously well planned. The story includes an explanation about how it was gathered. Reporters not only checked public records but also did it systematically by using computer print-outs of court dockets and comparing them with campaign disclosure information. The game plan may have included, at the outset, a commitment to which types of conduct would be reported.

How did the reporters know the lawyer kissed the judge? We know they were not there. In a situation of that kind, reporters will not accept one person's account. It is apparent that many people attended this gathering. The reporters got enough independent confirmation and then asked the lawyer and the judge.

This story states that there is a relationship between one lawyer and a judge: the lawyer's sister is the judge's clerk. Such a relationship can be proved with birth records, but it seldom is necessary. People are not likely to deny family relationships when asked.

This gathering and writing task moves up a degree of difficulty from the retirement land story. Rather than report to the public about a problem that is being addressed by enforcement agencies, this story reveals a problem at the highest level of enforcement, shows a lack of control, and calls for new laws.

Documents Used in This Story

Criminal case records. These records are filed at the courthouse and indexed by defendant. When a person is arrested and charged with a criminal offense, the record is open to the public. Such disclosure is necessary to prevent the secret incarceration of people. Also, the criminal court file shows the disposition of the charge, whether the defendant was convicted or found innocent, or whether the charges were dropped. This information is often used in investigative stories that survey the court system to learn of unfair trends in the administration of justice. Also, it is a valuable tool in doing a personal profile. If the subject of an investigation has been arrested, a reporter will want to note all of the facts in the file, such as where the person was arrested and with whom.

State campaign finance reports. Described earlier under *Campaign disclosure reports.*

GLOSSARY

Common pleas court.   A designation in Pennsylvania for a court that hears civil complaints.

Municipal court.   A low level court that hears mostly traffic cases.

Judicial board of inquiry.   The supreme court of each state has established such boards to receive complaints about judges, investigate the complaints, and possibly take action to remove a judge from the bench. The complaints the board receives and its investigations are not made public. However, if a board brings a complaint against a judge, it will be public record. Boards of inquiry set standards of proper behavior for judges.

Quid pro quo.   A Latin term that means something done in exchange for something else. It has the connotation of one favor requiring another in return. The investigative reporter often searches for the quid pro quo when he or she gathers information. A reporter may have just half a story about influence over government officials—a government official took some action that was an inordinate favor for a monied businessman or a businessman gave a large amount of money to a politician. In either case, the task is to find the matching pieces to complete the story.

Exercise: Writing an Investigative Story with a Hard News Lead

On July 31, 1972, Carl Bernstein and Bob Woodward wrote an investigative story for the *Washington Post* under pressure of deadline and fierce journalistic competition. We know exactly how that story was gathered and written because it is detailed in their book, *All the President's Men* and portrayed in a movie of the same name.

BUG SUSPECT GOT CAMPAIGN FUNDS
By Carl Bernstein and Bob Woodward
Washington Post Staff Writers

> A $25,000 cashier's check apparently earmarked for President Nixon's re-election campaign was deposited in April in a bank account of one of the five men arrested in the break-in at Democratic National Headquarters here June 17.

This straight lead states an unattributed fact as in a news story. Readers of the *Washington Post* at the time were familiar with the developing story of the break-in at the Watergate office building and the lead is presented as a further development.

> The check was made out by a Florida bank to Kenneth H. Dahlberg, the President's campaign finance chairman for the Midwest. Dahlberg said last night that in early April he turned the check over to "the treasurer of the Committee [for the Re-election of the President] or to Maurice Stans himself."
>
> Stans, formerly Secretary of Commerce under Mr. Nixon, is now the finance chief of the President's reelection effort.
>
> Dahlberg said he didn't have "the vaguest idea" how the check got into the bank account of the real estate firm owned by Bernard L. Barker, one of the break-in suspects. Stans could not be reached for comment.

The story proceeds with raw facts, including a quotation from an interview. There is no attempt to interpret the meaning or to point out any specific wrongdoing. The writer has not stated and will not state that presidential campaign money should not be in the account of a burglar. He is leaving that interpretation to the reader.

> Reached by telephone at his home in a Minneapolis suburb, Dahlberg explained the existence of the check this way:
> "In the process of fundraising I had accumulated some cash . . . so I recall making a cash deposit while I was in Florida and getting a cashier's check made out to myself. I didn't want to carry all that cash into Washington."
> A photostatic copy of the front of the check was examined by a Washington Post reporter yesterday. It was made out by the First Bank and Trust of Boca Raton to Dahlberg.

Still in the process of backing up the lead, the writer has cited a key interview and document.

> Thomas Monohan, the assistant vice president of the Boca Raton bank, who signed the check authorization, said the FBI had questioned him about it three weeks ago.

The reporters are chasing a story as the FBI is conducting an investigation. They show it here when the bank official will tell them no more than the fact that the FBI has talked to him. Readers are told through this information that there is no mistaking the significance of the check.

> According to court testimony by government prosecutors, Barker's bank account in which the $25,000 was deposited was the same account from which Barker later withdrew a large number of $100 bills. About 53 of these $100 bills were found on the five men after they were arrested at the Watergate.

Up to this point, the writer has been specific in details but now neglects to identify which prosecutors in what court testimony. He has sacrificed that information to protect his exclusive story and possibly his source. There has been no mention in this story that the checks in addition to the deposit information came from an investigative file of a local prosecutor in Dade County, Florida, because, in a running, competitive story, the *Post*'s competition would seize on the information immediately, possibly confirming it all with a phone call.

An overanxious reporter might have written a lead or a supporting paragraph stating that Barker got money from the Committee to Reelect the President to pay the Watergate burglars. As we read the story, that is what we surmise. But that could be untrue. We know only that the check was found in Barker's account. Barker could have gotten the money after it passed through several hands and without the knowledge of Stans and for some purpose other than the burglary. The $100 bills could be other bills. The reporters have not matched the serial numbers. They only know the prosecutors' testimony. And they only know that Dahlberg said the check was for the campaign. Perhaps he was mistaken. That is why the writer must tell only the facts one at a time. In this story the writer takes even more care, using the word *apparently* in the lead paragraph.

> Dahlberg has contributed $7,000 to the GOP since 1968, records show, and in 1970 he was finance chairman for Clark MacGregor when MacGregor ran unsuccessfully against Hubert H. Humphrey for a U.S. Senate seat in Minnesota.

The writer has summarized Dahlberg's background from campaign disclosure forms and previous stories from the files in the newspaper reference library, which draws his association closer to the national committee. In addition to keeping on file their own stories, individual reporters and newspapers will often keep campaign disclosure reports of major candidates.

> MacGregor, who replaced John N. Mitchell as Mr. Nixon's campaign chief on July 1, could offer no explanation as to how the $25,000 got from the campaign finance committee to Barker's account.
> He told a Post reporter last night: "I know nothing about it . . . these events took place before I came aboard. Mitchell and Stans would presumably know."
> MacGregor said he would attempt this morning to determine what happened.
> Powell Moore, director of press relations for the Committee for the Re-election of the President, told a reporter that Stans was unavailable for comment last night. Mitchell also could not be reached for comment.

The writer shows that attempts have been made to contact important participants in the story. If a participant had been reached but would not comment, the writer may have stated, "contacted by a Post reporter last night, he declined comment."

> In a related development, records made available to the Post yesterday show that another $89,000 in four separate checks was deposited dur-

ing May in Barker's Miami bank account by a well-known Mexican lawyer.

The deposits were made in the form of checks made out to the lawyer, Manuel Ogarrio Daguerre, 68, by the Banco Internacional of Mexico City.

Ogarrio could not be reached for comment, and there was no immediate explanation as to why the $89,000 was transferred to Barker's account.

This makes a total of $114,000 deposited in Barker's account in the Republic National Bank of Miami, all on April 20.

The same amount—$114,000—was withdrawn on three separate dates, April 24, May 2 and May 8.

This additional information is inserted well into the story as a related development. It could have been summarized in a paragraph after the lead to show that more than the circumstances of the Dahlberg check had been learned, then the details given later, but that probably would have caused confusion. Or, the reporters might have held this information for a second-day story, because it is significant in itself. But the *Post* chose not to hold back information because they either wanted to inform their readers or feared that their competition would beat them to the story.

In the story, the transactions appear to be a new mystery. The reporters know that they are describing the laundering of money—it is sent out of the country and back so that it does not leave a paper trail. But once again, they cannot state such a conclusion. They can only state the facts and let the reader surmise.

> Since the arrest of the suspects at 2:30 a.m. inside the sixth floor suite of the Democratic headquarters in the Watergate, Democrats have tried to lay the incident at the doorstep of the White House—or at least to the Nixon re-election committee.

The writer now is filling in the background and focuses the story for readers by telling what has been perceived by others. He has refrained from editorializing, but, as the person in control of the information going into the story, he wields his journalistic power to guide the readers.

> The burglary suspects were accused of breaking into the office to "bug" the offices by planting electronic listening devices.

That is why the subjects are called "Bug Suspects" in the headline.

> One day after the arrests, it was learned that one of the suspects, James W. McCord, Jr., a former FBI and CIA agent, was the security chief to the Nixon committee and a security consultant to the Republican Na-

tional Committee. McCord, now free on bond, was fired from both posts.

The next day it was revealed that a mysterious White House consultant, E. Howard Hunt, Jr., was known by at least two of the suspects. Hunt immediately dropped from sight and became involved in an extended court battle to avoid testimony before the federal grand jury investigating the case.

It may sound like the writer has editorialized by calling Hunt mysterious, but he explains this use in the second sentence. Also, there had been conflicting previous stories about Hunt's duties for the White House.

The writer then relates more historical background, more detail from the Dahlberg phone interview, and more background about Dahlberg, tapering off into least important details. In a breaking story, a writer does not have the luxury of a strong finish. The more important information is placed at the top in the traditional inverted pyramid form. Besides, a reporter doesn't know how much space a story will be given in the paper, and any exciting items left for the end, or bottom, may be chopped.

How They Got the Story

The retirement land story had the advantage of being in the past tense. While the problem was shown to be ongoing, the examples were of events that had already happened. In the lawyers and judges story, there was an incident in the past that was investigated for its social importance, and then new information was revealed that came from public records. The gathering and writing of that story was of a higher degree of difficulty than the land story.

The "Bug Suspect" story reached a final degree of difficulty—the high diver doing a triple flip—because it was hidden and immediate, and people were making an effort to keep it hidden. As each bit of information was revealed, the reporters published new information on a daily basis. They reacted to events and investigative breaks without having time to plan. Such a story is not only the most difficult to produce but also the most difficult to analyze for its sources.

It was revealed in *All the President's Men* (Carl Bernstein and Bob Woodward, Simon & Schuster, 1974) that the checks were in a file of the local prosecutor in Miami, who had subpoenaed them to find out if any local laws had been broken. Bernstein found them there when he was looking for telephone records that a source said had been subpoenaed in the same investigation. Bernstein got the information from the checks and called Woodward from Miami two hours before the newspaper deadline. Woodward interviewed Dahlberg by telephone, and then wrote the story, according to the book.

The *Washington Post* and the *New York Times* had earlier associated the Watergate burglars with campaign workers for Nixon, but this story for the first time showed the transfer of cash from the reelection committee to one of the burglars. Efforts by Nixon to cover up the committee's role in the burglary and then to try to conceal his White House staff's cover-up efforts led to his resignation as Congress considered impeachment.

How Woodward and Bernstein gathered the story is reenacted in the Warner Brothers' 1976 motion picture, *All the President's Men.*

GLOSSARY

Grand jury.   Unlike a jury that hears one court case, this group of citizens is impanelled as a jury to decide if there is sufficient evidence for the prosecutor to file criminal charges. Testimony before a grand jury is secret.

Subpoena.   If a crime is suspected, the government prosecutors can ask a judge to allow them to confiscate documents. A search warrant is used under the same circumstance to gather evidence, but a subpoena is usually used if there is knowledge of the existence of certain documents.

Prosecutor.   An official who represents the local government in court. This official may be called a district attorney or state's attorney. When he or she acts, it is for the prosecution.

CHAPTER EIGHT

Illustrating an Investigative Story

Investigative reporters know that the investigation itself and the work that went into gathering the information make the story a success or a flop. A weak investigation cannot be propped up by ornate newspaper illustrations or television visuals any more than a bad play can be saved with expensive costumes. Such an attempt only highlights the weaknesses of an investigation.

But there is a need to explain the investigation through means other than words. The pen is said to be mightier than the sword, and pictures and graphics in an investigative story make the pen even mightier. Illustrations will not stand alone, but they are powerful allies of the written word.

In the print media, newspapers, books, and magazines offer an opportunity to illustrate an investigative story with still pictures and graphics. In broadcasting, television offers the opportunity to show a person as he or she speaks and to have moving pictures explained by a voice as the viewer watches. Ideal television visuals show happenings—action pictures—and graphics of statistics that can be grasped by the eye in a moment.

Both readers and viewers want to experience the story by seeing the subjects of the investigation. If a surgeon performs dangerous, untested, unapproved surgery that cripples patients, what more powerful testimony could the television reporter present than a patient showing a crippling deformity and telling how it happened and how it feels? The emotion of the victim's story emerges and can be shared with the viewer.

Newspaper investigative reporters can barely hide their jealousy when they see the TV journalist deliver such emotional material. But they may also illustrate their stories with pictures and graphics. Each medium of communication has its advantages and disadvantages for investigative reporting, and after a study of each, one may choose a career merely from preference.

Print Media versus Broadcasting

Television and newspaper investigative reporters have found that the system of developing stories from tips and ideas is the same no matter how it is to be presented and that there is no substitute for accurate, thorough investigative work. They coexist as competitors, using the advantages unique to their media; or they work together and use those tools to investigate and expose a common target.

A newspaper has space to use more words than a television station has time for newscasting. There is space to keep a story running in the newspaper for weeks or months. The newspaper reader selects his or her own reading matter within each edition, but the television news editor must make that important selection for the viewer, broadcasting one story after another. Left with no choice, the viewer will change channels if he or she loses interest. Therefore, a running investigative story on television must be strong each day to maintain the level of excitement and keep the audience that will insure that it stays on the air. Also, a lack of visuals for a television investigative report may allow other stories that are perhaps less important but have better visuals to get more play.

Newspaper stories can be clipped, passed around, and put in library files. Weeks after an important story appears, a copy may circulate among interested persons and stimulate the reaction that the reporter wants. The television and radio broadcast signals head out into space toward some distant star. If people miss the news on television, only by word of mouth or a video cassette tape will they know what they missed.

In presenting a story in newspapers and television, reporters have found that some aspects of gathering information differ. Newspaper investigative reporters go about their work anonymously. The people they interview may not know them and have to be told which stories they have done to know that they are competent investigative reporters. Television reporters are like old friends. A contact has seen TV reporters expose wrongdoing. People relate to a TV reporter as a person who gives valuable information. What oppressed person wouldn't want a Mike Wallace to come to his or her defense? And what charlatan wouldn't be in fear if Wallace showed up at the doorstep? When the television reporter presents a story, the viewer may make a judgment on its accuracy based on past experience with that reporter. The newspaper reader will likely skip over the byline on the story and prejudge it by the overall reliability of the newspaper.

A television investigative report can seldom be handled by one person. A well-done television report is a combination of journalistic and technical achievement and is, therefore, much more expensive to produce. When television cameras are used, the budget may not allow for a crew to go to a location day after day to try to get "exactly the right shot." Television producers are inclined by budget restraints to look for the sure thing, such as a head shot of a person talking into a microphone in a prearranged interview.

It is not uncommon for newspaper and television reporters to work together. Television stations are inclined to pick up and run with stories that have been broken by the local newspaper. They often credit the newspaper and show a picture of the headline. If the two media are truly working together, television reporters may be given advance information about the story so that they can get the visuals that will support it, including taped interviews with subjects of the story. A combination investigative effort produces more impact. The television station appreciates the help, and the newspaper management appreciates the additional media exposure.

An investigative reporter sometimes looks to the publication of a book to overcome disadvantages of newspapers and television. A book has the space to tell a complicated story and makes possible the use of illustrations and graphics. But the publication of a book lacks immediacy. The time necessary to prepare and distribute a book means that it is unlikely that the book will be appropriate as part of a timely, breaking story. Some investigative books take years to gather and write but are useful for examining a controversial happening in the past, such as the assassination of a president or the career of a deceased public figure. For an investigative book to be successful, the subject must be of such broad appeal that people are willing to pay for the book. Television and radio broadcasts are free, and newspapers and magazines are inexpensive and may be bought for the other information they offer. A book must stand on its own, and it faces stiff competition to get a buyer's attention.

Magazines present an investigative story with pictures and graphics and space for the written word, the same as a newspaper. But, like a book, the time from writing to publication of a magazine story is more lengthy, and there is no opportunity for an immediate follow-up.

Little has been done by investigative reporters with radio. Even all-news or talk stations find it difficult to take time out from covering breaking news stories of the day to set aside time for investigative stories. However, any of the stories in this text could be done on radio. Pictures and graphics would be replaced by interviews and sound effects. For some of the stories in this text, a radio station could broadcast the sounds of a roadway, the school cafeteria, the bingo hall, the rap of a gavel that calls a public meeting to order, or the hospital emergency room.

Using Pictures

Television reporters can broadcast pictures and the voices of sources as they tell their stories—so the viewer is helped in ways other than the written argument to judge the veracity of the information in the investigation. If subjects look and sound sincere, television investigative reporters score an important victory in getting a point across. But what if subjects have an unattractive appearance? The television viewer might unfairly judge them, but the newspaper reader would not.

Investigative reporters of either medium can actually show documentation as well as the people and places mentioned in their stories. The television report can be illustrated with pictures at the same time a reporter is talking and explaining what the viewer is seeing: "This is the deed to the land that was sold by the city without bid to the mayor's business partner . . . and here it is today after it was upzoned and resold at a profit." And the television report has one more advantage. As the reporter speaks, he or she adds inflections to the words, stressing important points and even sounding shocked or amazed at the actions reported. And, if time is short, those verbal explanations to the viewer about the documentation may be eliminated—pictures can be shown while the reporter says, "The land was sold [picture of deed] without bids to the mayor's business partner, upzoned [picture of land] and resold at a profit."

In newspapers, magazines, books, and television, investigative reporters can attribute their documentation with both words and pictures. Newspapers, magazines, and books use photographs to illustrate a story. Television can show a document or illustrate the attribution with movement, such as showing a pencil circling a meaningful item on a list. The device of picturing a document is usually used when the document is the key to the investigation. The picture underscores the document's importance and accuracy.

Still photography is utilized by print media to show the characters or scenes involved in an investigative story, but pictures can best be used to prove the story. For instance, if the state licensing agency revoked the license of a doctor, but it is learned that the doctor is still practicing, an investigative story would be supported by a still or moving picture of that doctor leaving an office that has his name on it, or a sign advertising his medical services. If it is alleged that a city official is using city workers at his private property, what better proof could be had than pictures of city vehicles and workers at the scene? Poor upkeep of the county senior citizens' home could be illustrated by pictures of piles of trash and broken stairs. The picture in a newspaper can be studied, and the reader can glance at it while reading the copy. The television picture, on the other hand, is seen briefly and then is gone.

A Legal Question

Investigative reporters and the photographers who work with them have to take extra care to stay within the law when taking pictures. There is seldom a question of privacy when the photographer is standing on public property. But a newspaper or television station would not likely print or broadcast a picture that was taken by someone who walked across a private yard and shot a picture through a window. Photographers may also be banned from public courtrooms by court orders or standing rules, but a subject walking out of a courthouse has always been considered fair game for an ambush photo.

An investigative reporter avoids using a picture of a person who is unrelated to the story if it might put that person in an unfavorable light. A picture of an illegal-gambling hall that shows a man coming out of the door implies that he is a patron, when he could be the air conditioner repairman. As a safeguard, a TV technician may jumble the face of an uninvolved person electronically or a newspaper photo technician may cloud the face with shadowing.

Using Graphics

Both print media and television have graphics at their disposal to help tell the investigative story. The newspaper graphic can be held in the hand and studied. The television chart flashes by on the screen. Preparing graphics is an art, and newspapers, magazines, and television stations have staffs that specialize in this field. Investigative reporters provide graphic artists of their medium with statistics that help explain their story. For example, how much of the school budget is necessary and how much is wasteful? How much money was left for charity after the fund raisers took out their costs? These statistics can be shown in a pie chart.

How much did the traffic accident rate increase after the sheriff eliminated regular patrols? How much did the campaign fund of the mayor increase after he started giving tax breaks to developers? These statistics can be shown in a bar chart.

The television graphic can move. Just as television uses moving graphics on a weather map, it can show a pile of money dwindle as part of it is blown away by waste in government. A bar chart showing the number of accidents before and after patrols are eliminated need not be two bars standing side by side, as in the newspaper graphic, but one bar that grows.

MEMO

- Television and newspaper investigative research is similar, but the presentation of each differs.

- Pictures and graphics can aid an investigative story and even provide proof or substantiate findings.

- Magazines, books, and radio should not be overlooked as a means to present an investigative story.

What pictures and graphics could have been used to illustrate the newspaper stories that Bud Munn wrote about the mayor's partnership in the construction project and those projects that Gladys Tydings proposed about city workers and campaign contributions?

PROJECT

Write an investigative report for television based on the Eastchester investigation. How would it be illustrated with pictures and graphics? Would it be told best in a series of short reports on television news or in a more lengthy documentary-style report?

Case History: Oral Courier Develops a Career in Television Investigative Reporting

Oral Courier worked in a small radio station while in college and stayed on the job after graduation. At first, he did a little of everything around the station, both on and off the air. Oral found that reading the news suited him best. He had an afternoon shift—he would tear off a news summary from the wire service printer every thirty minutes and read it into a microphone. The radio wire service had brief stories from all over the world. When there was a foreign name in the copy, the wire service inserted phonetic pronunciations. With little effort from Oral, his newscasts had a polished sound that was almost as good as that of the network newscasters. He also rewrote the local stories that the news director gathered and made calls to update those stories. But the manager of the station wanted no one but the news director to gather the important local stories. After a few months on the job, Oral found that it did not present much of a challenge.

When the job of news director at another station opened up, Oral applied for it and was hired. That job took him to most of the important news happenings in the city and brought him in contact with city leaders. Oral believed himself to be more fortunate than reporters at the daily newspaper because they were limited to special subjects or beats, while he was able to experience a cross section of the news of the city.

After several years of developing the necessary expertise to cover political and economic stories, Oral convinced the program director at the public television station to let him do a local public affairs program in which he would interview people about the most important local events of the week. Oral had never imagined a future for himself in television and did not spend much time thinking about his television image as he prepared for each show. He was more interested in the content of the program. Partly because of that, his on-the-air style developed naturally, and he was received by viewers as a person who was interested in the subject he was discussing.

Then Oral accepted an offer to become a full-time television newsman at one of the commercial TV stations. His friends teased him, telling him that television reporters were people with pretty faces and little perception. But when Oral was covering breaking stories he had seen how television reporters worked. He knew that his friends' comments were not true. He found TV reporters to be competent and enthusiastic, and as talented as their print-media counterparts. He looked forward to his job in television as an opportunity to become a better newsman.

The job was difficult for Oral at first because he lacked experience in the technical aspects of television. But again he was successful, learning television production and broadening his knowledge of the city by working at the scene of breaking stories. Although covering fires, news conferences, and election nights was exciting, it was not as fulfilling as he had hoped. So he asked the news director if he could do several special reports on local community happenings that he found interesting. Those reports—neighborhood complaints about an incinerator, senior citizens petitioning for better bus service, people raising money for an animal shelter—ran on the late night news and were appreciated by the viewers and the people involved in the stories.

Then, late one night, while driving home from work, Oral looked into his rearview mirror and saw the grill of a huge truck that was following him at high speed. He slowed down and let the truck pass. He remembered hearing others talk about how they were becoming more and more fearful of being tailgated by trucks on highways and he thought of the possibility of a television project about that concern. He wondered why truckers were speeding and if the trucks were safe. He began to gather bits and pieces of information about the trucking industry and truck safety to determine if there was a story that would be appropriate for a television report. He got information about truck safety rules from the Motor Carrier Safety Bureau of the Federal Highway Administration. He talked to neighbors and coworkers to find if they also were fearful of tailgating trucks. When he talked to truck drivers, he learned that those who were employed by trucking companies had schedules to meet. They claimed that they needed to speed to make those schedules. They also said that they got tired from the long hours, and they complained that the trucks they drove were not kept in good repair by the trucking companies. Oral concluded that truck drivers were as worried as auto drivers about speed and safety on highways.

But an official of an association of trucking companies told Oral that he should not conclude that many trucks speed. An occasional speeding truck gives the others an undeserved poor reputation, he said. The idea that unsafe trucks are on the highways is also erroneous, he said, because trucks must undergo surprise safety inspections at state-operated truck weighing stations.

Oral contacted members of a trucker's union and developed them as sources. He found that they had different views. They scoffed at the idea that few trucks speed or that they are regularly inspected. "Everybody is going as fast as they can, and we always know when safety inspectors are at a weigh station," a driver told him. "The trucker who first sees them setting up will get on the CB radio and alert us all. 'There's smokies in the chicken coop,' he'll say, and we know right off there are safety inspectors in the weigh station, so we'll just get off the road and bypass the station."

Oral needed to learn which version was true, so he borrowed a hand-hand-held radar gun from a company that manufactured them. The radar gun had a digital number on the back. When he held the radar gun up on the side of the road as a truck approached, the digital miles-per-hour number clearly showed and a television camera could shoot a picture over his shoulder to show both that number and the approaching truck. He got some immediate shots of trucks running over seventy miles per hour in a fifty-five-miles-per-hour speed zone. But then the trucks that followed those were within the speed limit, and Oral realized that his crew had been spotted and the CB radios were probably buzzing about their activities, alerting truckers who must have thought they were police.

The question was not going to be resolved as easily as Oral had thought. He had to devise a new plan. He set up cameras twenty-five miles from the city on five different highways. Hidden television cameras recorded pictures of trucks from broadside as the trucks sped along the highway toward the city. The exact time was shown across the bottom of the screen. Twenty-five miles farther down the road in the direction the trucks were heading, another hidden camera was taping them. Oral spliced the video tapes together to show the same truck at different locations with the times showing. Most of the trucks had large signs to identify them, but reporters also looked for the Interstate Commerce Commission numbers on each truck. With a small amount of arithmetic, the speed of the trucks could be calculated: If a truck had travelled twenty-five miles in twenty minutes, it was averaging seventy-five miles an hour. Once the tapes were edited, the viewer could see that truck after truck was averaging over the speed limit on the stretch of highway.

Oral also wanted to determine if the trucks were unsafe, so he and his television crew began watching truck weighing stations on the highways. Oral interviewed the chief inspector in the state agency that examined the trucks to learn if he had an adequate staff and budget to enforce truck safety. The chief invited Oral and his television production crew to observe how his inspectors checked trucks. Oral and his crew got pictures of the safety inspectors as they examined trucks, and they noticed that the trucks were in good condition. But then, in the same way they had checked speed, they quietly set up hidden cameras alongside the first interchange on the highway as the trucks approached the safety inspectors, and they got pictures of those that turned off. Then they showed the same trucks as they were turning back onto the highway at the interchange on the other side of the safety inspectors. By putting cameras on an overpass, they were able to picture a caravan of trucks driving along a frontage road and bypassing the safety inspectors. By then, Oral had his own CB radio which provided a sound track for the pictures of the truck caravan. The CB radio crackled with trucker jargon that included warnings about the safety inspectors.

Oral used photographs of recent serious truck accidents for his report. While those photographs were stills, the television camera could be moved close to the picture and then scan around it to give the viewers a feeling of being present at the scene.

But Oral was not happy with the visuals for the story. He believed that his report lacked the element that had started it all. He wanted the viewer to share the experience he had when he looked into the rearview mirror and saw the truck bearing down on him. So Oral and his crew mounted a camera on the front seat of a car and shot pictures out the back window as they drove along the highway. When they slowed down, trucks would drive up close and then pass them. When they looked at the video tapes they had gotten, they and concluded that the view of the truck out the rear window was not as frightening as they had expected. While twenty feet at sixty-miles-an-hour was a split-second experience, when viewed in a picture, it was seen as a safe interval.

A director and cameraman suggested that the picture be staged. "We can get a truck cab and tow it with the car so it'll be closer," they said.

"Or why not just make it a still shot and back the car up to a parked truck in a truck stop? Nobody will know the difference."

The Argument for Staging the Shot

This is Oral's first attempt to do a big investigative story, and he wants to show that he can do such stories quickly and economically. If he continues to try to get an actual tailgating shot on the highway, he may fail over and over again and delay the project. If he stages the shot, it would have just as much viewer impact and would remove any danger that could result from going on the highway and exposing the television crew to the risk of a serious accident. Also, he is not staging something that he knows is not true. He knows that trucks are tailgating. He wants to show it with pictures that have impact. On a warm day in winter, newspaper and television photographers have been known to ask someone to pose for them by jumping into the water at the beach for a weather picture. Do they reveal if the shot was staged?

The Argument against Staging the Shot

Investigative reports should be true, because truth is what reporters seek. If readers learn that one of the pictures in an investigative report was staged, the entire project could be discounted. Persons who would seek to discredit the report because of their personal interests would leap at the chance of condemning it as a fake. The reputation of the reporter and the television station would be damaged. An investigative reporter would not stage a picture, just as he or she would not fake a document.

The Decision

The decision that Oral made was to scrap the original picture idea and convey the feeling of danger with a different kind of a shot. His crew took pictures of auto and truck traffic intermingled on a rainswept highway from the vantage of an overpass. It was scary to look down on traffic as trucks tailgated small cars, and the distance between them was put in a perspective from outside the vehicles.

The truck investigation series worked well for television because it generated action pictures. But Oral wanted to be sure that his report had solid documentation and that it was meaningful. He got statistics about the number of truck accidents from the state police that showed accidents were increasing. And he got some technical studies and interviewed experts from the state highway department that detailed how excess weight and speed combine to add to the cost of highway maintenance. Spokesmen for the trucking industry also were interviewed. They downplayed the significance of Oral's project and explained their side of the story. People could not be supplied with their everyday needs if it were not for trucks, they said. They described their business as highly competitive with long hours of hard work, and they said that as much as anyone else, they were interested in safety and maintaining the highway system in good repair.

The story ran for six nights on the news. It was the type of story that people told others about the next day. It caused them to turn to Oral's channel each night, and the audience increased through the week. Station management decided that an investigative series of that kind should be programmed each time ratings were being taken.

Some state representatives called for hearings on why the speeding laws were not being enforced, and enforcement officials pledged a crackdown. A "hot line" (separate phone number) was set up at the state police headquarters, and people were invited to call with complaints about trucks.

Oral started looking for new subjects to investigate and adopted the approach that there were no subjects television could not do as satisfactorily as any of the other media. He knew that television investigative stories did not have to be limited to consumer safety, so he began producing investigative reports about waste and corruption in government. Looking back over the development of his career, he saw that he had gone from reading the news to gathering the news and finally to making the news.

- How would you tell the story about speeding and unsafe trucks for print publication?
- Did the truck investigation go far enough?
- Are there other investigative ideas on the subject to be explored?
- Are there similar subjects for investigation that could be handled with the same approach?
- What should Oral do for his next project?

Sources Used in This Investigation

Interstate Commerce Commission (ICC): Regulates trucks, buses, and railroads and has public records of ownership and financial reports of companies. States have similar commissions that register and regulate vehicles and companies in commerce within the states.

Motor Carrier Safety Bureau. This bureau of the Federal Highway Administration, U.S. Department of Transportation, investigates and publishes reports of major accidents involving trucks and buses.

Exercise: Producing a Television Investigative Report

This television investigation, "Armed and Dangerous," was aired May 14, 1985, by CBS in Chicago. It was the work of Pam Zekman, Sandy Bergo, Jack Murphy, and Andy Segal, members of a standing team of investigative reporters. It won a Peabody Award for local television investigative reporting.

ANCHOR LEAD:	Police forces in many cities are being cut back. To take up the slack, companies and private groups are turning to private security guards. In Illinois, security guards outnumber police three to one. But the Channel Two Investigative Team has found that there are few or no requirements for security companies to weed out guards who may be armed and dangerous. Pam Zekman has a special report.

This introduction has a relaxed style; it states why the investigation is important and what it is about. The anchor was a TV newsman who regularly anchored the ten o'clock news. He read the words while the camera was close-up. He shared the screen with a logo that stated, "Special Report, Armed and Dangerous" and a picture of a police officer-style cap with a badge on it. Next, for two seconds a picture of a billboard occupied the entire screen: "Channel Two News Investigative Team." By

this technique, the station indicated that this story was special and aside from the usual news coverage of the station.

ZEKMAN: Twenty-six-year-old Michael Bellamy is paralyzed from the chest
          down.

As these words were spoken, the slide dissolved to a moving picture of a man struggling as he was helped into a wheelchair. The reporter didn't say, "This is Bellamy here, being helped into a wheelchair." We knew it simply from his appearing on the screen as the words were spoken.

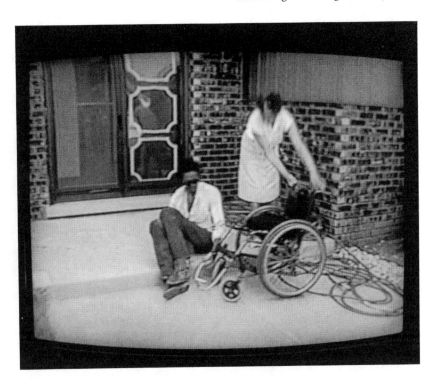

ZEKMAN: Five years ago he was brutally beaten by a fellow security guard in what Bellamy claims was an unprovoked attack. Experts say the incident should have been a warning to subsequent employers that the guard was potentially dangerous.

Note that the reporter did not conclude who was at fault in the attack and attributed the word "unprovoked" to Bellamy. The man struggled into the chair, and the picture cut to Pam Zekman seated at a desk with books behind it, an office atmosphere in which one would expect a researcher or investigator to work. Her personal dress was businesslike, an open jacket with a scarf.

ZEKMAN: Instead, he was hired by one company after another. Ultimately he murdered someone he was supposed to protect.

She leaned toward the camera, and the camera moved in as she spoke the next words.

ZEKMAN: Our investigation found that unstable security guards get jobs in Illinois because the state does not require employers to do any psychological screening or to review the guard's prior work record.

A still photograph of the front of a report was shown simultaneously with her next spoken words. As she said "recommended," the picture changed to an inside page, a chapter on re-employment screening.

ZEKMAN: Both types of background checks were strongly recommended by a national task force of experts in 1976.

Fulfilling a need to establish this report as authoritative rather than an editorial comment, the reporter used expert opinion as documentation early and showed the report to add support to the words.

Next, a man appeared, seated at a desk across from the reporter.

ZEKMAN: Cliff Van Meter was the executive director of the task force.

We knew that this was Van Meter because his picture appeared on the screen at the moment the reporter spoke his name. While we were look-ing at him sitting across from Zekman in his office, Zekman was still speaking in the context of a narrator. It would have been confusing if the Zekman in Van Meter's office turned to us and introduced Van Meter, because we would have had to grope with the incongruity of her bouncing from her office to someone else's. Then we heard Van Meter speak on camera from the interview taped in his office.

VAN   Background investigations, background screening, testing are
METER: critical, and I want to emphasize that that is before they go on the
          job.

The statements of the persons appearing were brief; the reporter placed a person on screen only to underscore the written report that appeared and to show that someone stood behind it. Another man appeared, and the reporter introduced him and gave immediate information about him.

ZEKMAN: Dr. Eric Ostrov screens Chicago police recruits and says that a minimal psychological test should also be given to security guards.

DOCTOR   The person with an emotional disturbance is a risk to the public,
OSTROV: he's a risk to himself, and he's a risk to his fellow officers.

A large amount of information can be conveyed in the time restraints of television through this technique. A new person was introduced, and his function described and opinions aired. It would have been a waste if after the reporter stated that Ostrov said minimal testing should be given, Ostrov appeared on screen and said, "Minimal testing should be given." Instead, he expanded on the idea, and more information was broadcast.

ZEKMAN: In 1978 George Purnell went to work for Amber Way Security.

As these words were spoken, a black and white photo of a man with his name, George Purnell, written beneath it, appeared as a slide on the screen. Then the name Amber Way replaced Purnell's name, and a company logo for Amber Way was included. This was the beginning of a gimmick used to emphasize Purnell's job changes. Each time a new company was named, Purnell's picture reappeared with a new company logo in the picture.

Next, the picture of a factory building was shown, and the camera moved slowly toward the entrance.

ZEKMAN: He was assigned to guard a vacant factory on the South Side.
          Purnell worked the late shift, relieving the early guard, Michael
          Bellamy.

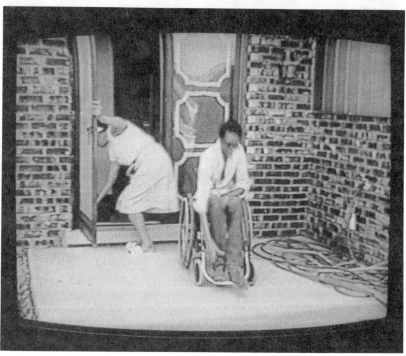

As soon as Bellamy's name was spoken, Bellamy was shown sitting in his wheelchair. He is the man we saw as the story opened. This time he was being helped through the doorway of his home, a continuation of what we saw earlier.

ZEKMAN: Bellamy says that one night they argued over whether Bellamy's radio was too loud, and Purnell accused Bellamy of getting him in trouble with their boss.

An argument is simplified, and the writer used the names of the two parties rather than "he" or "him" to help the listener. A reader would have an opportunity to go back and reread the sentences, but the listener/viewer cannot.

Next, the picture of a round clock wrapped in leather and held by straps was pictured.

ZEKMAN: He says Purnell was holding a steel watchman's clock, similar to this one.

For the first time, the reporter mentioned what was on the screen. It was

necessary to clarify that this was not the weapon, but something similar to it. A close-up of Bellamy followed.

BELLAMY: He was standing on the side of me and he swung it down like that [gestures violently downward], and then it hit me over the back of the head and I went straight to the floor.

The visual became a woman seated in a home.

ZEKMAN: Bellamy's mother remembers hearing the news about her son's condition.

LOIS The doctor came out and he told me that my son had been injured
BELLAMY: and that he would never walk again—in his life. That was a moment I never forgot.

As the woman spoke the words, "never walk again—in his life," her voice broke and she wept as she finished speaking. Merely telling that she wept does not convey the emotion of the television picture. Many a viewer wept with her. An arrest report then appeared on the screen.

ized by anyone to carry
rvisor, nor was he auth
he knew of no problems
ard at the factory. Aft
at Aggravated Battery c
. 79 in Br. 44-2. Arres
operty seized from arr
hecked clear, register

ZEKMAN: Purnell was charged with aggravated battery, but was found not guilty after testifying that Bellamy started the fight.

A picture of a personnel record appeared.

ZEKMAN: Purnell's personnel records show he was fired from Amber Way for insubordination.

Purnell's picture appeared again, this time with the name and logo of another security firm.

ZEKMAN: But two months later, he was hired by Titan Security. His employment records there say Purnell falsified reports about his patrols. A supervisor said it was a possible black eye for the company. He suggested firing Purnell.

As the reporter continued the narration, the camera moved in on the personnel record, and the words, "falsified reports," "possible black eye," and "firing" were highlighted as they were spoken.

EW: MAN NOT ON POST A
ervisor arrived. Could
Falsified client report
oted AT 2AM. (See ATTA

S: Not Available

Purnell's picture appeared again, this time with a new company and logo.

ZEKMAN: Purnell's next job was with B. E. Levy Security.

Three written reports were shown in one picture on the screen.

ZEKMAN: The president of the company would later describe Purnell's manner as "belligerent" and suggested that Purnell "avoid confrontations." His fellow workers said he is "insubordinate" and "too aggressive." His supervisor said Purnell "has a short fuse," "acts irrationally," and "should not be . . . a public safety officer." Purnell was fired.

As the quoted words and phrases were spoken, they were shown highlighted in the pages of the report.

The next shot showed Zekman seated beside a man at a desk. She had an open folder, and the camera was looking over her shoulder at the man. She spoke in her narrator role.

ZEKMAN: We showed Purnell's work records to a psychologist who screens
applicants for security jobs.

A close-up of the man appeared; his name, because it was not mentioned
by the reporter, was superimposed on the screen. He is Dr. Frank Rowe.

ROWE: His history of antisocial behavior is so chronic that I have no
doubts that even a minimal screen, psychological screen, would
probably have eliminated him from consideration.

Purnell was pictured again with another company name and logo. The
reporters used the same black and white picture of Purnell each time, and
each time it shared the TV screen with a different company logo to hammer home the repetitiveness of his behavior as he moved from job to job.

ZEKMAN: But Purnell went to work for CPP Security.

A doorway of an office building was shown.

ZEKMAN: He was assigned as the night guard at a Loop office building.

The camera moved inside the building, and people were walking through the lobby.

ZEKMAN: One night, Purnell could not find his brief case. He was mad and accused several people in the building of stealing it.

A still color picture of a young man was shown.

ZEKMAN: At one point he confronted 20-year-old Michael Lavin, who worked in the building, and eventually cornered him in the utility room.

Color pictures of a messy room and then of blood on floor tiles appear on screen.

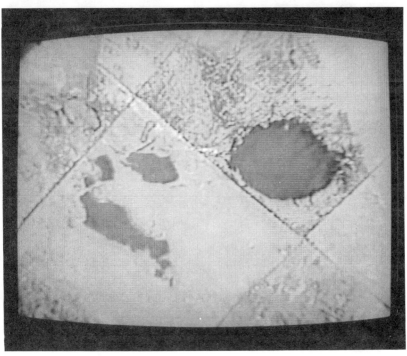

ZEKMAN: Lavin was hit in the head with a snow shovel [picture of shovel]—
beaten so brutally that the shovel was bent [picture of Lavin]. Lavin
died two days later.

Lavin's picture dissolved to a picture of the accused attacker. It was a
police mug shot.

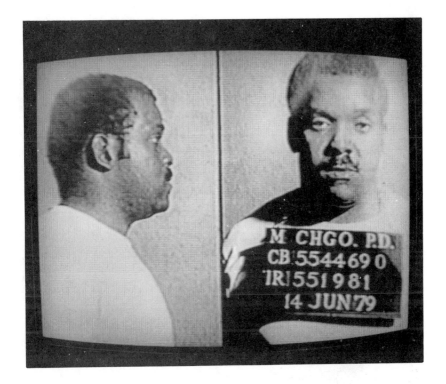

ZEKMAN: Purnell was convicted of murder—sentenced to sixty years. The
judge described his conduct as "monstrous." The prosecutor who
tried Purnell agreed.

A picture of a man in a suit and the name, Neil Cohen, superimposed,
appeared.

COHEN: He was a time bomb waiting to go off. Unfortunately for Michael
Lavin, he got caught in the explosion.

Close-up of a woman. She was not introduced, but her statement identified her.

BARBARA   If they had checked the company that hired him, had checked into
    LAVIN: his background thoroughly, had he taken some kind of
              psychological test, perhaps my son would be alive now.

Lois Bellamy, the mother of the other victim, appeared on the screen
without introduction.

     LOIS   That woman lost a son and I sympathize with her. But needing a
  BELLAMY: warm body, I guess that's why they hired him. And they got a dead
              body. It just doesn't make sense. Not at all.

These close-out statements by the two mothers addressed the problem
being explored by the investigation. Although this segment of the series
dealt with one man's behavior, the viewer was reminded that that man
was not the problem. In her office, Zekman summarized:

ZEKMAN: A spokesman for CPP Security said the firm could not comment because of a pending lawsuit. However, the spokesman said that the company is now one of the few that voluntarily give a psychological test to every new employee. Meanwhile, state officials say that legislation may be needed to force agencies to give those tests and check an applicant's prior work record. Tomorrow night, at ten, we'll tell you about a growing underground of unlicensed security firms.

The report took five and one-half minutes, including the thirty second introduction of the anchorman. The anchorman was not shown with Zekman, and it was obvious that the entire segment was taped and edited. It would be risky for a live reporter to narrate over tapes and slides in a report like this, because a stumble or delay in the narration would throw off the synchronization of the words and pictures.

All of the visuals used were produced for that specific purpose. There were no stock shots from the files, such as a police car going down a street or a picture of the skyline or courthouse, which would have served no purpose other than create movement.

How They Got the Story

Gathering this information appears to be little different from gathering a newspaper story. Care for detail was not sacrificed because the story had to be brief. Reporters got the documents and statistics, talked to experts and victims, and organized the material.

At the end of the report, the narrator mentioned that representatives of the company involved in the death would not comment because of pending litigation. That is a clue to a reporter who is investigating how the reporters gathered information for this story. Perhaps the family of the murder victim sued the security company and the business that used the company, and the information about the background of the guard came from the file. Or, the guard who was crippled may have filed a suit against the company that employed him, and information was obtained about the subsequent murder conviction of his assailant from that civil court file. Reporters would also go to the criminal court, pull the case files, locate the families, their attorneys and the prosecuting attorney, and call the state's attorney.

Because security guards are licensed, information would be available from the state licensing agency. The reporters would have gotten all of the information they could from any complaints filed and, if the state requires that a guard report for the record each time he changes employment, they would be able to trace the career of the dangerous guard. Then they could contact previous employers for their cooperation in making available his work records.

Pictures of the blood on the tile and the bent snow shovel could have come from criminal court files. After a conviction, there should be no problem in reproducing documents placed in evidence in the court case. The reporters went the extra mile when they found a clock similar to the one used as a weapon to fully illustrate the story.

If reporters in any medium were to investigate problems caused by increased need for security guards, they could design a project that might result in what the Channel Two Investigative Team found. We could think of it as an idea proposed in an outline:

Title: Armed and Dangerous

Subject: The problem of selecting, training, and controlling the growing number of private security guards.

Need: Security guards in this state outnumber the police three to one, and while they are often in the same critical situations as policemen, they have little training and are given poor supervision. Meanwhile, they are able to carry guns.

Scope: We will attempt to judge the quality of private security guards. Have they caused more harm than good? If the state is not doing a proper job of licensing and disciplining the security business, we will try to learn why.

Methods: We will research the backgrounds of guards to learn their training and if they have a history of violence. We will research the laws regulating private security firms and compare them with those of other states. We will try to find impartial experts in the security field and locate any studies that have been done.

Sources: We will check the indexes of area civil courts for lawsuits filed against security companies, pull those cases, and find the people and attorneys involved. We will pursue leads we get by checking the complaint files of the state licensing agency and any action they have taken. If we learn of a criminal charge against a security guard, we will pull criminal case files and get as much information about it as possible. We will talk to any victims of abuse by security guards.

Presentation: Depending on how much information we get, we plan a four or five part television series of five minute reports. We expect to have taped interviews with victims, experts, and prosecutors. We will present our written documentation both by the spoken word and with pictures.

CHAPTER NINE

Investigating Consumer Abuse

Investigative reporters are almost always appreciated by their readers but never more so than when they expose a widespread consumer fraud or abuse. Consumers may be abused by misleading advertising, unscrupulous salespeople, poor quality or unsafe merchandise, and overpricing. Consumer abuse ranges from gray areas of interpretation to outright theft by those operating outside the law.

Some newspaper columnists and radio and television programs wage an ongoing battle against abuse of the public. They try to resolve immediate problems. Investigative reporters step into consumer reporting when a particular fraud is rampant, and they take a long-term look. They seek out victims of the fraud and get them to go public with their personal experiences; they talk to experts or legitimate operators; and they track down and expose those individuals or companies that are repeat offenders. Investigations extend to government if certain agencies that are supposed to be protecting the public against a particular fraud are not doing the job.

Reporters may go one step further and take on the role of victim by responding to advertisements or phone solicitations and reporting on what happened to them. They might go undercover as a sales trainee to expose what appear to be fraudulent or misleading sales tactics.

Investigative stories about consumer fraud may tell of victims, name the names of perpetrators, and demand action from public officials. The stories never entirely eliminate potential fraud, but they warn consumers to be on guard.

The fly-by-night repairman or "chimney shaker," the fast-talker who skips town with a deposit, and the mail order hoax are familiar targets of such exposes. The fraud scheme may even be a sophisticated financial plan like an illegal pyramid or Ponzi scheme. People who operate such schemes can be arrested and prosecuted if caught. They prosper because they usually move from place to place or from one scheme to another. Investigative reporters cannot hope to catch all of them, but their mission is to educate the public and therefore ruin, for such illegal operators, what was a lucrative racket.

Not all consumer abuse can clearly be defined as fraud. Consumer protection stories may involve overpricing, misleading advertising, and inadequate or unsafe products. Usually, the most effective means of exposing such consumer problems is a survey to judge the amount of risk facing a consumer. While a survey may expose some fraudulent operators, it is most useful in showing the amount of consumer abuse within an industry.

Reporters investigating a product can compare one product with another and reach conclusions about the superiority of a product by using technical experts and scientific tests. Investigations can range from testing automobiles to counting the number of peanuts in a chocolate bar. In an investigation of services, reporters check on prices and competence. They might ask, for instance, if several income tax preparation services produce the same bottom line when the same figures are submitted to them.

Consumer abuse is not limited to private business or individuals. Government also may be in the role of a direct abuser of the consumer when administering public programs, like unemployment benefits or welfare assistance. The public seeks help from the news media when government is cumbersome or unfair. In investigating those consumer complaints, reporters have the advantage of public records to survey.

Most consumer investigations involve private businesses. The fly-by-night consumer racketeers do not have a Securities and Exchange Commission filing or other corporate documents. Chances are, they are not even incorporated but attach business advertising signs to the side of vehicles with magnets so they can quickly be changed and a new business name displayed. They don't leave a forwarding address. They attract lawsuits, but because they are highly mobile and use various names, even locating them to respond to a civil suit is difficult. Also, consumer racketeers do not have public contracts. These require the posting of bonds and proof of performance.

But investigative reporters have ways to expose consumer racketeers.

- They find the extent of the problem by talking to agencies that hear consumer complaints.
- They learn some of the technical aspects of the particular consumer problem by finding professionals in the field who can educate them.
- They seek out people who have suffered from the fraud and listen to

their stories. Usually such people are willing to go on the record, because they have tried other means of getting satisfaction and have gotten none. Reporters have nothing to promise them but that their stories may warn other people who could be taken in by the fraud.

Reporters can find the extent of a problem and victims by contacting agencies that hear complaints, and those that can give background information and opinions.

Better Business Bureau. Ask people where they would go with a complaint about a consumer injustice and usually the first place they mention is the Better Business Bureau. It is so well known that people think it is a government agency. Better Business Bureaus are private organizations funded by businesses to ferret out bad apples that give business a bad name. A Better Business Bureau may be helpful to consumers by giving advice and reporting on the status or record of a business, but it has no arrest powers and cannot shut a business down; it can only turn the complaints over to government agencies. Better Business Bureaus and similar organizations can be helpful to reporters by telling them of the types of complaints they most often get. They are usually quotable sources about how a particular fraud scheme is worked.

Legal assistance groups. Some private organizations are funded to provide legal assistance to persons who are unable to pay for lawyers. They hear complaints and help people with legal matters inside and outside of court. Investigative reporters looking for victims of a certain fraud may contact these groups to find out if they have had any complaints. Information obtained by a lawyer from a client is confidential, but the lawyer may be persuaded to contact the client/victim to see if that person would like to talk to reporters.

Courts. Even the little guy can go to court and get satisfaction for a small injustice. The court system has provisions for small claims court or *pro se* court in which a citizen can file a suit without a lawyer for small amounts of damage. These court files are open and treated like any other lawsuit. Investigative reporters have learned that such complainants make excellent interviewees for stories of consumer abuse, because they know that a person does not travel to the courthouse and file a complaint, for example, against a plumber for $30 for the money alone. He or she is hopping mad and ready to tell anyone about it.

Congressional offices. Some U.S. senators and representatives keep offices or special personnel to handle complaints from their constituents. They refer complainants to that government agency which might best be able to help them. They might also write a letter to the party complained about in the hope that the two parties can get together and resolve their problem. Investigative reporters know which legislators are crusaders in certain areas of consumer abuse, for instance, auto safety, problems of the elderly, insurance, or real estate sales.

State and local government. In the administrative branches of state and local government there may be offices set up to hear consumer complaints. They have names like the Mayor's Office of Consumer Protection, or the Governor's Consumer Action Office. They get more complaints than they can handle and are usually helpful to investigative reporters. They often handle complaints by tenants about landlords and landlords about tenants, and reporters may choose to investigate either or both.

Citizens organizations. A large class of consumers—homeowners in a neighborhood or subdivision, tenants, condominium owners, automobile drivers, sports fishermen, amateur gardeners—may band together in an official association or loose-knit organization. These groups are helpful to reporters not only in steering them to victims of a certain alleged fraud but also in providing them with factual knowledge of the subject. Reporters look for help from wherever they can find it. If they are investigating someone who is selling poor quality flower seeds by mail order, they might turn to a gardening group for help.

Business and professional associations. Numerous associations exist for each segment of business and for individual professions. They are helpful in providing information about those frauds that either prey on their businesses or professions or that travel under their guise. Real policemen don't like people who are selling advertising for a phony police organization. Real bankers don't like con men who say they are bank investigators and ask people to draw out their money and give it to them. And real mail order sales companies don't like people who place mail order ads and then don't deliver. It is obvious that such frauds make consumers fearful of the legitimate operators. Business and professional associations may have campaigns against such practices and will be eager to help reporters.

Federal government agencies. The Federal Trade Commission is an enforcement agency empowered to sue companies involved in unfair business practices. The Food and Drug Administration (FDA) not only enforces standards for food and drugs, it educates consumers. The U.S. Post Office is a source for information about mail order fraud.

Another revealing source of information for reporters researching a consumer fraud story is the reformed "con artist," a person who once swindled people and now will go on the record to tell about it. Reporters believe that it's unwise to make alliances with criminals, but if a criminal claims to be reformed and gives legitimate advice to people about how to avoid being swindled, his or her value as a source would be unquestioned. A story exposing carnival game cheats could use the advice of a former carnival game operator. However, the confidence man turned consumer advocate is a rare find.

With help from the sources listed above, investigative reporters are able to produce a story such as the retirement-land sales story. To produce a story by more active participation, reporters will use other means:

> *Working inside the scheme.* If reporters are allowed to go to the extent of getting a job as a sales trainee for some fraudulent scheme, they would stop short of actually going out with a sales team and becoming part of an effort to defraud people. In a short time in the training process, they would learn what the sales or service people are told to do and their attitudes toward the victims.

> *Doing a planned survey.* The best consumer investigations do not expose only one fraudulent operator. They make the public aware of widespread hazards. Reporters use surveys to show that not all sales in one category are fraudulent or unfair. If the story were about the sales promotion of unworkable selling opportunities or franchises, the survey-type investigation would show the good with the bad. Reporters would find as many instances of such sales as they could. The survey would show that while a certain number of people were "ripped-off" by a franchise salesperson, others profited from their investments. It would try to show how to detect the difference between a legitimate opportunity and a fraudulent pitch.

Let's say a newspaper has decided to do a survey on furnace repairmen. A home with a furnace is chosen. Reporters have the furnace inspected by several experts and they conclude that it is safely operating. Next, furnace repairmen are selected at random and asked to come to the home and check the furnace. They might give opinions ranging from nothing wrong with the furnace to "it's going to blow up any minute." After each repairman's visit, experts check the furnace to confirm that it is still okay. Whatever is said by all persons involved is made a part of the story, and readers are left to draw their own conclusions.

Local laws may prohibit recording a conversation without participants' permission, which introduces a problem for radio and television reports of such set-ups as the furnace repairmen. Reporters should be knowledgeable of the recording or "wiretap" laws in their state so that they don't violate them. Those laws were created to protect people from having their private phone conversations listened to and taped, and some state laws are stricter than others. In an investigative report by CBS's *60 Minutes,* a set-up scenario was videotaped without sound and then played with a voice-over narrator in order to abide by one state's recording law. The confrontation interviews, however, were taped for sound, because the reporter first asked the interviewee for permission to do so.

When does such an exercise by reporters cross the line between responsible reporting and pulling off a stunt? Reporters can generally defend what they do if it is legal and fair and when the action they take is appropriate to the seriousness of the investigation. Writing and broadcasting also entertain, so no one sits in judgment over flamboyant reporting. The degree of entertainment usually fits the media that is used. The supermarket tabloid has a different approach to journalism than the metropolitan daily newspaper of record. But when reporters and editors make decisions about whether to use theatrical means to prove a point, they will consider whether the same information could be proved and illustrated equally as well by more traditional reporting. If a newspaper or broadcast station chooses the option to use too much showmanship, the stunt might be remembered, rather than the message the reporter is trying to convey.

GLOSSARY

Chimney shaker. A fraudulent repairman who approaches a homeowner and says he just happened to spot a chimney problem from the street. If he is allowed on the roof, he shakes a perfectly good chimney until something breaks. The term is also used for any furnace repairman or salesman who uses scare tactics.

Pyramid scheme. Consumers are solicited to join a plan where they are rewarded when they get other people to join. The plan grows with money from the large number of people at the bottom going to the small number of people at the top. It works well until there are no more people willing to join. Then the last people to be solicited, the people at the bottom of the pyramid, lose.

Ponzi scheme. A person claiming to be an investment expert takes money from people and immediately gives them a large amount of cash return. Then they give him more money to invest for them. The scheme collapses because the so-called investment expert has not been investing the money, but instead, has been using one investor's money to pay another investor's dividends. Finally, the Ponzi scheme confidence man takes a large amount of investment money from his circle of happy investors and skips town.

PROJECT

Have you ever felt that you were cheated, swindled, defrauded, or ripped-off? Write about your experience. Submit your story to the class for discussion about how that particular consumer problem could be investigated and exposed. Then write an outline on how you would proceed with an investigation.

Case History: Gladys Tydings Investigates a Consumer Problem

A consumer columnist at the *Daily Metro* noticed an increasing number of complaints about auto repair shops. The columnist alerted the city editor and suggested an investigative project. The city editor saw an interesting story in the idea, but he believed that the assignment was rather routine and suitable for a novice. He also thought that a woman was more likely to be victimized. Gladys Tydings, the newest reporter on the newspaper staff, got the assignment to check auto repair garages to find out if they were doing unnecessary or shoddy repair work.

Gladys realized that auto repair is the kind of consumer investigation that is done from time to time by newspapers and television stations, so she researched past investigations of auto repair garages. She looked for such stories in the annual indexes of major newspapers around the country which she found in the public library.

Gladys was surprised that so few stories had appeared, but she contacted the reporters who had done them and asked them how they went about it.

She learned that in a typical investigation, a good distributor cap on an engine would be replaced with one that was cracked, and the car would be taken to a few garages for repair estimates. Many times, mechanics would say the engine needed a complete overhaul at a cost of hundreds of dollars. But when it was time to write the story and mechanics were contacted for comments, they would say that what they quoted was only an estimate. When they did the actual work, they found that it wasn't such a big job after all. The estimate was too high and the customer would not be charged. The story then would lose much of its impact, and readers would be faced with the question of whether the mechanics did or did not intend to defraud the car owner.

Several reporters told sad stories of being accused of making errors in their reporting and having to run retractions even when they were sure they were correct. The mechanics would insist that the engine did need the work, contending that the repair problem was not the distributor cap alone. Complaints would come to the editors from auto repair garages by way of the advertising department. Officials throughout the entire auto industry and in local service stations, repair garages, and car dealerships often complained that the stories were unfair because they painted an entire industry with the same brush.

This was enough warning to put Gladys on guard. She realized that she would have to have a well-planned, flawless investigation of auto repair garages to succeed.

She looked at the state statutes and talked to government regulators and consumer advocates; she learned that there were few laws to protect consumers from fraudulent or overpriced auto repairs. To the contrary, the laws seemed stacked against the consumer. She learned that when she signed a work authorization form in a repair garage she signed beneath a paragraph of small print that stated the garage could keep her car until the bill was paid even though she may find she was overcharged.

Consumer advocates told Gladys that they received more complaints about auto repairs than about anything else—it was at the top of the list. She learned that the major concern of car owners was that when they turned their car over to a mechanic, they were at his mercy. They had no way of telling after the work was done if the repairs really were necessary. Poor workmanship and overcharging were other major concerns.

Gladys took her plan to the editors. She would get an outside expert to examine cars and guarantee that when she took them to an auto repair shop they were not in need of repair except for one small defect that would be inexpensive to fix. She might have to pay the expert, but it would be better if she could get him to help without pay. Then critics could not say he was in the newspaper's employment and therefore did what they wanted. After repair work was done, she would have the expert mechanic examine the car again and report on what had been done. The story would name names. Of course, to do all that, the newspaper would have to pay for the actual repairs so that there could be no retort that the mechanic had only made an estimate.

Gladys also proposed that the reporters call not only on independent garages and small service stations but also on the garages of major auto dealers, franchised transmission, brake, and muffler shops, and even repair shops of big retailers in shopping malls. The investigation would be a survey, she said, so the story would include the mechanics who did a good job as well as those who did a poor job.

The editors were anxious for a well-done, fair story that could be documented with expert opinion. So, even though it was going to cost more than they thought, they okayed the project.

The first task for Gladys was to find an expert. She knew this person should be someone not active in the auto repair business who could not be accused of playing favorites, so she approached high school and college auto repair instructors. The job of selling them on the idea was not easy. They were not in the auto repair business, but they placed students in auto repair jobs and did not want bad relationships to develop with the auto repair industry.

Gladys had to go fifty miles outside the city to get a school instructor to be the expert. He agreed to serve as the expert for the project without charge, because he wanted to promote the new auto repair program at the school. Because the expert was so far away, Gladys felt secure that word of the project would not leak out to repair shops in the metropolitan area and alert them in advance.

Working with the expert mechanic, Gladys set up tests for transmissions, starters, and brakes. What is more foreign and baffling than the inside of a transmission? What is a person to do if the car just does not start? Are mechanics taking advantage of the importance of brakes? In each of these auto operations, the expert designed a simple malfunction that could be repaired for less than $20.

Gladys had decided to use American-made cars, recently out of warranty, so she could take them to the shops of new-car dealers. She got friends and other reporters to loan their cars in exchange for a complete tuneup and checkup. She then had to decide where to take the cars. She divided the metropolitan area into sections and chose at random one new-car dealer, one independent repair shop, and one franchise or retail outlet in each area. She listed fifty-two stops and would adhere to the order in which they were placed. The expert mechanic would not be told where each car was going, which would further insulate him from the criticism of favoritism.

The expert mechanic told Gladys about an old ploy in transmission repairs: the mechanic would "drop the oil pan," dip into it with his fingertips, and say there were metal filings in the transmission. Then he would tell the customer that the transmission was "burning itself up" and needed to be replaced. The expert said there was nothing wrong with the transmission on her car except for a detached vacuum line, so any metal filings found would be meaningless.

Gladys enlisted the help of other reporters to carry out the project more quickly. They established a rule that they would not tell mechanics about any specific problems that needed repair, because the mechanics might later say the reporters had entrapped them by specifically asking for certain repairs. All the reporters were to say was, "It's not running right." Each time, they would ask for the worn or damaged parts that had been replaced, but they would ask for these parts when they picked up the car so that the mechanics would not suspect there was something unusual going on.

As she made the first stop, Gladys wondered if all her preparation would net responses worthy of a story, but she proceeded as planned. Gladys told the mechanic, "It's not running right." He gave the car a test drive and then put it up on a rack. He lowered the oil pan and said, "There's metal filings in your transmission. It's eating itself up from the inside. You are going to have to get a new transmission." Gladys could hardly keep from laughing out loud. It was almost word for word what the auto repair instructor had predicted. But she kept a straight face, had the work done, and paid the bill of over $600.

The editors were shocked at the price and would be shocked again and again as twenty-six of the fifty-two repair garages either did unnecessary work or grossly overcharged for the repairs, causing the repair costs for the project to top $7,000. But the editors kept their part of the bargain and dipped into their operating budget to pay for it.

After all the stops had been made, the reporters made the rounds of all the shops, told the mechanics or shop owners what they had done, and asked for responses. Some said that the car must have malfunctioned on the way to the shop—but the reporters had taken the old parts back to the expert to have them checked and he found them still okay. There was no way for the repairmen to talk their way around what had been documented.

The reporters also interviewed the mechanics who did jobs correctly. Three of them had charged nothing for the minor repairs. Underscoring that fact in the story made the survey more valid. The work of the honest and skilled mechanics further proved the others to be incompetent or dishonest.

The results of the survey showed that the abuse was spread throughout the industry in all types of shops, the big places as well as the small. Also, Gladys dispelled a preconceived idea that women were deceived by mechanics more than men. One of the male reporters had the highest score for drawing unnecessary repairs.

Along the way, Gladys learned that there was no licensing of mechanics in her city, county, or state and that there was no federal control of auto repairs. Anyone with a wrench could hang out a sign and claim to be an auto mechanic. She researched the laws in other states and learned how those laws were enforced. She got opinions about the problem from auto consumer groups, garage owner organizations, and auto mechanic associations that she found in the *Encyclopedia of Associations.*

After all information was gathered, others in the city room joined to produce the final product. There were graphics to prepare, and it was decided that each part of the series would include a drawing of the malfunction that had been inserted in the car by the expert mechanic. This would help the reader with scant technical knowledge to better follow the adventures of the reporters. Pictures of the "hero" mechanics who had done the work free were included. The story made no effort to establish that any mechanic deliberately misdiagnosed the repair problems, because the reporters had no evidence to separate ignorance or error from fraud and theft.

The lead of the first-day story of the four-part series read: "A motorist has a 50-50 chance of getting a fair deal from an auto mechanic in the metropolitan area."

Gladys and the other reporters kept notes of exactly what they and the mechanics said, so the story contained colorful exchanges of the type that every motorist has experienced:

> Told that his car would need a new transmission, the reporter said, "But it only has 16,000 miles on it."
>
> "Miles don't mean a damn thing," said mechanic Herman "Buddy" Wrenchman.

It was a story that readers remembered and appreciated. From then on, if colleagues in the city room had a question about a car, they came to Gladys first.

MEMO

- Consumer stories that indicate fraud must be carefully planned.

- Fairness and balance can be achieved in a consumer fraud story.

- A well-planned, far-reaching consumer survey can change preconceived ideas.

Documents Used in This Investigation

Annual newspaper indexes. Every newspaper keeps back copies of issues. They will usually clip and file individual stories by subject matter or proper names. Reporters routinely call for clips on the subjects they are writing about to learn what has been published before and to get background on the subject. The clip and file system has been computerized at major newspapers, at least for the most recent articles. Also, major newspapers index their stories and issue them each year in book form. If a student does not have access to newspaper clip files, he or she can get the information by looking in the directories in public libraries. Directories give the date a story ran, the page, and the column. Then the student can look at that issue on film in the library.

Encyclopedia of Associations. This index, found in libraries, lists about 70,000 business, professional, and consumer associations. It includes organizations for such specialized fields as dog catcher, bird

watcher, and zoo keeper. It even includes the Investigative Reporters
and Editors Inc. at University of Missouri School of Journalism.

PROJECT

Design a survey to research a consumer abuse problem. Think through carefully
how such a project could be fair and yet not easy to challenge.

GLOSSARY

Consumer advocate.   A general title for persons in government offices or private organizations who hear complaints from consumers and act in their behalf.

Entrapment.   A police arrest could be discharged if the judge found that the crime for which a person was arrested had been suggested by the arresting official. "Entrapment" in the gathering of a news story would be similar. Readers would have cause to dismiss the validity of a story if the subjects were told to do something wrong by reporters and then were exposed for what they did.

CHAPTER TEN

Investigating Private Businesses

There seems to be no question that the media should investigate government operations because it is necessary to provide accountability by elected officials to the people who elected them. But when reporters start digging into private corporations or the conduct of professionals, the public may want to know why.

Reporters do not limit themselves to investigations of government operations when the public interest is the issue. The safety of airplanes, the price of food, dangerous medical practices, poor investment by banks of pension money, and misconduct in management of utilities are important subjects for investigative reporters.

In other countries, including some we call Western democracies, the government owns banks, airlines, electric and telephone utilities, and even broadcast stations. In some, prices are regulated and medical care is nationalized. In the United States, the government does not operate these important services but, as an alternative, reserves the right to regulate them.

Therefore, the reporter's responsibility extends into the private sector to monitor whether government is properly regulating those businesses that it is empowered to regulate. This responsibility also includes checking on those companies that contract to do business with government to assure that the public is getting what it expects from those contracts.

Public documents are readily available because the government requires disclosure. Disclosure of financial information is required of companies that sell stock to the public; of transportation companies seeking routes; and of insurance companies. Waste management companies must disclose information about landfills to environmental control agencies.

Disclosure of background information is also required of individuals seeking public licenses, like tavern owners and independent truckers. We say that a dog is licensed, but actually the dog owner is providing disclosure that he or she owns a certain dog. When professionals, like real estate brokers, take tests to be licensed, they are disclosing their knowledge to the government. Other disclosure is obtained by government agencies when they inspect private facilities that must be licensed, such as nursing homes, day care centers, and restaurants. Owners of factories must open their doors to disclose the premises to safety inspectors, who then file reports.

When one company or person sues another company or person, the two parties have left the private sector and have asked the government to mediate the dispute and grant a judgment. They disclose in a court file what otherwise might be private business. Also, when companies or persons buy property or issue a mortgage, they want that information disclosed to protect their interests if original documents are destroyed, so they record it with a government agency. This public records system provides reporters with ample documentation for important areas of the business sector.

For the purposes of investigative reporters, business can be divided and analyzed in sections. For clarification, we will first separate not-for-profit organizations from for-profit businesses, and then dissect the for-profits.

Not-for-Profit Businesses

A not-for-profit business is much misunderstood. It may be to the advantage of the not-for-profits to be misunderstood because the public perception is that they are charitable institutions. Some are, but others are businesses that are controlled by individuals. The not-for-profit status is an arrangement with the Internal Revenue Service. The company declares that it will not make a profit, and it files a tax return with the IRS that shows how it spent the money it took in. This return, IRS 990, is designed to disclose that information, and the return is made public by the IRS. The law requires that companies make copies available to the public, but by getting it from the IRS, reporters do not alert the companies that they are examining. Also, states require that not-for-profits file an annual report of officers. Copies of these reports are available to the public.

A not-for-profit company declares a public purpose, such as furthering education or science, or providing health care. It's difficult to list types of businesses that are not-for-profit, because the same operations may be carried out through a business organization that is for-profit. The organizers have a choice. For example, those hospitals and colleges that are not publicly owned and tax supported may be either for-profit or not-for-profit organizations. But neighborhood groups and ethnic associations are usually not-for-profit.

When investigative reporters look at a not-for-profit organization, they want to determine if those people who control it are taking advantage of the not-for-profit status by siphoning off the money to other operations they control. Those who control a not-for-profit might take advantage of their positions and lease property from themselves at a high rate or enter into contracts with for-profit firms they own to provide services that normally would be done by the not-for-profit staff. This would obviously subvert the idea of the not-for-profit status and would be contrary to serving the public interest.

Charitable institutions or foundations require more disclosure than other not-for-profits if they are raising money to aid people outside their organization. If someone sets up an organization to help hungry children in a foreign country, the state may require disclosure of exactly how much money went for that charitable purpose. Reporters want to learn if charitable organizations are associated with for-profit fundraisers, who then use the charity name to raise money, returning only a small portion of the money to the charity.

For-Profit Businesses

We will start with the smallest and move to the biggest corporations in analyzing for-profit businesses for the investigative reporter's purpose.

Paper Corporations

It is not unusual to find a corporation that does no business. It has no office, operates no store or factory, and has no employees. It may be controlled by one or more people who are not officers but are stockholders who are the beneficiaries of the profits. It may have income, but the money flows through from enterprises of other corporations. The paper corporation might have a function, such as to get a contract or to lease back property to another corporation. If preference is given to women or minorities in awarding a government contract or certain persons are prohibited from getting a government contract because it would create a conflict-of-interest, a paper corporation might be created as an intermediary to disguise the true involvement and fulfill the requirement. When the term "paper corporation" is used it has a negative connotation. It should be understood that there is nothing illegal or improper about forming a corporation for a single function as long as that function is not improper.

Professional Corporations

These corporations are formed to make a person's professional operation such as lawyer, accountant, doctor, consultant, etc. independent of his or her private life. Because a person is responsible for his or her professional conduct, it seldom matters in the telling of an investigative story whether an act was done by a person or by a person through a professional corporation; but this separation will be seen in indexes of court cases and other public documents.

Partnerships

Partnerships may be formed to operate small businesses or to invest in large ventures. General partners control the business and are responsible for its operations, while limited partners are not active but may share in the profits as would stockholders in a big corporation. Although they are not called corporations, partnerships are required to register the same as corporations in most states and to disclose their general partners. Most information about partnerships will come from court cases. Partners turn to the courts when they get angry at each other, and if a partnership fails, the partners may end up in a long court battle or in bankruptcy court.

Private Corporations

These corporations run stores and factories, construct buildings, and provide financial services. But because they are privately owned, they do not have to make financial disclosures to the public. They do have to disclose financial information to the government for income tax purposes, but that information is private.

What are these businesses, and why should a reporter investigate them? They include the company that owns a pornographic bookstore, the operator of a private waste dump, the builder of a subdivision, owners of a bar or nightclub, a travel agency, a trucking company, an auto repair garage. Any of these might be the object of repeated complaints or be in the news because of controversial activities.

While business accounts are private, an investigative reporter is equipped to examine such private corporations through the large number of public records they leave behind.

Court cases. The civil courts are the back alleys of the business world. While small businesses make every effort to achieve a good reputation with their customers and the public as a whole, they will roll up their sleeves and slug it out in the courts. Businesses sue other businesses for unpaid bills or undelivered promises. Employees and customers sue for any perceived wrongs. Those files are public records and include testimony taken under oath. It is rare to find an active business that has not been either the plaintiff or defendant in a court case.

Real estate records. Small businesses often own the buildings from which they operate, and they get loans on the property when in need of cash. Public records of ownership and mortgages may provide important information about small businesses. If they rent, the ownership records will show who the landlord is, and that person may be willing to talk to reporters about the business being investigated.

Licenses. Most retail businesses need a license to operate and are inspected by local authorities. Inspection reports of food establishments are usually public record. Also, a business must get a license for its vehicles such as delivery trucks. If all other efforts fail to disclose ownership, or it appears that owners are being hidden in the corporation papers, such licenses may reveal the true owners.

Public contracts. If a business is not a public nuisance that has caused a demand for a newspaper investigation, the need for the investigation may be stimulated by the number of public contracts it gets. Just as a reporter in a previous example checked the bidding process to see if a government agency was working well, reporters can trace that process to find out if a business is doing proper work and also to gain insight into its ownership and operations.

Published reports. A company that is active in business will post signs, circulate advertising, and be listed in business directories. Reporters will check those items when investigating a business. Even a phone number can be important. The association of two companies can be shown if they share a telephone listing.

Public Corporations

These are the big guys, the businesses that take the most heat. They include the oil companies, auto manufacturers, food distributors, defense contractors, airlines, and hotel chains.

Like small companies, big corporations also have a history of lawsuits, real estate records, public contracts, and licenses. They are more likely than small businesses to have public relations offices that are prepared to handle inquiries and combat dissemination of unfavorable information. But, most important, their financial information is not secret. They are classified as public corporations because their stock is offered for sale to the public. That means they must comply with financial disclosure under the Security Exchange Commission Act (SEC). On an annual basis, these companies report to the SEC. The SEC operates reading rooms for public research of company disclosures.

Big companies also report to special regulatory agencies. Insurance companies must file financial information with states, and their records are public and readily accessible. Transportation companies file with the Interstate Commerce Commission. Broadcast companies have information on file with the Federal Communications Commission. States regulate utilities and require disclosure when rates are set. Federal and state governments require disclosure from banks and savings institutions. Reporters must learn what agency regulates the business they are investigating and the extent of disclosure it must provide.

That information is of great value when reporters are investigating the general practices of a type of business service, for instance, the auto insurance industry, credit card companies, funeral directors, and exterminators. Such projects mean researching as many of those companies as possible and learning how they are regulated, talking to officers about their operations, and reading trade publications.

If the business being investigated requires its operators to be individually licensed, a look at those licenses might be productive. States license health professionals, real estate and insurance sales people, private detectives, exterminators, barbers, beauticians, and many other professionals. Routine complaints on file about such professionals will probably not be open to the public, but if the agency brings a charge against a licensee, the nature of the complaint and what was done about it should be on the record.

Other sources of information about businesses are employees and former employees. Employees who are fired or who leave a company with bitter feelings usually can be persuaded to talk about it. Their names can be found in the course of checking the lists of court cases involving a company. The information these people provide, however, is not documentation. It is often hearsay or exaggerated claims that must be documented elsewhere. It is treated by reporters as information from a tipster.

GLOSSARY

Plaintiff/defendant.   The defendant is the person who is placed in the position of having to defend him- or herself in court from an allegation. The other party in the case is the plaintiff, the person who creates the lawsuit by making a complaint.

Trade publications.   Businesses and professions usually have at least one magazine or newspaper that is directed toward their specific field. By reading a library index of publications, reporters can find that particular magazine that covers the business field they are exploring. There are magazines or newsletters for public officials like prison wardens, airport managers, and public works engineers; for businessmen like jewelers and plumbers; and for professional people like lawyers and hospital administrators. Some groups have many publications, and some are directed at subgroups within the profession, for example, publications for lawyers may include specialized publications for trial lawyers, probate lawyers, copyright lawyers, bankruptcy lawyers, and so on. The publications are extremely frank, because the writers and editors assume that no one outside that business will read them. They sometimes contain letters that are almost confessions about how a customer, a competitor, or Uncle Sam was tricked!

Exercise: Finding a Property Document

Media investigations often involve property ownership. Property ownership is generally thought of as a private matter, so it surprises some that so much information about private property transactions is available. Reporters, students, and others may readily get such information.

The purchase and sale of land and the buildings on it, mortgages on property, liens against titles, contracts to buy property, restrictions and easements, and some leases are recorded with counties in each state. That function may be controlled by the office of the county clerk or by a separate elected or appointed county office called the registrar of deeds, recorder, or lands officer.

Students of American history and fans of Western movies are familiar with the idea of a prospector staking out a claim. Owners of property want proof that they own the property, so they stake out their claim by recording their ownership with the county. Some states specify what must be recorded; others make it optional. Technically, just about any document can be officially recorded with the county for a fee.

The bank or other agent loaning money to a property owner will want it known that it has been promised a piece of that property up to the value of the loan if the loan is not repaid under conditions of the contract with the land owner. The lender records that fact so that the land cannot be sold unless the loan is revealed to the buyer.

Buyers also want assurance that the property they buy is free of liens that they don't know about. If contractors work on a property and do not get paid, they place a lien on the property for the amount owed them.

If a lawsuit is filed that has a direct relationship to the property, it will be recorded. Such a lawsuit might be a building code violation filed by the local government, a condemnation suit by a government agency seeking to acquire the land, or a pending foreclosure by a mortgage holder.

Land recording offices were set up as a part of the government early in the history of this country. They were designed for relatively simple operations. Land parcels were seldom smaller than forty acres, and usually ownership changed only when parents died and left the property to their children. Indexes of land ownership changes in the county then were handwritten in books, and copies of the deeds were tied up with ribbons and stored in a safe.

Then came subdivisions and condos. The land offices were overwhelmed. They had to develop more sophisticated means of recording and storing information. But even though most offices are modernized, the basic system has remained much the same. Most land offices still use a grantor-grantee recording method.

The record shows what happened to the property, not what happened to the property owner, so one must think of the record from the viewpoint of the property. Owners come and go, but the property is constant. The property owner—the grantor—grants a part of his or her equity in the property to the lender when the grantor gets a loan. The same idea applies to a lawsuit or lien; the property either gives up something or invites such a possibility. The grantee gets the property or a promise of equity in the property through a loan, lien, lawsuit, or option to buy.

Usually, grantors and grantees are indexed in separate books by years. If reporters investigate an individual, they check the grantor-grantee books for each year for the person's name. Next to the name would be the name of the other party in the transaction, the type of transaction (such as transfer of ownership or mortgage), the date of the transaction, a brief description of the property involved, and a code number. That number refers to another index system which tells where a copy of the actual document is stored, so more information or a copy of the document can be gotten.

Knowledge of the grantor-grantee system is basic to research in a land recorder's office. If the known owner of a property is traced in the grantee books, then the name of the person who granted the property can be found and that person's name can be checked in the grantee books to see when and from whom he or she got the property. Often land is turned over quickly; one person buys the land for the purpose of transferring it to a second person. The previous ownership and the duration of the ownership can be important to an investigative reporter.

Over the years, grantor-grantee books have been put on microfilm to preserve them and make them more readily available. More recently, the land records offices have become computerized. In urban areas and resort cities, where there is a large turnover of properties, the system may be computerized or partially computerized. Reporters can put the name of an individual into the computer system and any transactions involving that name will pop up on a screen. It is likely, though, that reporters will have to deal with a variety of recording techniques because counties have not attempted to put historic documents on computers, and most computerized systems do not go back farther than the mid-1980s.

Some recorder's offices may use another system, the tract system, and some may have both systems. The tract system is used when one wants information about a specific piece of property and does not have knowledge of prior ownership. Then one looks up the property through a legal description. The entire country is neatly divided into sections for this purpose. Sections, which represent acreage, are numbered, and then subsections within those sections are delineated and numbered. A property description might read: "The South one-half of the Northeast one-quarter of Section 10–30–15." The land recorder's office has record books with a separate page for each property. The books are organized by subsections within sections. Reporters researching a property find it on a section map and then locate the book the property is listed in. There they find all the transactions on the land from the time the area was first settled. The names of grantors and grantees are listed, the types of transactions, the dates, and code numbers to direct them to the actual documents.

Subsections are further divided into subdivisions. We may think of a subdivision as a place in the suburbs with winding streets and barbeque pits, but subdivision started out as a term used in land records. Each subdivision may have a separate book of its own. The correct subdivision and lot are found on a map, then the lot number is located in a book where a chronological list of the transactions involving that lot is found. In recent years, condominium books have been added to the shelves of the recorder's office; condo property in the tract system is also listed by number.

Some counties use a tax description number for all land parcels in addition to the other indexing. By using those numbers, a researcher can shortcut the tract and section systems. If a property can be identified on a map and its tax description number found, that number can be put into the land record's office computer and property transactions will be shown. The tax description number can also be taken to the treasurer, assessor, or tax collector's office where the current owner will be identified. That name can then be used to find information in a grantor-grantee record system.

The idea of a land records office evokes the image of a stifling government office where dust and cobwebs are forever encroaching. In reality, these offices are usually pleasant places. They are in constant use by local real estate professionals and lawyers. The larger offices are frequented by researchers of all ages. Some are employed by credit rating companies to look for liens, law suits, and foreclosures. Others are searching for property they might obtain in a foreclosure auction. These offices are generally operated in a do-it-yourself fashion, with no restrictions and no questions asked. Reporters who learn to use the facilities can blend into the crowd with little problem.

Finding a document is one thing, but understanding it is another. If reporters own homes of their own, a deed and a mortgage will not be foreign to them. But the face of a land document is confusing because of their often old-fashioned style. Some deeds are written in wording that befits Old English script. But most of these documents are standard forms with the blanks filled in, and once they are understood they can be recognized. Reporters usually get a copy of the document they think is important, hand copy it, or take thorough notes, and then take the information to a friendly expert for help in interpretation. Unless the copy has to be certified for legal purposes—and reporters won't need that—the cost of copies will be small.

An important notation on a document that may need interpretation is the tax stamp. To support the operation of the land offices, a tax is charged on the transfer of a title. The charge is based on the dollar amount of the sale. The tax is small, in the range of $.50 to $1 per $1,000 of the sale; the stamp is affixed to the deed and recorded with the document. Reporters can determine the price a person paid for the property by finding out the tax rate at the time of the sale. But many counties write the price of the sale on the recorded transaction, making mathematical calculations unnecessary.

We know that reporters are not looking at land records for the usual reasons. They are looking for public wrongdoing in the ownership of property or transactions related to it. They need not feel guilty, because Internal Revenue Service investigators may be working in the same offices for the same reasons. Because of that, the subjects of investigations may want to hide their ownership. Land may be placed in the name of a nominee. A nominee is a person selected to "hold" the land for the real owner. The real owner has a contract with the nominee for transfer of the property that is not publicly known. Another means of concealing ownership is to list the property in the name of a trust or a corporation; the ownership of the trust and corporation does not have to be revealed.

In an investigation that involves property, research of other than land records may be needed. Some public places are regularly inspected for safety by a city agency. Property owners also have their buildings inspected by various local agencies. Owners usually have to get building permits and submit new facilities to a thorough building inspection.

The amount of property tax paid may be important to an investigative story. Those records are public and show not only the amount assessed but also whether the owner has paid or is delinquent in paying the tax. These records are found in county government in an office that may be called assessor, treasurer, or tax collector. A check of building permits, zoning applications, inspection reports, and tax bills may turn up names that reveal the hidden involvement of persons not listed in the land records office.

PROJECT

Go to the land records office of your county government and find a land record that could be a part of the investigative project you are outlining. Submit a copy and an explanation of its possible meaning to your investigation when you submit your investigative project outline.

CHAPTER ELEVEN

Investigating Health Care

Reporting on health care involves looking into government and business and even crosses the line into emotional and religious issues. It is viewed with such importance that some newspapers and television stations and networks have specialists to provide health care information to the public and report on happenings in the health care industry.

Investigative reporters may choose to view health care in a dispassionate way, researching a story of body maintenance and repairs as they would a story about automobile maintenance and repairs. But the stories will have great personal impact and will be emotionally received. Because of their broad impact, health investigations require the most skill of all investigative reporting.

In an investigation of health care, reporters may choose to look only at the cost aspects and leave the technical stories to specialists. But medical competence and procedures may also be investigated if reporters are willing to take the time to understand the science of a particular area of health care to the degree that they can accurately simplify and transmit it to readers.

We will examine investigative reporting of health care in three categories: (1) cost; (2) competence of practitioners and facilities; and (3) whether practitioners are working "outside of licensing"—outside the scope of their training and the limitations of their licenses.

Cost

We look at waste in government, and we know that government passes that unnecessary cost to the taxpayers. As long as taxpayers are willing to pay, government spenders have no reason to economize. However, if operators of a business want to succeed or even survive, they must run a leaner operation and draw their expenses only from the income that the business produces. But health care professionals and facilities are between government and private business. They have little incentive to be efficient whether they are tax supported, for-profit, or not-for-profit if they are mostly paid by insurance plans. "Don't worry about it, your insurance will cover it," the clerk in the health care facility tells a patient. But somewhat like the tax spender, the health care provider who overcharges insurance companies passes the cost to the private individual by making higher premiums necessary. Reporters may respond by taking on a mission to guard that public expenditure by exposing waste in health care facilities.

A health care facility may also overcharge patients. If it is a for-profit company, rather than waste money on unnecessary services, it skimps on expenditures and takes the money out of the operation in profits. If it is a not-for-profit company, those persons who control it may devise ways of taking money from the facility through schemes to lease back equipment or contract for services through companies they own. Such arrangements drive up the cost of health care without improving the services.

Reporters can use the traditional tools of investigative reporting to produce stories.

Financial Reports

Hospitals, nursing homes, and other health care facilities that are funded by Medicare and Medicaid must make public financial reports to the U.S. Department of Health and Human Services. Not-for-profit companies must also make public financial reports to the U.S. Internal Revenue Service. For-profit companies that sell stock must file public financial information with the U.S. Securities Exchange Commission.

Patient Billing

Another telling financial document from a health care facility is an item-ized bill. The bill is a private record, but a patient who believes he or she was overcharged will be willing to show it to a reporter. A bill for publicly paid medical care, such as care for welfare recipients, may be public record after the patient's name and other personal information has been removed.

When hospital patients see an itemized bill, they are usually alarmed. A bill might list one aspirin at a cost of $2. Patients know that they can go to a drugstore and get a bottle of aspirin for $2, so they believe that the hospital has overcharged them. That may or may not be true. The hospital spreads the costs of *all* of its services over all patients. In the itemized breakdown, the cost of the aspirin includes costs of the time that it took the nurse to walk across the room and hand the pill to the patient; that portion of the nurse's salary and benefits, including the cost of a parking space provided for her in the hospital parking lot, the laundering of her uniform, and so on. Minuscule costs attributed to purchasing and handling by others in the hospital would be factored in. This method of cost analysis can be studied by investigative reporters and applied to other service operations. It is alarming to the person who pays the bill if he or she takes it at face value, but for reporters, it is a handy means of investigating costs.

Surveys

Each day in every hospital and nursing home bed sheets are washed and replaced (we hope!). The cost of doing laundry per patient should be about the same in comparable facilities. If it is not, questions will present themselves for reporters to answer, and a story would be forthcoming. Other clear-cut comparisons would achieve the same goal of getting a handle on costs. The variation in the amount and quality of medical care and the food served would make those comparisons inappropriate.

Another method of surveying costs in medical facilities is to separate all those items that are not medical in nature from the cost of the nursing care, medicine, and medical procedures—like emergency room care and surgery. That would leave all else that figures in a hospital bill, such as administration, supplies, janitorial services, and food services. Those two separate accounts would show what proportion of the health care dollar is going to services other than medical within a facility. Those figures can be compared with figures from other hospitals or nursing homes to determine which spends the most in areas that might be considered most vital. Findings from statistics are never conclusive, but they bring up the questions that must be answered, and the answers will become the framework of a story.

Competence

An investigation of competence in health care would include looking into the facilities and the professional people who practice health care. Conclusions about competence are difficult to reach, but reporters have investigative tools to help them.

Inspections

Hospitals and nursing homes may be the most regulated enterprises in the United States. Aside from all the financial disclosure required, health care facilities host a parade of inspectors who file reports for the public record. Among the most powerful are state health agencies and local health departments, which are empowered to close down facilities or prevent their receiving Medicare and Medicaid patients. They inspect both the medical practices and the housekeeping of a facility. The local building department and fire department inspect the facilities themselves for safety. Food is inspected by specialists in the local health department.

Medical Licensing

Professionals who work in a health care facility or who are independent practitioners are individually licensed and regulated by the state. The medical professions are usually licensed by a separate agency or division within a state licensing agency. The state regulators hear complaints about practices other than the prices charged and can take away licenses. Such decisions are made by boards of practitioners who are licensed and experienced in the same field as the medical professional who drew the complaint. The decisions are never final, because the medical practitioner can appeal to the civil court system to have a ruling overturned. Doctors, nurses, pharmacists, and dentists are regulated by the states. Technicians, nurses aides, psychologists, and other health care professionals also may be licensed by states. Complaints against medical practitioners filed with the state by individuals are not public record, but if the state brings a complaint of its own and sets a hearing, charges are usually public. Reporters usually find that an individual who complains to the state is willing to complain to the newspaper and, therefore, make what was private a public complaint. Either way, reporters know that a complaint without a finding must be treated the same as a tip; it must be checked out before it is considered to be fact.

Big hospitals have boards that will dismiss from their staff a medical practitioner they believe to be incompetent or not up to their standards. Those actions are private, but court records can be obtained if the practitioner goes to court to overturn a ruling by a hospital, as they most often do.

Investigative reporters first make sure that a medical practitioner is licensed when he or she claims to be a professional by displaying a sign or advertisement. Reporters check with the state licensing agency and the university at which the person claims to have studied. Professionals whose licenses have been revoked in one state may relocate to another state. And some may be complete frauds who never had licenses or medical education and who fake their skills and credentials. A background check may reveal that a professional is licensed but is practicing medical procedures that are outside the scope of the license; for instance, a podiatrist who does not limit his or her practice to the foot, or a physical therapist who does surgery.

Lawsuits

Investigative follow-ups of complaints, such as those in lawsuits, are productive in learning about poor health care. But reporters seldom use information from a court file of a malpractice suit without further investigation. Plaintiffs in malpractice suits often make wild, unsubstantiated charges, and the medical person who is the defendant may want to wait until there is a trial to answer them. Also, the trial may never be held because the doctor's insurance company might rather settle than go to court.

Some doctors are in the front line of malpractice jeopardy by working in the emergency room or in especially difficult areas of surgery, so a large number of malpractice complaints does not always mean gross incompetence. But malpractice suits can be important in describing medical procedures and identifying patients who can then be interviewed by reporters. Specific allegations may also be found, such as routinely using a procedure that has been discredited by medical experts. This would cause reporters to pursue the story much as they would if they had gotten the information from a tipster. Opinions of professional associations, government health agencies, and medical university experts help produce a story about a poor medical practice.

Public Facilities

The government runs many kinds of medical facilities. Their records, except for individual medical records, are public. On the federal level, the Veterans Administration and the military operate hospitals. Also, there may be city, county, and state hospitals for persons unable to pay for other health care. States and local governments also run hospitals for the mentally ill. These facilities vary in the degree of quality of care. Investigative reporters have exposed and corrected appalling conditions in these and have documented political interference in what should be professional operations.

Outside of Licensing

Careful reporters refrain from using the word *quack,* often heard in connection with poor medical care. Its use is limited to untrained, unlicensed persons who sell medical cures, and even then one should be careful. Anyone can give medical care. Unlicensed medical care might range from giving advice to a friend with a cold to posing as an expert and claiming to know more than others about curing some ailment. When that wide range of "medical" advice is considered, it can be understood why it is difficult to define what is improper outside of medical licensing. A weight-loss club that promotes exercise or the promoters of a diet with vitamin supplements are in the health care business, but they are not licensed as medical practitioners and they are *not* "quacks."

Investigation of most unlicensed medical practices calls for the same procedures as consumer investigations. But the seriousness is compounded if the victim shuns licensed medical care for a salesman's pitch and then suffers more health problems. Also, the sick person who is victimized by an unlicensed medical practitioner may suffer a tragic drain on funds that could have been spent for proper medical care. Remedies sold by someone outside the medical establishment are seldom cheap. Machines or computer analyses may be used which require the patient/victim to return again and again for costly treatments or to be monitored.

Reporters find that it is difficult to thoroughly discredit persons who sell such cures because they have followers who want to believe. They will tell them that the medical profession and the government are persecuting them because they know a simple remedy that they don't want the public to know. Patients/victims of a medical fraud may also be convinced that a seller is deeply religious and that the cure is being suppressed by an irreligious medical establishment. As irrational as it may seem, such arguments are an important element in the sales pitch to insulate the salesperson from criticism. When newspapers or television stations then expose the fraud, the unlicensed practitioner tells clients, "You see what I told you—now the medical profession has gotten the media to persecute me."

Associations like the American Cancer Society and the Arthritis Foundation, which raise money for research, provide information about unproven, dangerous, and fraudulent practices in the areas of their concerns. The U.S. Food and Drug Administration rules on whether a drug is dangerous or worthless, but the rules can be circumvented by the sale of a food item shaped like a pill or in a tea bag and therefore not a drug. Or by having patients receive treatments by traveling to a foreign country.

Only an overt, obvious sham may be labeled as quackery. If the "miracle machine" can be proved to be an old World War II bombsight bought from army surplus, or the "secret plant of the Amazon Indians" can be proved to be ground-up maple leaves, investigative reporters can make some headway in educating the public.

MEMO

- Investigative reporters have access to the financial information of most health care facilities whether they are tax-supported, for-profit, or not-for-profit.

- Reporters need assistance from medical experts to reach conclusions about the competence of medical care.

- "Quackery" is not easily defined or proven.

- Complaints in malpractice suits are unsubstantiated charges that are not considered fact even if the complainant wins a judgment.

Case History: Bud Munn Investigates a Health Care Facility: Part 1

The information that got the story rolling was contained in a memo from the *Daily Metro* reporter who covered the county building. It was passed along to Bud Munn. The newspaper's court reporter had been told by an attorney that one of his clients, who was suing a hospital where he used to work as a janitor, mentioned that janitors were being used to help out in the surgery room. Janitors did not wield surgical instruments alongside the surgeon, but they would on occasion be asked to help move patients from the surgery table to a gurney, then take them back to their rooms without allowing the janitors to wash their hands or put on sanitized smocks. When Bud told the story to his friends in the newsroom, they laughed at the improbability of such a thing happening in these times in a metropolitan hospital.

But then Bud learned that the city police and fire departments had recently stopped taking accident victims to the emergency room at that hospital because of its poor facilities. There had been rumors of bizarre happenings at the hospital, a small, privately controlled, not-for-profit facility. The patients were mostly welfare recipients who were referred there through a chain of walk-in clinics in low-income neighborhoods. Bud drove by the hospital building and saw that it was old and shabby.

Bud realized that proving that the hospital allowed janitors in the surgery room would be difficult. He could not propose such a story on the word of the disgruntled ex-janitor who was suing. He anticipated that the hospital administration would deny that such a thing could have happened, and then, even if Bud got the newspaper editors to print such a story, it would not have much impact. Readers might scoff at the janitor's charge just as Bud's colleagues had laughed about it in the newsroom.

Bud thought that this might be an ideal circumstance for an undercover job. If he could be hired as a janitor and report the story from the inside, readers would be more likely to believe it. His experiences might make for exciting reading, he thought.

The idea stimulated debate among the editors. There was no question that the threat to the safety of patients in the hospital was an important story and that a report of an undercover experience would be exciting. The main discussion centered on whether the story could be gotten by means other than a reporter getting an undercover job. If the hospital were dangerously operated, there must be more to find there than the janitor story, one editor surmised, and the story could be gotten through traditional investigative reporting methods. Also, the legal implications of a reporter getting a job in the hospital were not clear, they concluded. One thing was clear—if a patient in the hospital were harmed while the reporter was there and he could in any way be blamed, the legal consequences for the reporter and the newspaper could be great, and the publicity would be harmful. The idea was much too risky, the editors ruled.

Bud began to work up another idea. The newspaper could do a sweeping survey of hospitals that had a large number of welfare patients by having reporters go undercover as exterminators. They could put together a team of reporters and photographers and
get into the hospitals by offering them a free demonstration of exterminator services. Then they could view the conditions and get pictures. In preparation for a presentation of the idea to
the editors, Bud read the inspection reports of the state health department, which were public records. By looking at the inspection reports and finding what violations were found in each hospital in the past, reporters would know what to look for. Bud also researched how exterminators work so that the reporters would be able to pull off the charade. But the idea had flaws—Bud found that anyone who uses toxic chemicals, such as an exterminator, must be trained and licensed. To pose as an exterminator would be illegal. The newspaper would never allow a reporter to break any law. Some of Bud's investigative stories had caused new laws to be created; he didn't want to break laws. He knew also that entering hospitals by means of such a subterfuge might be construed as invasion of privacy, and so he decided to abandon the idea without proposing it to his editors.

Bud realized that he would have to get inside the hospital by means of documents, interviews, surveys, and surveillance, perhaps without actually setting foot inside the hospital buildings. While he was exploring the idea of an undercover reporting, he had requested information from government agencies. In addition to inspection reports from the state, he requested the hospital's IRS 990 report (for a not-for-profit organization) by filing a Freedom of Information Act request with the U.S. Internal Revenue Service.

The IRS responded, providing Bud with a copy of the hospital's financial report. Bud noticed that the hospital officers received very high salaries, higher than salaries of officers of other hospitals in the city. That's strange, he thought, because the hospital was small and had always been thought of as poor. And then, one line on the form caught his eye. During the year covered in the most recent report, the hospital paid "$368,000 for the goodwill of the Revolving Door Clinic."

Bud checked the newspaper clip files each time a new name came up in an investigation. He had already checked the clips for stories under the hospital's name. Now he looked for the Revolving Door Clinic and the names of the officers that were listed on the financial report. The only mention of the Revolving Door Clinic was eight years before, when it was listed in a story about campaign contributions to the governor. The story noted that Revolving Door Clinic and two doctors had contributed $300 to the campaign. The two doctors were the same two doctors who controlled the not-for-profit hospital. They sat on the board of directors and under the hospital's by-laws could appoint the other directors.

Why was the hospital paying so much money for the "goodwill" of the clinic? It appeared to Bud to be a financial trick. He was told that goodwill, in a business transaction, meant the value of a business aside from its hard assets such as buildings

and equipment. Did it also mean that the clinic was selling its referrals? Either way, it appeared that this was not an arms-length transaction, because the doctors were both buyers and sellers. But what and where was the Revolving Door Clinic? Bud had no address from the campaign contribution story of eight years before, and there was no listing in the phone book.

Bud went to the public library, got telephone books from eight years before, and found the address of the clinic. In the telephone books for the following year, there was no listing. He drove to

the location and saw that it was a vacant lot with some trash and rubble on it. It appeared that a building had been there but it had burned down or had been torn down. Goodwill from a clinic demolished years ago? Bud knew that he was starting to pull together a story of financial fraud. He was also able to get corporation records from the state for that year, and they confirmed that the two doctors were the owners of the clinic, which was a for-profit business. The money that was listed as a payment for goodwill of the clinic had in reality gone out of the not-for-profit hospital into the pockets of the doctors.

Bud did personal profiles on the two doctors. The older of the two

had been in partnership with the father of the other doctor. When the father died, his son continued in his capacity at the hospital. Bud checked the probate files of the doctor who died
ten years before. It showed numerous corporations owned in partnership with the doctor who was still living and was now a partner of the deceased doctor's son. One of the corporations was called Specific Land Acquisition, Inc. and was listed along with other information in the memos that Bud was compiling.

Even though he was the only reporter on the story, Bud thought it best to put all of his information in memos and store them in orderly files. He also started a chronology of events and dates he had gathered in his investigation so far, going all the way back to the older doctor's birth and school records. Bud had long since abandoned the typewriter he had brought from the police beat years ago and used the *Daily Metro's* computerized system. He kept memos both in the computer and in computer print-outs. It was no problem to insert new information into the memos and the chronology.

While he continued his orderly compiling of facts, Bud worked on other facets of the expanding investigation. He
had gone to the hospital to look at the building early in his investigation and had written down the license numbers of cars in the parking lots—cars of doctors, hospital workers, and some of the patients. Part of the task was easy because the doctors and top administrators had their own parking spaces marked with their names. He got the names of the owners of the other vehicles from a check of the plate numbers through the state motor vehicle licensing division. Then he compared those names with the medical licensing agency to learn if they were doctors, nurses, or licensed medical technicians. That information went into his memo file on the personnel of the hospital. He also saw trucks of companies that brought supplies and was able to start a list of contractors because most of them were marked with signs.

Bud made friends with the original source—the janitor who said he was used in the surgery room. The ex-janitor had worked for the hospital for about one year, and it amazed Bud how observant his source had been. "The janitors know what goes on where they work," he said. "People almost always ignore us, but we see and hear things and then talk about them on our breaks. What they're doing at the hospital is bringing whole families in and having all their tonsils taken out the same day. That's why they used us to help move the patients out of the surgery room. They've got to get them in and out of there as fast as they can so they can keep running up the bill with public aid."

Bud had no medical training. The janitor did not pretend to have medical knowledge. Both believed that the procedures were improper.

But how could a reporter and a janitor go against the opinions of licensed medical doctors? The answer would come from medical experts that Bud found in professional associations, government agencies, and universities. They said that tonsillitis was not contagious and that the odds that there would be a need for an entire family to have their tonsils out the same day were astronomical; "trillions and trillions to one, I suppose," one expert said, "if not just completely impossible."

Bud had names of patients from the license plates. He called them and told them that he was a reporter from the *Daily Metro* doing a story about the hospital and wanted to know if they had any complaints about the care they received. Some were satisfied, even thankful that they got the treatment. Bud chose to not tell them that they probably got unnecessary surgery and were subjected to dangerous unsanitary conditions. He could imagine a storm of protest over a reporter second-guessing a doctor and interfering with the doctor-patient relationship. But there were a number of patients who were not happy with their care. Bud went to their homes and talked to as many family members as possible.

A patient's medical records are private. If Bud believed there were important facts for the story in a patient's medical records, he asked the person to get those records for him or to sign an authorization allowing him to get the records. However, welfare payments were public records after the patients' names were removed from the billings, Bud learned.

When Bud researched a major story, he always checked the court indexes and land record indexes at the county building. He would write down the names of people and corporations involved in any way in the story inside the cover of his notebook. Then he would scan records for those names to learn about any transaction that might provide a little more information about the person or corporation. He also did property searches of locations that he knew were important to his story. He searched for transactions involving the ownership of the land the hospital occupied and soon found that Specific Land Acquisition, Inc. owned the property on which the hospital was located. He remembered the name of the company from the probate case file of the doctor who died and whose son was now a partner. The corporation appeared to be an effort to hide the true ownership of the property. Other hospital board members would not know that the two doctors who set the amount to be paid for rent were also the landlords.

Bud went back to the IRS 990 financial report and found the amount of rent paid by the hospital, compared with rents paid by other hospitals of comparable size and location, and found the rent to be much higher than any of the others. Through this process, he had an indication of another way in which the doctors were enriching themselves. He had accomplished that breakthrough in the investigative story in a way that makes his work exciting. He had pieced together two separate, concealed bits of information just as he had done with the Revolving Door Clinic and found a new illustration for his story.

Bud worked long days and late hours on his story. When he wasn't talking on the telephone with sources and experts, he was digging through public records or watching the hospital from across the street. Even when he was supposed to be away from work, his mind was racing with thoughts about the hospital story. He was turning over information in his head and formulating new ideas about where he might find more information. He had a feeling that all of his years of learning on the job had prepared him for this point in his career so that he could produce an investigative story that was difficult and of extreme importance to the community. He was determined that he would not fail to deliver.

MEMO

- A reporter can overcome a lack of scientific or technical knowledge by consulting with experts.

- A complicated investigative story may take the full concentration of a reporter over a long period of time.

- When a reporter is unable to get information from one method, he has alternatives.

Documents Used in This Investigation

Inspection reports. State and local agencies inspect health care facilities. Some have teams that specialize in nursing home or hospital facilities. Their inspections and approval are required for a health facility to be eligible to receive public funds. They inspect housekeeping, not medical treatments. Doctors and other medical professionals are responsible for the medical care. A nursing home or a hospital may be considered a motel where the medical profession brings its patients for more convenient care. The owners may or may not have medical training. Inspection reports are usually checklists of violations and indicate if the complaint has been satisfied.

Private medical records. Medical records may be bills or detailed reports. They are private records that belong to the patient. With his or her cooperation, they can be valuable, reliable documentation. Some otherwise private medical records are made public when they are filed as part of a malpractice suit against a medical practitioner.

Public aid payments. Records of medical bills that the government pays are usually public if they do not invade the privacy of the patient by revealing his or her name. If an investigative reporter is researching the methods of one or more doctors in a facility, an itemization of the charges can be revealing. A question such as, Where are the most tonsillectomies performed? may be answered by a computer run of bills to a public agency—bills that can be requested with a FOIA letter.

Old telephone books. Public libraries often have old telephone books. Some have put them on microfilm or preserved them through other means. The listing of a now famous person may be there and former addresses of people being profiled may be found there. Public libraries may also have out-of-town telephone books, even of overseas cities.

GLOSSARY

Arms-length transaction.   If two sides of a business transaction are separate in their interests and influence, the transaction would be considered "at arms-length." Otherwise, if the public interest is involved, a reporter might want to show that it was closer than arms-length and therefore insider trading.

Exercise: Finding and Understanding Court Records

It may seem to us petty and personal when one neighbor sues another. So, why is it a matter of public record? The two parties could not reach an agreement, so one of them, by filing a lawsuit, asked the government to intervene. When government intervenes, the people have intervened. All of the people, therefore, have a right to know the decision of the judge or jury who represent the people and how that decision will have a bearing on their lives. Any lawsuit, no matter how insignificant, could affect reviews by the court of the conduct of others. In order to understand the decision, the public must know the facts of the case.

The facts are placed in court records, available for all to examine. The task of the investigative reporter is to find those facts that are important and to interpret their meaning.

Investigative reporters do not look through court files in order to study the law. On occasion, reporters may produce a story about the justice system and will survey court records for signs of some imbalance in the manner that the law is being administered. But usually reporters are on a fact-finding mission—they are gathering information about people and institutions revealed in the files, often in sworn testimony.

Approaching the court system for information and going to the land records office are similar in some ways, but the social issues and private disputes that enter the court system are not as easily marked off for reference as are land boundaries. Reporters are faced with a complex system in which new information is added daily. Out of it, they must locate the right documents.

To understand a complex court system with many branches, first examine a small court system such as one in a rural county that combines its functions into one records system and maintains one or two courtrooms. Every lawsuit filed in that court will be indexed in a clerk's office by the names of the plaintiff (the person complaining) and the defendant (the person being complained about). The case is assigned a number, and a docket sheet is created. As the case proceeds through the courts, the docket sheet is marked with the date of any court appearances and what happened to the case that day. Motions may be filed, arguments heard, the case continued, the case dismissed, or a ruling made. If the case is appealed to a higher court, records would be found in the state appellate or supreme court.

A civil case is filed if a person or corporation sues another person or corporation. The cause for the suit can be any suspected wrongdoing. A criminal charge is brought by the government under statutes that specify exactly what wrongful act the law enforcement agency believes a person committed. The government also may bring a civil action against a person or corporation for alleged wrongdoing outside the criminal statutes. The files of a civil court case reveal what might otherwise be private information about the parties involved.

As a civil court case proceeds through the lower court, a file is created—an expandable envelope designed to contain legal-sized sheets of paper. The file placed on a shelf in the court clerk's office, and each time there is an official paper filed in connection with the case, it is placed in the file. By looking for the name of the plaintiff or defendant in the index and taking the case number from that index to a clerk in charge of the files, reporters can examine whatever is in the case file.

Some files bulge with information, taking up two or more of the big envelopes. Certain documents are contained in a file:

1. *Complaint.* This is the original document—the one that got the case into court. A person or a company complains about another person or company. The complaint tells, in the opinion of the complainant, who did what to whom. It should include such specific information as dates and locations involved in the incident or condition that the complainant, or plaintiff, is complaining about. It must be under-

stood that a complaint is merely an allegation by the plaintiff. The dates and locations of an incident are valuable to reporters as information, but not as fact. The complainant lists the individual(s) or company at whom the complaint is directed—the defendant(s).

2. *Answer to complaint.* The persons or corporations named as defendant in the complaint have an opportunity to respond within a certain period of time. They will probably deny the accusation. They may even file a countercomplaint in which they turn the tables on the complainant and put on record their grievances related to the same incident or condition. However, there may be an admission to some of the facts concerning an incident. If a person complains (plaintiff) that a neighbor allows his dog to run through a flower garden, the neighbor (defendant) might deny that and counterclaim that his fence was damaged by the complainant, causing him to be unable to keep his dog confined. Through this counterclaim, a reporter learns that the defendant acknowledges ownership of a dog and says he has a damaged fence.

3. *Interrogatories.* Each side may direct questions at the other under certain rules of law. Often, these questions are in a standard form that provides information—names, ages, dates of incidents, status of insurance policies, and place of employment, if those matters relate to the complaint.

4. *Answers to interrogatories.* The person questioned is allowed time to respond and places the answers in the court record. The information is brief, but it gives the reporter basic information about the parties involved in the suit.

5. *Motions.* The defendant is likely to file an argument, or motion, asking that a judge dismiss the suit. His or her attorney may put the argument in writing in the file, and the attorney for the plaintiff will be given an opportunity to reply to that argument. The battle of the written word continues, and the judge studies the written arguments. Some of the motions may contain documents that will interest the reporter. For instance, if taxi companies are being sued to stop a fare increase, the companies might file a summary of their financial records to support an argument that the increase is justified. Those previously private records are then made public.

6. *Discovery.* Each party in a lawsuit asks the other to submit, for the record, certain information believed necessary for the court to make a decision. Either side may protest this intrusion and cause the file to be filled with more written arguments, or they may comply by submitting the information. As a part of discovery, depositions may be taken from individuals involved in the suit. A deposition is sworn testimony, but instead of being testimony on the stand in a court-

room, it could be taken in the presence of attorneys and stenographers in a law office. A sworn, written deposition may be of extreme importance to a reporter, because while the party gives testimony about one matter, he or she inadvertently gives information about other matters.

7. *Findings.* The idea of the battle of words in the court file is to keep the matter out of court and cut down on expenses at the county courthouse. When the case finally goes to trial, much of the work has been done, and the trial can proceed with each party knowing where it stands. It is more likely that the two parties will reach an agreement before the case comes to trial. Many people have insurance which pays for the costs of lawsuits and any damages. Those companies may know what is a reasonable settlement in a legitimate suit and may convince the plaintiff that the amount offered is fair. Or, the original complaint may be dropped because the plaintiff realizes that the cost of pursuing the case is more than he or she can hope to win. If there is an out-of-court settlement, the two parties inform the judge, who will dismiss the case. There will be a record in the file that the case was dismissed on agreement of the parties, but it will not necessarily state the terms of the settlement. If it matters to the story, reporters may contact the attorneys or parties involved and ask them for the details of the settlement. But if they won't tell, the reporter is stymied, because the settlement has slipped into what might be call the "black hole" of private records— the argument is no longer a matter for the government to rule upon.

8. *Transcripts.* If the case goes to trial, another document is created—a transcript of the proceedings. While the words spoken in the trial are public information, reporters cannot expect to be supplied with a free transcript of the work of a court reporter. Transcripts are costly to reproduce. If a newspaper or TV station will not entertain the idea of spending hundreds or thousands of dollars for a transcript, reporters may be able to get one from a friendly attorney. If a case is appealed, and most large-dollar or high-visibility cases are, a transcript of all or part of the lower court trial may have been prepared and paid for by the party appealing, and it will be in the higher court clerk's file or available from the judge in the higher court.

Criminal court files may be researched by reporters investigating individuals; they are found by searching the indexes in the court clerk's office for defendants. Criminal court case files are indexed in the same way as civil cases. A file cites the criminal violation that the person is charged with and may contain the police report concerning the arrest, or a summary of a more complete file found at the police department. It will show when and for how much a defendant posted bond to be released. The disposition of the case, which could be a finding of guilty or not guilty or a withdrawal of charges by the state, is shown in detail. Reporters may be shown a "rap sheet," or list of arrests of a person, by the police department. "Rap sheets" are not reliable and are not held out by the police as documentation. But a "rap sheet" gives dates to check and confirm with the more accurate criminal court files.

The court system of a large metropolitan county may be broken up into various divisions. For criminal cases, there may be courts for felonies (the more serious crimes) and for misdemeanors (lesser crimes). Or there may be separate court systems for narcotics and traffic cases. The civil cases might be divided into a domestic or divorce court, a probate or inheritance court, and perhaps a housing court. Each would have an index system and filing system that enables reporters to find the name of a plaintiff or defendant and get a court file. In the more personal matters of divorce and probate, a party to the suit may ask the judge to seal the information about personal assets that has no bearing on the court decision. Reporters must then ask the judge to break the seal on the information. Some localities have juvenile courts, and state laws prohibit them from providing information about the arrest of a juvenile.

The enforcement of criminal statutes and the judgment of civil matters are mostly in the hands of local government, with the U.S. Supreme Court sitting in final judgment. But the federal government has its own legal system. The federal courts act in those matters that cross state boundaries or violate federal law. Also, the federal government operates the bankruptcy courts. Bankruptcy was on the minds of the founding fathers when they wrote the Constitution. Right up there with the authority to print money they granted the federal government the right to preside over bankruptcies. A reporter investigating a business that is in bankruptcy court will find all of its financial records on public display.

Whether reporters are seeking a court file in local or federal courts, they should have no problem gaining access to the information. Similar to the land records offices, the court clerk offices are designed to accommodate the public. Attorneys, paralegals, and researchers make daily use of the facilities and are provided with places to sit and work. Reporters can carry on research without having to reveal why they are looking at a file.

PROJECT

Search the indexes of a local court clerk's offices for lawsuits that would be important to your investigative project outline. Find the file, write a summary of the case, and include it in your outline.

Case History: Bud Munn Investigates a Health Care Facility: Part 2

The hospital investigation, started by a tip from an ex-janitor, grew to such an extent that the editors of the *Daily Metro* assigned two other reporters to help Bud Munn. An investigation of an allegation of unsanitary medical practices had grown into a complicated story of financial wrongdoing and medical incompetence.

The reporters called on former patients and searched in the state controller's office for medical payments to the hospital through the public welfare program. They substantiated charges that the hospital brought in entire families to have their tonsils removed. The reporters talked to as many of those family members as they could locate. By pulling records, talking to patients, and discussing their findings with medical experts, the reporters found and proved a pattern of overbilling and unnecessary surgery.

At this point in the investigation, it seemed almost incidental that the hospital used janitors to move patients in and out of the surgery room, but Bud continued to pursue that allegation as well. The janitor who was Bud's original source had sued the hospital he had worked for in federal court for damages under the federal wage and hour law, which prescribes certain rules for minimum wage standards. He claimed that he was owed money due to excess hours he was forced to work without overtime pay. He told Bud that other employees suffered such exploitation also, but they needed the jobs so badly that they were afraid to complain or to join him in the suit.

But those people talked off-the-record to the reporters. By meeting with those employees who still worked at the hospital, the reporters learned about the day-to-day happenings inside the buildings. They talked to the janitors, nurses aides, and clerks. Bud knew that the hospital administration must have learned of the reporters' activities, but there was no way that he could avoid having them know about his investigation at that time without hindering his ability to get more information. He thought they probably would have no idea how much the reporters knew and that they would be unable to hide anything that had happened because of his widespread sources.

While one of the reporters was watching the building one day, he saw a group of men in jogging outfits run out the side door and down the sidewalk. There was a man running along with them who blew a whistle and yelled at them. The group looked like a sports team, something one would not expect at a hospital. After running several laps around the block, the group ran back into the unmarked side door from which they had come.

Bud contacted one of the inside sources the reporters had developed and asked what was going on. The sources wanted to help in every way, but they often needed to be prodded with such questions because they didn't always know what was important to the reporters. The source said that the hospital had built a health club in one of the hospital buildings. It was used by the doctors, their families, and their friends, but never by the patients. The hospital administration had hired a professional trainer to give workouts. They had built an indoor basketball court and sauna and the facilities of a health club, such as lockers, showers, and a hospital employee to supply clean towels.

Bud knew that the installation of the health club facilities would have required substantial remodeling of part of the building and that the hospital would have to get building permits. Permits could not be avoided because the licensed electricians and plumbers the hospital hired would require permits before they could make water and electric utility connections.

Bud got the building permits from the city building department offices and found that a sketch of the floor plan for the proposed health club facilities was included in the file. He showed the sketch to some of the hospital employees, who confirmed that it had been built as shown. The building permit also showed an estimate of the cost of the work, and it listed the names of the contractors who did the work.

But Bud wanted to know where the money to build the facility had come from. He checked with the health systems agency in the state where medical facilities operators must apply to get approval for large expenditures for improvements or equipment. He learned that the hospital had applied for and gotten a grant from the U.S. Department of Health and Human Services. They had labelled the new construction a "physical therapy unit for patients" in their application for federal funds.

Meanwhile, one of the other reporters tracked down a medical doctor who had been an intern at the hospital several years before. An introduction was supplied by one of the current employees who knew the doctor, and two reporters went to talk to him.

"Yes, I saw them using janitors to help move the patients in and out of the surgery room, but I was a newcomer and I couldn't very well make trouble over it," he said. "I'm not even sure that there is any specific rule against that, but I can tell you that the hospital was extremely understaffed, and there are probably rules that would cover the number of staff members. The janitor had to be doing somebody else's job."

Bud found the requirements for hospital staffing in the rules set by the state health department and checked their inspection records to see if there had been any complaints. But he found none. He learned the names, though, of the persons at the nursing stations on different shifts from the inside sources. He also had his sources look at the timecards that were posted at the employee entrance and note who was working each day. Checking the names against the licenses of registered nurses and nurse's aides with the state, Bud learned that nurse's aides were being used to do the job of nurses.

He now had the accounts of four janitors or former janitors who told him that they were used to move patients from the surgery room. He had located them through his growing network of sources. When the janitors were called to help in the surgery room they were not given time to wash up or put on clean clothes. They might have been loading a laundry truck in the parking lot, for example, and have dust all over their shoes and clothing. They would be told to roll the patient back to his or her bed. Often, another patient was being pushed into the surgery room as they left.

Bud noticed that there was an item on the patient bill of $50 for "recovery room." He learned from health care inspection reports and medical experts that the recovery room was where a patient was taken during the dangerous period immediately after surgery so that his or her vital signs could be monitored. Taking a patient to a bed in a regular hospital room and leaving the patient there unattended was dangerous, Bud realized, but billing for care in the recovery room when there was none could be considered fraud.

Bud decided to go into the hospital and see for himself, even though he had not received approval to do this from his editors. He wanted to see the name tags of the nurse's aides who were working as nurses. He had learned from his sources which patients were due for surgery; so, getting the room number of a patient who was in surgery, he waited in the room until the patient was brought back from surgery. The hospital employee who brought the patient back to the bed and left him there unattended did not challenge Bud's presence because the employee was a janitor.

It was time for the close-out interviews. The findings of the reporters were presented to some of the doctors who had been bringing their patients to the hospital and who had them undergo what was alleged to be unnecessary surgery. They defended the surgery they did, stating that they disagreed with traditional medical practices and believed mass tonsillectomies to be proper preventive care.

But the hospital administrators and directors who were the target of the investigation refused to grant interviews. Apparently, the doctors who had been interviewed told them what the reporters were going to ask. Unable to get interviews, Bud submitted a list of questions in writing, including questions about ownership of the land occupied by the hospital and the purchase of goodwill from a clinic. He made sure that his list of questions informed them about the extent of the investigation that the newspaper was about to report to give them an opportunity to respond. But they did not reply.

- What information should be published in an investigative story?
- Did the firsthand viewing by the reporter confirm the use of janitors in the surgery room sufficiently to use it in a story?
- Is this story best told in one report or a series of reports?
- Should the story be killed or limited because hospital officials could not be interviewed?
- Are there other areas of the investigation that should be pursued before it is ended?

These questions call for editor decisions rather than reporter decisions. Reporters gather the information accurately and tell the editors how they got it, but the editors make the determination. When editors and reporters debate issues, reporters usually fight to use everything they have gathered and the editors are inclined toward restraint. In this situation, the editors were kept informed of the progress of the investigation and believed it to be important enough to assign more reporters to it. They should be enthusiastic, but each aspect of the story would be carefully examined.

There probably would not be much argument about using the information on purchasing the goodwill of the clinic, because it is well documented. However, because the doctors involved in the transaction would not comment, the story as it has been gathered would not have much detail. If there is a hospital board that approved the expenditures, reporters might try to get them to reveal what they thought they were getting when they bought the "goodwill." A question that might be debated is how strongly the newspaper might describe the situation to indicate that the hospital got little or nothing for its money. However, the story could at least show the inside dealings of the doctors. The editors would probably decide that the transaction should be described fairly to allow readers to draw a conclusion of their own about the propriety of the deal.

If there is no hospital corporation rule, local law, or federal regulation that prohibits the doctors who control the hospital board from secretly paying rent to themselves, the newspaper may be able to show how much higher the rent payments are than they would be at a fair-market rate. A comparison with other rents paid in comparable rental markets may be needed, along with expert appraisals. The rent also may be compared to what the hospital would pay on a mortgage if it purchased the land outright at a fair-market price.

The possible fraud in the federal application for a physical therapy unit could be stressed because of the amount of documentation. If the hospital administration stated in its application for funds that it was going to use the money for a patient physical therapy facility when it actually used the money for a private health club, it would be a blatant example of what the reporters want to show. So many different people had used the facilities that reporters should be able to find several who would talk about it because those users probably don't know that anything is questionable. They were invited to use the facilities and would have had no knowledge of how the construction was funded, so they can't be faulted. The definition of a "physical therapy unit" would have to be determined from federal and medical spokespersons. Readers must know with precise documentation that a basketball court and a sauna are not a hospital physical therapy unit to be funded with money set aside for medical care.

The editors could debate about how far the newspaper report could go in alleging fraud by the hospital in billing for a recovery room visit when there was none. The use of janitors to move patients is related to this debate, because they told of bypassing the recovery room. The documentation of janitors used in the surgery room and bypassing the recovery room is limited to personal accounts; however, if several janitors go on the record and the newspaper also has the account of the doctor who had been an intern, there could be a strong argument for using it. Sworn statements from these people would give the editors an added feeling of security. Such statements are often taken by lawyers in relation to a lawsuit and then used by a newspaper. For instance, the attorney for the janitor who is suing the hospital might take such statements; but in this case, the janitor's complaint is about hours and wages and has nothing to do with janitors being used in the surgery room. Also, the information gathered by Bud when he entered the hospital room without permission of the hospital or the newspaper editors would be of little value. He may not want to even tell of his experience for fear of being fired or reprimanded by his employers. All he saw was a part of the scenario being reported. He doesn't know if the recovery room was bypassed. Maybe the doctors decided not to operate on the patient that day and returned him to his bed. A solid investigative report will need more than a quick observation. But, seeing for himself made Bud feel better—he knew that his sources were not lying to him.

Unless there is written documentation, it would be difficult to prove that nurse's aides were being used in place of nurses. If the hospital were cooperative and would provide an official list of all hospital medical employees or timecards, it might be shown that too few were employed to meet the standards; but without this documentation, statements about who was where at what time are hearsay.

The information about tonsils of entire families being removed on one day is the most useful. The reporters have medical bills, accounts of patients and employees, medical experts calling the practice improper, and the response of the doctors defending it. It could be held out as an example of overbilling for unnecessary surgery. And if the only motive for the surgery was to run up a bill, it is clear why the janitors were needed to move patients quickly and bypass the recovery room.

Perhaps other questions should be answered or other leads pursued before the story is written. The emergency room equipment that caused the police and fire departments to eliminate the hospital from their emergency room lists could be compared with equipment in other hospitals. The hospital's other equipment and facilities could be evaluated. The backgrounds of the doctors who brought patients to the hospital for the questionable tonsillectomies could be delved into. Have they been sued or had complaints filed against them with the state licensing agency?

A large unanswered question is, How could such a hospital exist with all of the government control and inspections that are funded to prohibit such practices? Who is supposed to be checking for fraud in public welfare medical billing and why did their system not question the mass tonsillectomies? Who should inspect the buildings and equipment for maintenance and housekeeping and why were the facilities allowed to become so unacceptable that the police and fire departments stopped taking emergency patients there? Does anyone in IRS ever look at the financial reports to determine if a not-for-profit organization is abusing its tax-exempt status with inside deals?

The final decision about what will go into such an investigative story will differ from one newspaper or TV station to another. The *Daily Metro* editors decided to run the story as a two-part series.

Follow-Up

The story had such impact that families of patients in the hospital had them removed and taken elsewhere. The city Board of Health called an emergency meeting the next day and brought in the hospital administrators. When they were unable to give a satisfactory account of their conduct and procedures, a date for a hearing on a possible revocation of their license was set. Meanwhile, because the number of patients dropped and so many licensed nurses and other medical professional resigned, the hospital was forced to close.

Bud knew that he had to be absolutely correct in his story because of the great amount of damage it could do to the hospital and doctors, both financially and to their personal reputations. Any carelessness on Bud's part could mean a huge court judgment if the doctors or the hospital won a libel suit. But he was confident in the accuracy of his facts and had no prior experience with the hospital that would have caused him to maliciously attack them.

The U.S. attorney from the district started an investigation and within one year indicted the hospital's top five officials. It turned out that what the reporters found was only a small part of the overall fraud at the hospital—the tip of the iceberg. With subpoena powers, the federal government found millions of dollars in fraud and was able to get convictions of those indicted. Bud and the reporters who worked with him were commended by the U.S. attorney, who stressed the fact that the stories and convictions stopped others who might have been committing abuses in the same way.

MEMO

- An investigative report need not disclose all of the wrongdoing. It should cause the public to respond and government agencies to act.

- Even regular government supervision and inspection may allow huge amounts of fraud and abuse.

- An investigative report must be fair and accurate because of the public response and damage it can cause to the subject of the investigation.

- Interviews, documents, surveys, and surveillance may be as effective as getting information undercover.

PROJECT

Create fictitious names for the hospital, doctors, and other persons and places involved in this story and write the first paragraphs of the story. If this is to be a series of stories, write the first paragraphs of the first part. What pictures and graphics could be used in a newspaper report? A television report?

GLOSSARY

Board of health.   A local agency that administers rules and provides a variety of inspections of facilities that provide health care.

Hospital administrator.   A professional manager who specializes in operation of hospitals.

U.S. attorney.   The chief prosecutor for the federal government.

U.S. Department of Health and Human Services.   The agency that administers federal health care grants and Medicare and Medicaid payments. It also provides the public with health care research information.

CHAPTER TWELVE

Investigative Reporting in Washington

Investigative reporters in Washington have a broad responsibility to reveal important information hidden from the public by the government. While reporters anywhere may accept that responsibility, Washington reporters have two special callings: to reveal threats to the constitutional balance of power and to monitor the conduct of government in its dealings with other countries. History has taught Washington reporters that the next major investigative story could fall into either of these categories, happen anywhere in the world, and involve any level of government. In the last seven decades, Washington reporters have developed stories from the most unpredictable locations.

- In the 1920s, private businesses secretly paid high-level government officials to allow them to remove oil from a remote government land reserve in Wyoming called Tea Pot Dome.
- In the 1930s, widespread loafing by government employees in jobs such as the Works Progress Administration (WPA) were exposed.
- In the 1940s, a Washington scandal involved the use of a military ship in a war zone to transport the president's dog.
- In the 1950s, a story centered around a coat that a White House aide received in return for influencing regulatory agencies to drop an investigation.
- In the late 1960s and early 1970s, reporters exposed coverups of U.S. military atrocities in Viet Nam.
- In the 1970s, an investigation of a burglary in the Watergate office building revealed the use of presidential power to suppress political opposition.
- In the 1980s, Washington reporters disclosed details of a secret deal

involving arms sales to Iran and covert aid by U.S. officials to Central American counter-revolutionaries.

Each of those important stories was critical of the administration in power and, consequently, reporters were faced with a powerful opponent. When investigative reporters in Washington go up against an incumbant administration, the information and legal interpretation that the administration controls may be used to thwart their efforts to reveal the truth. For instance, the attorney general may advise that release of certain information would be detrimental to the public safety or to national defense. However, reporters may believe that the administration is depriving the public of that information because it does not want voters to know about it. Also, an administration may transfer or fire suspected informants in an effort to make people afraid to talk to reporters.

But the two-party system has aided Washington reporters in gathering and publishing investigations of the incumbent administration. If the White House and Congress are controlled by different political parties, information about one may be gotten from the other. If reporters are investigating an agency controlled by the White House, congressional investigative agencies like the General Accounting Office and investigators for congressional committees may become allies of the reporter. If congressional conduct is the subject of a story, reporters may find that information will flow from White House sources with the knowledge of their superiors.

A major newspaper investigation often stimulates a congressional investigation. Reporters continue to dig for new leads and information as congressional investigators prepare for hearings. They will talk to some of the witnesses before and after the government investigators, making it difficult for them to present anything but the full story.

Investigative reporting in Washington may be examined in four areas: (1) local or regional, (2) national, (3) international, and (4) special interest.

Stories of Local or Regional Importance

When a Washington decision involves such actions as deciding the route of a federal highway, the location of a military base, or whether to provide financial help for a particular farm crop, there may be intense interest in the area affected. The newspaper and broadcast stations there will want their Washington reporters, if they have them, to cover the story. Because the local newspaper or broadcast station will want more than perfunctory coverage of the government process, reporters will investigate the influences involved in the decision. They will want to learn who are the lobbyists for or against the proposal and how they influence officials. Have they made campaign contributions or given favors? Do legislators, their staffs, or government agency administrators who made recommendations have private financial interests that might have swayed their decisions? Who suggested the proposed site? Were alternative sites well researched? To try to answer those questions, reporters will look at campaign disclosure forms of the elected officials, financial disclosure forms of elected and appointed officials, information that lobbyists must file, and published studies of government agencies involved. Such stories may lead back to the local area where reporters will check legislators' business ties to see if they might profit from the particular action and research ownership of land that may increase in value because of the federal project. The question reporters will want to answer is whether this isolated government action is taken in the interest of the public or to benefit private interests.

Stories of Nationwide General Interest

A federal project or legislation may affect more than a particular area—it may restructure the tax laws, require safety devices in automobiles, or effect some change that will affect all citizens. Investigative reporters will want to learn if there are hidden interests blocking the legislation or pushing it for their own benefit. They will look into recent financial dealings of the key government persons involved.

Reporters in Washington also try to judge how well important government programs are working and how carefully the federal government is regulating industries. Stories in those categories include the condition of the savings-and-loan and banking industries and the inspection of meat producers. An important function of the federal government is to provide loans and insurance to the public. Reporters want to know how well those Washington-based programs are functioning. Social Security, Medicare, and Medicaid are federal insurance programs that affect almost everyone, and many people have direct loans or loans insured by the Federal Housing Administration (FHA), Small Business Administration (SBA), or Agriculture Department. Reporters start out with statistics and reports of government agencies, talk to consumer and business representatives, study the law, and then locate people who have the stories that best illustrate whatever problem has been perceived.

Some major questions they ask are:

- Are rules of the loan or insurance programs unfair to some segments of the population?
- When local governments administer these programs does the federal government check on them?

- Are the programs being overbilled by recipients because they know that government monitoring is lax?

Some stories of national scope involve waste of tax dollars in the operation of government. The Defense Department budget and the operation costs of the General Services Administration, which maintains federal buildings, have been particular investigative targets. Because of the size of those budgets, reporters usually study individual contracts or determine the actual amount of one item, like a screwdriver, and show that the government paid ten times as much for it as an individual would pay in a hardware store.

Stories of International Relations

The Central Intelligence Agency (CIA), the State Department, and the Defense Department and associated military services are among the federal agencies that have international responsibilities. They also maintain a greater degree of secrecy than other agencies. Reporters have found that dealing with them usually means filing a Freedom of Information Act request that may produce little or no information. Officials of those agencies argue that their actions and secrecy are for the benefit of the country, but often, when the public has learned about what some of these agencies have done in international dealings, they do not approve.

One method Washington reporters have used to get information is to interview employees who have left those services. In the Persian Gulf War of 1991, reporters complained that they were too restrained by the military in their coverage of the war. The military argued that it was for the safety of the reporters and to avoid giving the enemy information. But reporters found that the restrictions spread even to interviews with military personnel about their opinions and morale. After the war, investigative reporters began to reconstruct the happenings in the war by talking to military personnel who returned. They were able to develop stories that were not the one-sided "official" reports of the victors.

Stories of Special Interest

Business and science reporters investigate and report on stories of general national interest, but they may also focus on narrow subjects for the limited readership of publications for specialists. A journal for bankers, for instance, is likely to keep an investigative watch on the operations of the Federal Deposit Insurance Corporation and the Federal Reserve Board. A journal for pharmacists, as another example, might want to closely monitor the Food and Drug Administration (FDA) and the Drug Enforcement

Administration (DEA). Those reporters, and others for publications directed to special readerships, also follow legislation that involves the profession of their readership in hearings before various congressional committees. They will investigate influence on the legislative process much the same as the reporter following legislation of local interest.

Advantages of Being an Investigative Reporter in Washington

Washington reporters use the same tools of investigative reporting as other reporters, but due to the concentration of government offices in one place, they have many advantages. Regulatory agencies require a large amount of disclosure. For example, the Securities and Exchange Commission gets information from publicly traded businesses, the Federal Communications Commission from licensed broadcasters, and Labor Department from a variety of businesses for pension plans. These agencies have reading rooms in Washington where public disclosure files may be examined. Other agencies with reading rooms are the Federal Election Commission for campaign contributions; the Department of State, where one can get unclassified information about foreign relations; and the Department of Transportation for information about highway, waterway, and air transportation.

Another advantage for reporters in Washington is the information readily available from the General Accounting Office. The questions GAO tries to answer for Congress are similar to those asked by investigative reporters. According to the *U.S. Government Manual,* the GAO asks:

- Are government programs being operated in compliance with applicable laws and regulations, and is the data furnished to Congress on these programs accurate?
- Do opportunities exist to eliminate waste and inefficient use of public funds?
- Are funds being spent legally, and is accounting for them accurate?
- Are programs achieving desired results, or are changes needed in government policies or management?
- Are there better ways of accomplishing each program's objectives at lower cost?

The GAO provides free copies of its reports to the public, and a local reporter can receive them by mail. Some public libraries have indexes of all GAO reports. The reports are brief summaries that point out problems. They seldom name names, but they are used as investigative guidelines by reporters who expand on them with more detail, specific facts, and interviews, so that they may include different perspectives and opinions in their stories.

Washington reporters also have access to the Library of Congress, the national library of the United States. For researchers, this is the most comprehensive library in the country, with books on all subjects and in foreign languages. It has the personal papers of American presidents, historical photos, and recordings. Investigative reporters will be especially interested in the telephone directories from every city in the country, daily newspapers on film from major and not-so-large cities, and business directories for different trades and different areas of the country.

But do reporters in Washington really get their stories from government reading rooms and the Library of Congress? Usually they get only supporting information from those sources. Washington investigative reporters maintain networks of inside sources in government. It is from them that they get leads that may produce the next Tea Pot Dome or Iran/Contra story. While local reporters may breeze through a government office talking freely with the clerks, Washington reporters do much of their work on the telephone with anonymous sources. Reporters in Washington have learned that they can become the repository of gossip similar to office gossip and that Washington, D.C., is like a town with one big company. The common employer is the government, and people call reporters because they want to talk about it, examine it, and help keep it running right.

- Should reporters be allowed more access to defense-related information?
- Where should the line be drawn to define whether it is in the public interest to conceal government actions?

PROJECT

For each of the seven examples of investigative stories since 1920 given at the beginning of this chapter, list why they are or are not important to the public interest.

Case History: Gladys Tydings Reports from Washington

Soon after the *Daily Metro* published Gladys Tydings' story about the misuse of money that had been set aside for disadvantaged school children, Porky Barrows, a U.S. representative from the newspaper's circulation area, asked her to come to Washington to testify before a subcommittee of the House of Representatives that he headed. The subcommittee was examining waste in federally funded school programs.

Gladys, in the role of an expert witness, testified about her findings. It was an opportunity for her to have a platform other than her newspaper to reveal shortcomings in the monitoring of some government programs. For Barrows, it was an opportunity to get some favorable media exposure.

Gladys's testimony was reported by the *Daily Metro* and a local television station. When she returned from Washington, she answered questions on several local radio talk shows. The *Daily Metro* received positive publicity from these follow-ups to the story. The paper found it worthwhile to have an investigative reporter develop a story about a public problem and then help the government remedy it. The publicity enhanced Gladys' reputation and gave her a small measure of fame that could not have been achieved with a newspaper byline alone. Congressman Barrows asked her to join his staff. The offer was tempting because Gladys had been caught up in the excitement of Washington. It seemed everyone there was involved in much more important government functions than anything she had experienced. But at that time, she was working on the story about bingo, and she had other story ideas in mind. She decided that she was more interested in investigative reporting.

Barrows became one of Gladys's sources. He told her that he had learned through Washington contacts that a large company was "wining and dining" some top military officials to get them to recommend their paint for Department of the Navy contracts. Barrows said he had talked to a former employee of the company who had documentation that two admirals assigned to the Pentagon and their families had been provided free trips to Las Vegas by the contractor. They were given credit cards and allowed to charge their flights, rooms, meals, and show tickets. The paint company had had the Navy contract for several years, Barrows said, but the contract was coming up for renewal. It would be put up for bids again, and the paint contractor was trying to influence the decision of the admirals who would recommend the specifications, he said.

The story was outside of Gladys's experience and would normally be handled by the Washington bureau of the newspaper. But there also was a question of whether the *Daily Metro* should pursue it at all. Gladys told Barrows that because there was no local angle to the story, the editors would probably pass it up. But Barrows told Gladys that if she were to expose the conduct of this government contractor, he would hold hearings in Metro City on undue influence on government contracts. He said he also knew that a small Metro City company that qualified as a disadvantaged business was interested in bidding on the contract.

With that information, Gladys was able to win over the editors. Actually, they did not need convincing. They believed the time was right for their paper to emerge as a force in national investigations. However, they believed that because the information that would prove the allegation was in private documents of the contractor, it would be impossible to prove. Once again, Barrows was ready to solve that problem for Gladys. The ex-employee who was his source had filed a suit against the company, and his lawyer had requested some of the company financial records, which were then placed in the court file. The ex-employee alleged that he was fired because he would not participate in bribing public officials.

The court file was in a courthouse in Arlington, Virginia, where the Pentagon is located. It was similar to courthouses elsewhere, and the court clerk's office was open to the public. Gladys pulled the file and got copies of the vouchers for the expenditures that the admirals had submitted. But the only information the Department of the Navy would give her about the admirals was brief biographical sketches, and neither of the admirals would talk to her.

To broaden the story, Gladys wanted to do profiles of the two admirals. She found some color pictures of them in a naval publication in the Library of Congress. As she looked at the pictures, she got an idea. Pinned on the coats of each man were rows of military campaign ribbons. By getting another publication, a directory of campaign ribbons, Gladys was able to show when and where each man had served. She also attempted to talk to the paint contractor, but a spokesman for the company refused comment because, he said, any statement could affect the lawsuit of the ex-employee.

When the story ran, Gladys contacted the Department of the Navy and asked for their reaction. Three days later, they stated in a short news release that they would investigate the allegations.

Gladys realized that the story was not a major scandal for Washington. The *Daily Metro's* Washington reporters helped her find her way around Washington to gather the information, but they cautioned her that such practices as gifts to influential Pentagon officials were common. "They all do it—take a few freebees from contractors," Nat Beltway said. "I doubt that anything will come of the navy investigation. It's hard to prove that the Las Vegas trip really influenced the awarding of the contract."

Congressman Barrows carried out his promise of holding hearings in Metro City, and those hearings were reported by the local media. No official action was taken against the admirals by the Department of the Navy. But several months later, Barrows tipped Gladys to the story that the original contractor who had tried to influence the admirals lost the $1.8 million paint contract to a disadvantaged small business, and that company would produce the paint in Metro City and would provide local jobs. Barrows put a statement of thanks to Gladys in the Congressional Record. He proclaimed that she had provided an important public service.

Barrows was re-elected and got more important committee assignments. Two years later, Gladys got a call from Nat Beltway in Washington. "Here's one for you. You know your friend, Barrows? I heard he's been getting honoraria from the banking industry, and he's the head of the banking committee." Beltway explained that an honorarium was a payment for a speaking engagement. The banking industry held numerous conventions around the country, Barrows was flown to the meetings to make a few flattering remarks, and was paid $10,000 each time. "You know they wouldn't have him do that if he voted against their pet legislation," he said.

Gladys checked Barrows' ethics statements and found that he had gotten paid for twenty such speeches from the banking industry in one year. The ethics statements of all of the congressmen were published in the *Report of the Clerk of the House,* an annual publication that also lists the staff payroll and expenditures. She also noticed that Wiley Stewge was listed as a legislative aide. This was a thought teaser. She knew she had seen that name in connection with some story she had worked on, but she could not place it.

Gladys had another question that troubled her more. Because she had become friendly with Barrows, and he had been a source for other stories, should she overlook the possible story and remain loyal to him in return for what he had done for her?

The Argument for Yes

Reporters must be trusted by readers and sources. Many times, reporters will make deals to protect a source by not revealing his or her name or certain aspects of the story. For the sake of getting bigger stories, reporters often work with sources who are questionable. Public prosecutors do the same; they often make deals with their informants. Any story now that would embarrass Barrows would mean he would be lost as a source and might become a valuable source for one of Gladys's competitors. Perhaps at some time in the future, Barrows would provide Gladys with a story even better than the paint contract story. Gladys should look for those bigger stories and not try to report every little impropriety of a government official.

The Argument for No

No dedicated investigative reporter would allow a breach of ethics to go unreported because of some personal involvement or bias. If Barrows is lost as a source, other sources as good or better may be generated by the story. Gladys should stand apart from questionable politicians. It could be said that if she allows only one small transgression to go unreported, she is part of corruption of the legislative process. This is as important a story as Gladys has ever covered—a monied, special interest group may be subverting the wishes of the public in legislation vital to the economy.

The Decision

Gladys decided to launch into a full investigation of Barrows. She studied his campaign contributions, financial disclosure information, and office payroll. When she found the names of people and businesses with whom he was associated, she got information about them by looking for licenses, lobbyist registration, financial disclosure, and lawsuits that involved them. She also talked to as many people as she could find who knew Barrows, including his opponent in the last election. "Why should I talk to you?" his opponent asked. "Those stories you did helped get him re-elected. Don't you know he's been wheeling and dealing and feathering his own nest ever since he's been in office?" Gladys explained that she had no particular loyalties and would report any story that needed reporting.

Gladys also talked to some Washington watchdog groups, citizen-funded non-for-profit organizations that research and report on votes and activities of members of Congress. One said Barrows was high on their list of legislators who were swayed by special interest groups with money to spend.

Gladys's thorough search of records led her to the bankruptcy court, where she found in the court indexes that Wiley Stewge and a company he owned, called Metro Paint Concoctions, had filed for bankruptcy. That was the company Gladys had helped to get the navy paint contract. The file was huge. The company and Stewge personally owed millions to various people, the largest debt being a $750,000 government loan from a federal government disadvantaged business loan program. It appeared that the paint venture had been a disaster after all and that Barrows was helping out Stewge by putting him on his payroll.

Gladys found some former employees of Metro Paint who had not been paid. One was the whistle-blower Barrows had provided as a source about the other paint company. He said that Barrows had gotten him the job with Stewge as a reward for giving Barrows information about the admirals. The source was upset now, though, because of what he found Stewge doing. He said that Stewge had gotten the disadvantaged business loan as an advance to pay for the costs of producing the paint for the navy, but he never paid his bills and manufactured paint that was of such poor quality that the navy refused to accept it. "That paint was for battleships. If they would have used it, every ship in the navy would have rusted away," he said. After the navy refused the paint, Barrows helped Stewge sell it elsewhere. They funnelled that money and the money from the loan to companies they owned, and then Stewge filed for bankruptcy so the bills could not be collected, he told Gladys.

Even without having conclusive evidence that Barrows was financially involved in the paint deal, Gladys felt ashamed that she had played a part in the scam. What hurt the most was that she was sure that she had been the victim of a set-up. She was more convinced when she got Stewge's application for the disadvantaged business loan and checked it out. It showed a post office box in Metro City, the same box that had been used by the paint business. She was surprised to learn that a post office box used in commerce is not private information. By calling the local post-master, she was able to find out in whose name the P.O. box was listed, and it was Barrows. She also talked to the trustee appointed by the bank-ruptcy court. He gave her the names of companies that received large payments from the paint company before it filed for bankruptcy. She traced the ownership of those companies back to Barrows' financial disclo-sure statement. During that search of records, Gladys found that Stewge and Barrows were associated in other companies. Sometimes they shared office space or a telephone number. Stewge's companies would get govern-ment contracts with the help of Barrows. A check of Stewge's public records showed that his palatial home had been placed in the name of his wife to protect it from creditors.

"Washington is a lot like Eastchester," Gladys told Beltway. "There was a lot of corruption in Eastchester, but only a few people profited. I want to expose the few corrupt here for the sake of those who are really dedicated."

Because Stewge was working in Barrows' office, Gladys called there to arrange an interview to get comments about her findings. She said she wanted to talk about Barrows' association with the paint contract.

"What do you think she knows?" a worried Stewge asked Barrows.

"It doesn't matter," Barrows replied. "It's Gladys Tydings. I know how to handle her!"

- Could Gladys have avoided the embarrassment of being used by Barrows?
- Should Gladys have stepped aside and let another reporter handle the story?
- Will Barrows be able to handle Gladys?
- How should the questions in the interview with Barrows be orga-nized?
- What kind of a rebuttal would you expect from Stewge and Bar-rows?

Documents Used in This Story

Report of the Clerk of the House/Report of the Secretary of the Senate. Each year, these publications list the expenses of the members of Congress and reproduce their financial disclosure statements. The books are found in government libraries throughout the country.

Federal campaign disclosure statements. The Federal Election Commission enforces the law about the limits and prohibitions on contributions and expenditures in elections to federal office. It requires disclosure and makes public the amount of money, who gave it, and how it was spent.

Post office box. The U.S. Postal Service will make public the persons or companies who establish a post office box if that box is for commercial, not private, use. Another item on public record is the holder of a postage permit. In squares printed where stamps are affixed to letters are numbers that can be used to identify the sender. Reporters use this means to identify the sender of mass mailings of "hate literature" who is not otherwise identified in the literature.

PROJECTS

1. Write the lead paragraphs to the story as Gladys would after she interviewed Barrows and Stewge.

2. Outline an investigative idea that would be Washington based or national in scope.

GLOSSARY

Congressional Record.   A document published by the U.S. government that contains the daily discussions in Congress. Summaries of the daily proceedings on the floor of the House and Senate and their committees and subcommittees are included. Legislators also introduce published articles or make statements about persons or causes on the floor of Congress so they may be placed in this public record.

Lobbyist.   A person outside of government who works for the passage of legislation. The clerk of the House and the secretary of the Senate require public disclosure of the source of funds received by lobbyists and how they spent them to influence legislation. The disclosure reveals free trips or other gifts. Contributions to political campaigns are disclosed in reports to the Federal Election Board. Also, many states have laws that require lobbyists to register and disclose information about efforts to influence state legislators.

Subcommittee.   Panel of legislators who investigate, discuss, and hold hearings on the need for legislatin. Congrssional subcommittees are created for specific areas of interest. They make recommendations to a full committee of legislators, which then sends proposed legislation to Congress. All subcommittee meetings have public transcripts that are printed and available to the public.

Pentagon.   The large five-sided building that houses the Department of Defense. Reporters speak of the Pentagon as if it were a government agency, but like the White House or Capitol Hill, it is the location of certain government offices.

Watchdog groups.   Washington jargon for citizens organizations that are organized for the purpose of watching the conduct of government officials. They often work with the media to expose alleged wrongdoing and may file lawsuits in behalf of the public. An example of such an organization is Common Cause, which describes itself as a citizens lobby devoted to making government at the national and state levels more open and accountable to citizens and to improving government performance.

Exercise: An Investigative Story of International Scope

This investigative story from Washington was reported and written by Patrick Sloyan for *Newsday,* a daily newspaper serving the New York City area. It was published in May 1991, two months after the end of the Persian Gulf War. Reporters in the war zone complained that access to information and interviews was too restrictive. When military officers returned, Sloyan interviewed them to get a better account of what happened.

One Last Pasting

Two days after President George Bush ordered a ceasefire for Operation Desert Storm, U.S. Army tanks, helicopters and artillery destroyed one of Iraq's surviving Republican Guard divisions, in what American military officials now say was the biggest clash of the gulf war's ground campaign.

This straight news lead summarizes the story. It is presented no differently than a news story being filed as a dispatch from overseas.

The battle occurred March 2 after soldiers from the 7,000-man Iraqi force fired at a patrol of the 24th Mechanized Infantry Division.

The second paragraph informs readers that the newspaper has not made a generalization in the lead—it has specific facts to support the lead.

During a four-hour assault just west of Basra, the 24th, known as the Victory Division, blasted 247 Iraqi tanks and armored fighting vehicles and set ablaze 500 military transports—including towed artillery and a dozen transports carrying FROG battlefield rockets—according to U.S. commanders.

The source of the information in the first three paragraphs is cited.

More than 3,000 Iraqi troops were captured in the battle, which the military referred to at the time as one of a series of "small engagements."

The writer has contrasted his information with the official version.

Although the number of Iraqi troops killed is still unknown, *Newsday* has obtained Army footage of the fight showing scores of Iraqi President Saddam Hussein's elite soldiers apparently wounded or killed as Apache helicopters rake the Republican Guard Hammurabi Division with laser-guided Hellfire missiles.

The report continues by mixing details of the battle with specific sources of the information.

"Say hello to Allah," one American was recorded as saying moments before a Hellfire obliterated one of 102 vehicles racked up by the Apaches.

"There was just destruction all over the place," said Lt. Col. Patrick Lamar, the 24th Division's operations chief, who coordinated the attack. Lamar said the Hammurabi was at two-thirds strength, or fielded at least two brigades, when it was hit on Highway 8. "We went right up their column like a turkey shoot," he said in an interview.

Although the Iraqi units fired back, U.S. losses were negligible. The 24th Division lost a single M1A1 Abrams tank. One Bradley Fighting Vehicle was damaged and one soldier wounded.

In explaining the details of the battle, each military unit and each weapon has been identified with precise accuracy as in a scientific story.

The story has not implied any judgments on the part of the reporter/ writer. The quotations may be read with satisfaction by some and outrage by others. However, because the information produces questions about the propriety and necessity of the attack, persons responsible are identified and given an opportunity to comment.

According to U.S. commanders involved, the March 2 attack was approved by Desert Storm commander General H. Norman Schwarzkopf after Maj. Gen. Barry McCaffrey, the commander of the division, reported that a scouting patrol of his 64th Armored Regiment had come under fire from Iraqi forces. Two rocket-propelled grenades—a weapon fired by an infantryman's rifle—and a single round from a Soviet-made T72 tank were fired at the patrol, according to division records.

This paragraph is bracketed by two phrases of attribution to show that it reports the official version in both statements and written reports.

Word of the battle is still filtering through military channels, where there is widespread controversy over Bush's decision to end the war without destroying the Republican Guard.

But aides to Schwarzkopf in Riyadh, Saudi Arabia, and senior military officials at the Pentagon denied the assault was a political decision. "It was a tactical decision by Schwarzkopf," said a senior member of the Joint Chiefs of Staff.

McCaffrey has emerged as one of the most aggressive Army battlefield commanders of the war. "Give McCaffrey six inches and he'll take six miles," a Desert Storm officer said.

The story has entered into the politics involved and the reporter/ writer, who has identified all of his sources about the battle, has found it necessary to attribute more sensitive comments to partially identified but unnamed sources, who apparently would not talk freely and critically unless they were assured their names would not be used. Partial identifications are made so that readers may know how to assess the comments. Readers want to know if the comments are from the "man on the street" or someone who is likely to be privileged to inside information.

Under Bush' ceasefire orders, allied forces were to permit Iraqi units with their tanks and other weapons to pass unharmed through American lines. But conditions of the ceasefire also allowed Desert Storm commanders to "respond aggressively" if attacked.

This summary of the circumstances at the time is used as investigative reporters would—to cite rules or law for comparison to the happenings they report.

Army Gen. Colin Powell, chairman of the Joint Chiefs, defended McCaffrey's action. "They fired on us," Powell said of the Iraqi division during an interview. "It was their mistake."

No one can figure out why they fired on us," said Lamar, "They were just stupid."

The writer continues to use the device of alternating between the official proclamations and explanations of why the actions were taken.

Nevertheless, Bush's ceasefire guidelines anticipated some continued Iraqi shooting because of poor communications between Baghdad and troops in the field. "Before we initiate [aggressive offensive action]—unless it's under duress—we are trying to use the loudspeakers in the language that they understand to tell them that a ceasefire has occurred," Marine Brig. Gen. Richard Neal, operations director of Desert Storm, said the day the ceasefire went into effect.

Although McCaffrey's division was equipped with loudspeakers mounted on helicopters, they were never used to broadcast word of the ceasefire. "There wasn't time to use the helicopters," said Lamar.

The viewpoint that there was improper action becomes stronger as the reporter/writer counters each official statement with detailed accounts.

Instead, after the 6:30 a.m. attack, McCaffrey assembled attack helicopters, tanks, fighting vehicles and artillery for the assault, which began at 8:15 a.m. According to Lamar, the attack ended after noon, with the wreckage strewn over a couple of miles of Route 8, the main Euphrates River valley road to Baghdad.

A senior Desert Storm commander said details about the post-ceasefire attack were withheld at the time even though officials in Riyadh and Washington knew the extent of the damage shortly after the battle ended. U.S. headquarters in Riyadh reported the clash as one of a series of "small engagements," and the Pentagon said fewer than 200 vehicles had been destroyed after the 24th Division was engaged by a "reinforced battalion."

"We knew exactly [what the damage was] but it didn't look good coming after the ceasefire," the Desert Storm officer said.

Pete Williams, press spokesman for Defense Secretary Dick Cheney, denied there was any effort to suppress details.

The writer has chosen to allow readers to draw their own conclusions by first learning the facts of the story. Another approach to writing an investigative story with a hard news lead is to conclude strongly at the top of the story that there are allegations of wrongdoing and a coverup.

The conduct of ground operations will be reviewed in two days of hearings before the Senate Armed Services Committee. Today, the panel will look at the 1st Marine Division; tomorrow, the 24th Infantry Division will be reviewed.

More details of the combat action were contained in ten concluding paragraphs of the story.

Newsday chose to publish this story at a time when Senate hearings were getting underway, which gave them a "news peg" for the story and opened their coverage of the hearings. By having a story that precedes hearings, the newspaper not only gets a jump on its competition but also may provide new information for discussion in the hearings.

CHAPTER THIRTEEN

Investigating as News Breaks and Re-Creating an Event

It may seem to be enough that the investigative reporter pursues tips that might lead to investigative stories, examines the news stories of the day for any possible follow-up investigations that would reveal hidden aspects, and plans the larger, meaningful investigative series. But he or she may also be needed to employ unique investigative techniques in covering major news stories.

There are special times in a news-gathering organization when all reporters are called upon to concentrate their skills and energy on one story that is of immense and immediate public concern. Those unpredictable times include a natural disaster, such as a hurricane, tornado, or flood, a serious national event, such as a military action or the assassination of a public figure, and a local accident of great consequence, such as a shipwreck, plane crash, oil spill, or mine collapse. When those news stories break, reporters will not need to ponder the importance of the story. They gather spontaneously around the news desk to learn the few facts that are known and exchange ideas with other reporters and editors about how the story might be covered, and then depart, headed in all directions. At the time of such a news event, reporters, who have for weeks or months slipped into a routine, realize again the importance of their jobs and sense a reinforcement of their career choice.

One might assume that the investigative reporter would be left out of the excitement of covering such stories. After all, the investigation usually comes *after* the breaking news story is reported. Then the investigative reporter arrives and meticulously examines the scene and establishes the chronology of events. But when a major story develops, the investigative reporter has several ways to find an immediate important role. One is to join in the street coverage of the story, just as a military specialist would pick up a rifle in an emergency and march with the troops. That may be necessary in some smaller newspapers or broadcast stations or during times when the newspaper or station is temporarily understaffed. But other choices may be more productive. Street, or day-to-day, coverage of a breaking story usually involves reporting on the extent of the damage, rescue work in progress, efforts to counter the damage, and official pronouncements of those in charge. And there will be stories of individuals involved in the news event and assessments of its overall meaning.

Supporting Roles

As the day-to-day coverage develops, the investigative reporter often is relegated to what might be called a supporting role, one in which he or she uses investigative skills to assist the reporters on the scene. Such support might include locating a person who needs to be interviewed and finding background information about persons important to the story. Names from a public payroll, addresses from a voter registration record, identification of a property owner from land records may be important to the pursuit of the story. The circumstances of each individual news event will make different demands upon the investigative reporter, but usually familiarity with documents will be his or her most valuable contribution.

Anticipating the Follow-Up

The investigative reporter may start work immediately on the stories that are sure to follow the emergency. Was there adequate warning of the natural disaster from persons responsible for monitoring weather or other natural conditions? Was the emergency response of the police, fire department, and health care agencies immediate, and were they well prepared? An experienced investigative reporter will anticipate these and other questions before they are asked and while the event is still in progress.

There are several advantages to getting an early jump on the follow-up.

1. During the course of the news event, the reporter can observe what's happening rather than having to go back and reconstruct events that may be important to a subsequent investigative report.
2. Documents can be acquired during the coverage of the news event that may be withdrawn from public disclosure later because of government investigations or lawsuits.
3. Persons who talk freely at the scene of a news story may become more reticent later.

4. The competition may not be foresighted and anticipate follow-up stories because they are concentrating on day-to-day coverage.

5. During major stories, reporters often work themselves into exhaustion over days or weeks of coverage. As the day-to-day coverage becomes less important, readers are just as much in need of information as before. The investigative reporter who got an early start will fill that need.

Concurrent Investigations

The investigative work itself may reveal information of such importance that the reporter or the news organization will take the lead in coverage. This happens because reporters and editors are faced with an obvious question: If the investigative reporter is gathering important information for a follow-up, why hold it back? Somewhere in the unwritten code of the journalist is a pledge to the readers or listeners that only in very unusual circumstances will news be withheld. News would not be withheld only because the news media wanted to program it over a longer time to sell more papers or get better listenership. Therefore, as the investigative reporter gathers information concurrently with the day-to-day coverage, his or her employer may want to publish or broadcast it immediately. A decision will be made on the importance of the investigative findings and the completeness of the information. Such stories may become of such importance that they eclipse the day-to-day reports of the competing media.

In practice, when a major news story breaks, the investigative reporter combines the above functions, acting mostly on instinct to gather all the information available and either contributing it to the breaking coverage or storing it for the ultimate follow-up.

The assassination of President John Kennedy in 1963 is a major breaking story of historical significance that illustrates the supporting role of an investigative reporter. Reporters did not identify, locate, and accuse Lee Harvey Oswald of the assassination, but when he was arrested, they found out as much about Oswald as possible from public records and interviews in order to supply their readers and viewers with timely and correct information about a man who before that day was unknown to them. While there may not have been an official attempt to hide such information, reporters did not wait to receive it in an official government release. To wait for such a government investigation and release of information would invite a sanitized version, which perhaps would not be a flagrant misrepresentation but would eliminate information that might be embarrassing to certain government officials or agencies. Instead, reporters searched for military records, gun registrations, and court records involving Oswald. They interviewed acquaintances for more information that would give them ideas for other documents to seek. And even though the public saw Jack Ruby kill Oswald on television, they still needed to know who Ruby was and how he was able to breach police security, so reporters chased down those facts.

When Senator Edward Kennedy drove his car off a bridge at Chappaquidick, Massachusetts, in 1969 and a young woman campaign worker who was with him drowned, the circumstances were not quickly known. Reporters did not know if Kennedy was concealing information about what happened that night, but they recognized that there would be a temptation for concealment. The political repercussions would be great, and it would be advantageous for Kennedy to control the dissemination of information. With that in mind, they scrambled to gather information independent of government agencies. They examined the scene, talked to any witnesses they could find, and then compared their findings with Kennedy's statements. They reported numerous discrepancies in Kennedy's account and caused him to revise his story.

Not all misstatements in news stories are a conspiracy to hide the facts, but information may be twisted at the source to make one person or group more heroic or more villainous than another. Or the facts may be exaggerated as they are retold. Other times, there are honest mistakes made in haste. The presence of an investigative reporter at the time of an event can limit those reporting errors. If an investigative reporter had been present during the encounter between David and Goliath, would reports today make Goliath quite so large and David quite so small?

Re-Creating the Event

In gathering information about Senator Kennedy and Chappaquidick, reporters were re-creating the event soon after it happened. Reporters also use their investigative skills to go back in time and clear up any errors in historical events. Decades after the assassination of President Kennedy, the public remains skeptical of the official versions of what happened that day in Dallas. The circumstances have been reinvestigated and reported in newspapers, magazines, books, television, and motion pictures. To compile those reports, investigative reporters have re-created the smallest physical details of the incident on the streets of Dallas, such as the location and speed of the Kennedy car, the size and velocity of the bullets, and the distance and angle from which they may have been fired. Reporters reexamined autopsy reports and the composition of materials. When such reporting becomes highly technical, reporters and editors often need the input of a scientific expert.

Investigative reports about the Kennedy assassination have not agreed and have not been conclusive. But many have disagreed with the conclusion of the Warren Report that Oswald was the lone assassin, and they have offered other theories.

The investigative reporter's favorite tool, the document, may live for hundreds of years. Daily logs written by Christopher Columbus on his voyages have been preserved, and still in existence are documents from lawsuits that were filed by people making claims on Columbus's discoveries, which provide accounts that differ from his version. Military historians search for official government documents, letters, photos, and maps, and visit the sites of past battles to get new information and insights. An investigative reporter often will try to learn something new about an infamous crime by going over police reports, finding witnesses years later, and examining the scene. Depending on the time that can be spent on such a project, a reporter will create a written chronology of events as they are known and compare times and distances to try to determine which accounts are most reliable. The result of such an investigation might be to create some interesting new details that give a fresh lead to the retelling of the story or even indicate that the wrong person was convicted.

PROJECTS

1. Name a recent major breaking news story. What follow-up stories could have been anticipated?

2. Is there a news event of historical significance that you believe should be more carefully examined? How would you get information about the event?

Case History: Bud Munn Stays Ahead of a Breaking Story

Bud Munn knew no regular hours in his job of investigative reporter, but he had established a routine. He would arrive in the newsroom about nine in the morning so that he could return phone calls and set up appointments for the day. After an hour or so of reading the local newspapers and looking over the stories on the national news wires, he would leave and make interviews, read government files that he had requested, or search the courts and county building for documents pertaining to whatever he was investigating. He would return by early afternoon to organize the material he had gathered and make phone calls to ask questions to clarify the information he had gotten. When it was time to close out an investigation, the day would be longer and more hectic. But a news event would disturb any routine even more.

One such event occurred in the early morning hours of a summer day. When Bud arrived in the newsroom, the news gathering operation was already in high gear. Reports had reached the news desk from the overnight police reporter that the basements of downtown buildings were flooding. There had been no rain, so the flooding probably came from some underground source. Reports of water rising in basements were coming in from office buildings and shops as they were opened. Reporters who were early to arrive in the newsroom went to the scenes of the flooding to view it and to talk to those who first discovered it. Other reporters headed for the police and fire stations, which they had learned are the prime sources of information in almost every emergency.

Although there would be enough time to assemble and write the stories of the flood, reporters kept their central news operations informed of what they learned so that those findings could be shared and followed up by others. Reporters in the flooded buildings relayed the reports of witnesses that the water had burst through barricaded basement doors that led to an underground tunnel system. Because basements of shops were used to store merchandise and business records were stored in the basements of corporation headquarters, the cost of the damage was immediately assessed as high and widespread. Reporters found no instances of injuries or deaths, but some witnesses told them they feared that people may have been trapped by the sudden eruption of water.

Bud's reaction was to find as much information as possible about the city's underground tunnel system. This process is called backgrounding. Whatever Bud learned would be important to the breaking news story, and it also would give him the basis to launch an investigation. First, he checked newspaper clips and learned that the tunnel had been built about one hundred years before and contained a small-scale railroad system that had been used to haul coal to the building furnaces and to remove the ashes. Later, when modern furnaces were installed, the tunnel and railroad were used as a delivery and messenger system. When that use became a commercial failure, the tunnel was taken over by the city, sealed off, and used only for telephone and television cables.

The history of the tunnel was set out in a series of yellowed newspaper stories that had been clipped as far back as the 1920s and stuffed into an envelope marked "tunnel." The stories detailed the construction and various rehabilitations and included exact measurements of the height, width, and thickness of the walls and the underground depth. One of the stories also contained a map of the underground system. Bud noticed that at several points it passed under the bed of the river along which the downtown area of Metro City had been built. Bud realized that it was likely that the walls of the tunnel under the river had collapsed.

The city hall office building had flooded and was closed. Temporary headquarters were set up in a public works garage, but most of the city officials had gone to a site at the river bank near a downtown bridge. City officials had already concluded that the tunnel break was under the river.

A whirlpool in the river near a bridge marked the place where water was being violently sucked to the bottom. At this location the tunnel passed about twenty feet below the river bottom. This site would become the focal point for news coverage. Already, Oral Courier had arrived with a television crew and was broadcasting live reports.

During the day, city officials held news conferences and told their theories about the tunnel break and flooding. The situation seemed to be somewhat under control now, because it was determined that the water in the basements of the buildings had risen to the height of the river and would rise no higher. The water would not spill over into the streets. Also, it was established with more certainty that, unless someone had been in the tunnel at the time the walls broke, there were no deaths or injuries.

The mayor held a news conference. He said that the walls of the tunnel beneath the river apparently had eroded over years of abandonment and disrepair, and he stated that older cities were experiencing a problem of not having enough money to keep what he called the infrastructure in good repair. The infrastructure includes the basic underpinnings of the cities, such as bridge supports, sewers, and water systems, he explained. He called on the federal government to provide more money for cities to repair their infrastructures.

City workers now battled to locate and plug the hole in the tunnel. Reporters pulled together the information for the first-day story. And while it was only speculation, they passed along hearsay from workers at the river site that a barge that morning may have struck pilings in the river bed and set off vibrations that caused the eroded tunnel walls to finally give way. (Pilings are wooden poles banded together and driven into riverbeds near bridges to provide bumpers so that barges do not ram the bridge supports.) Reporters tried to find witnesses to such an occurrence. Also, some of the city supervisors working on the emergency operations suggested that when the new pilings were driven into the river bottom, one or more may have pierced the tunnel. This seemed unlikely, because the work had been done months before.

The first-day news coverage by print and broadcast media centered on estimates of the damage, first-person accounts of the water breaking through into buildings, and city efforts to locate the breach. The *Daily Metro* did a well-researched sidebar on the problems of the infrastructure in older cities.

Meanwhile, Bud prepared a Freedom of Information Act request, what could be called a "blanket FOIA." The letter asked for information regarding city work at the river site, inspections of the tunnel, and work connected with the pilings. Because City Hall was closed, Bud had to deliver the request to the city public works director at the scene of the emergency work. The city would have ten days to respond under the state Freedom of Information Act. The public works director laughed when Bud handed him the letter, telling Bud, "We've got our hands full. Don't you think this request could be called 'unduly burdensome' to our department?" But Bud wanted to get the written request on record to speed up the process for the investigative work that he anticipated would follow as soon as the emergency ended. He knew that an event of such proportion would be remembered and reported for months to come. There would be questions that would have to be answered, and investigative reporters would be competing for information. Bud's FOIA would put him first in line for the information.

The second day of the story, basements were flooded but the water was not rising. City work crews with divers had located the breach in the tunnel wall, and the major concern now was how to plug it. Bud continued to look for more information about the pilings. Because he could not get minutes of the city council meetings from the closed city offices, he got them from the public library. He was looking for minutes that documented the approval of the work to replace the pilings. He had to scan the volumes to locate the minutes because they were not indexed, but knowing the approximate time of the work, he figured that the council action would have preceded it by several months.

It took Bud about an hour to locate the council vote in the minutes. He found that the job was not done by city workers; it was contracted to a private company. The extent of the work was described briefly in the minutes—eighteen piling groups in the river at different bridges were to be replaced, and the work was to be funded with city and *state* money. Bud called the state transportation department and located the engineer who supervised the project. He asked general questions about the project and then asked, "Does the state have a file on the work?" "Yes, we have each document the city has," the engineer said. Bud went immediately to the regional office of the transportation department and viewed the public file. Bud knew that while many operational government documents may be obtained only through Freedom of Information Act requests, others are placed in public inspection files that are available at all times. State, federal, and local laws in addition to the FOIA spell out the circumstances under which a public file is created, and Bud knew that his state maintained such files for projects that were open to bidding.

The state file was huge, but Bud had a system for attacking such a volume of documents. Rather than reading documents as he came across them and taking notes, Bud organized the material. In this file, he knew there would be information about the city and state specifications for the job, government agency approval for the work, the bidding process, the grant of the contract, the contract itself, the inspections of the work in progress and when completed, and finally the payment for the work.

Usually, a public agency allows a reporter to make copies of the documents so that he or she doesn't take up space in the government office reading them. But Bud decided that the file was so large that copying would be an overnight chore and the cost of copies would dent the budget of the newspaper. So he read the file, took notes, and marked a few of the more important pages for copies. He found wording in the contract that was designed to protect the city from any liability from damages. This would be important, he surmised, if it were shown that the work on the pilings caused the tunnel to break. That was the theory Bud was pursuing, and he believed his theory plausible enough. But he feared he had come to a dead end when he found that the contract required that the pilings be replaced in exactly the same spot where the old pilings had been located. If the old pilings had not caused damage to the tunnel, how could there be damage caused by new pilings as they were slipped into the same holes in the river bottom?

The job of investigative reporting had given Bud knowledge of many areas of society, government, law, and science. In the course of his job, he had been called upon to understand complicated technical and legal processes, some of them obscure. He had become an expert-for-a-day in such particular knowledge as the chemical composition of foods served in schools, the appeals process for government bidding practices, certain techniques a brain surgeon used that resulted in a malpractice suit, rules regulating bill collectors, and the difference between a trustee's deed and a deed in trust. In each of these cases, every detail was important so that a factual story would be produced. Now it was pilings.

For years, Bud had walked across the bridge near the offices of the *Daily Metro,* glanced at the pilings in the river, but took no note of them. Today, Bud had to know everything there was to know about pilings. He called the company that got the city contract. They acknowledged that they did the work, but would make no further comment. Bud then found two associations of maritime contractors in the *Encyclopedia of Associations* and called them for information. The directors of these organizations had a wealth of information and were eager to talk about their business. Bud knew that as long as individual companies or persons were not mentioned, such organizations were willing to instruct people about what they did. That is one of the reasons for the existence of a professional or business association. Bud learned that pilings had to be replaced about every twenty years. While pilings were well preserved under water, the top part exposed to the air decayed more rapidly. And, it was cheaper for a contractor to put new pilings next to the old pilings rather than in the same location, because they break off under water as they are removed, and it is difficult for a crane to remove the stubs.

Bud also checked with government agencies that oversee the waterways. He thought first of the U.S. Coast Guard and located the office that approved new construction in waterways. Bud was told that a permit has to be obtained before construction can be done in or over a river. If pilings had been replaced in the river, no permit was necessary. But if they were relocated, a permit would have been needed. Bud got the Coast Guard official to check, and he found that no permit had been issued. Bud asked one of the spokesmen for the Coast Guard if he was familiar with the company that did the piling work. The spokesman said that he believed the company had recently been convicted of bid-rigging and price-fixing in government contracts that involved work for the Coast Guard. Bud contacted a computerized legal research service and had a nationwide search made for any lawsuits involving the contractor. The search revealed information about the convictions, which were in a federal court in Florida. At that time, a story about the conviction of a company in another state that may not have anything to do with the tunnel flooding did not seem worth pursuing. Bud did not propose such a story, because not only would it lack a direct link to the flood story but also it would have been swallowed up by the day-to-day coverage of the city's efforts to find the leak and plug it.

When we review what Bud did during the early days of the flood story, he appears to be a most organized investigator and reporter. Anyone present in the city room at the time of the story, however, would have gotten a different impression. In reality, the various ideas and follow-ups did not work themselves to conclusion so that Bud could move on to the next step. For instance, while he drafted an FOIA letter, the phone rang. It was an expert on pilings returning his call. Simultaneously, a clerk dropped materials on his desk that he had requested from the reference room, and then he had to run to the FAX machine to get some copies of pages sent from the public library. On the way across the city room, he ran into another reporter and asked him a question about the city operations at the river. Back at his desk, he placed a call to another pilings expert whose name he had gotten from the first expert. An editor came up to his desk and asked about the dollar amount of the pilings contract, causing him to dig for his notes, which were buried in the papers on his desk. The phone rang again. It was information for the story he was working on before the tunnel flooded.

But there would be more chaos in the coverage of the flood story. A new element was added when the city held a news conference and announced that it was firing several high-level officials for ignoring warnings that the tunnel was collapsing. A crew of cable installers had gone into the tunnel weeks before and notified the city that the tunnel wall was leaking at a spot under the river. The notification set off a flow of inter-departmental memos, but no one took action. Reporters rushed to cover the new aspect of the story, and Bud helped to locate and interview the fired workers.

More background about the company that got the pilings contract was needed. Bud asked an editor to contact Gladys Tydings in Washington to see if she could help nail down the facts about the bid-rigging conviction and confirm that there was no Coast Guard permit to relocate the pilings. He told the editor he still believed it possible that the pilings caused the damage, but they would have to have been moved in violation of the contract and Coast Guard rules.

The editor and Bud talked at the center desk in front of a television set. "They weren't supposed to be moved?" the editor asked. "But, of course they were moved. Look!" He pointed to the TV screen. There, behind Oral Courier, who was doing a live stand-up report at the river bank, were stubs of old pilings protruding from the water. Because of the flooding, the whirlpool had lowered the water and exposed the stubs. They appeared to have broken off at the water line. The new pilings were about eight feet farther away from the bridge. Bud wanted to break the story and accuse the pilings contractor of breaching the city contract and causing the tunnel break. But actual technical measurements of distances and water levels were impossible for Bud to make, because the documents were not readily available. Also, the contractor still refused to comment. Bud and the editors decided instead to confront city officials with the newspaper's findings. When they did, the city admitted it knew that the pilings had been moved and blamed the contractor. The story was published with the city confirmation and a mention that once again the company would not comment.

Now under attack by the city, executives of the company that drove the pilings decided to call a news conference and defend themselves. They said they had done nothing wrong. They had gotten verbal approval from city inspectors to relocate the pilings, they said. Reporters asked city spokesmen to identify the person who gave that approval, but they would not. Bud, however, had the name of the on-site inspector for the city who had filed duplicate reports with the state and found him at the work site, where he was assigned to the emergency plugging operation. The inspector confirmed that he had given verbal approval, but he said it was only after a series of okays from his supervisors.

Bud now had a new development to write about, but first he attempted to talk to the higher-up city officials the inspector said gave their approval. "Look, the city is in a very touchy situation here," one said. "There are sure to be lawsuits. Already we have been interviewed by the city attorney, because his office will have to defend the city from liability. The contract may say that the contractor has to pay any damages he causes, but when you get into the discussion about who gave what approval, then the issue gets clouded. The inspector should not have talked to you. If you guys at the newspaper are good citizens, you should protect the taxpayers from any liability and keep this thing quiet. We are self-insured. The taxpayers are going to have to pay if we get stuck with huge claims. The contractor probably has insurance."

In fact, Bud had already found that the specter of lawsuits was causing doors to be closed to him. Citing the prospect of possible litigation, city attorneys asked the state to close their public file. It was becoming obvious to Bud that the response to his Freedom of Information Act request could properly exclude any materials that the city felt would be involved in a court case.

There was little weight given by editors to the argument of the city to hold up on the story. Everyone at the newspaper agreed that a journalist should not be placed in the camp of one party involved in possible litigation by holding back information. Not only was that story printed but another story about the federal bid-rigging conviction of the piling company was also printed. As Gladys pulled together the information from Washington, she questioned city officials and learned that a city ordinance prohibited the city from entering into a contract with a company that had a recent bid-rigging conviction. The story asked how the company could have received the contract.

But company officials still proclaimed they were innocent of any role in the tunnel break. The pilings were relocated, the company spokesmen said, in effect, but we challenge anyone to prove that is what caused the tunnel to break. Such proof was the task that Bud and other reporters at the *Daily Metro* would attempt. By now, the leak was plugged, and water was being pumped from buildings. There needed to be wrap-up stories that would summarize what happened and include any new information that could be gathered. The event would have to be re-created for the reader.

Bud got a map from the city building department, which was now back in operation in the city office building. The map showed the exact location, within fractions of an inch, of the underground tunnel. The newspaper recruited a private engineer who had no involvement in the project to help reporters locate with surveying instruments the placement of the new pilings. The length of the pilings, their circumference, and the number of poles in each cluster were known from the contract specifications Bud had gotten earlier from the state. The density of the wood was learned from the contract, and the density and thickness of the walls of the tunnel were learned from old city building permits. The amount of power needed by a piledriver to hammer the poles into the river bottom was obtained from the manufacturer of the piledriving machinery. Experts were found and quoted.

The story concluded that the pilings had been moved to a point directly over the tunnel, and that the length of the poles and the power used to drive them was enough to penetrate the tunnel walls. The story presented the information as fact, not as an indictment of either the city or the contractor. However, the conclusion reached in that story and other investigative stories about the tunnel flooding was quite different from the earlier official version that indicated decaying infrastructure. Instead, those stories pointed to human error: miscalculation and dereliction of duty in both the private and public sector.

Two weeks passed, and the city finally acted on the FOIA requests. On a first in, first out basis, Bud was first to get documents, but he received only a partial disclosure. The city had chosen to release information about the failure of those fired city officials to act on the report of the tunnel leak. But that information was to produce another important story. Bud was able to detail a series of buck-passing memos and to lace the story with observations about how the city administration had become so overloaded with paperwork that it was strangling its effectiveness. Later, other information was provided by the city to comply with the FOIA, but perhaps as much or more would be concealed pending seemingly endless litigation. Most of the information that was supplied was "old news," but only because the reporters had already gotten it through their own enterprise.

MEMO

- An investigative reporter often must become knowledgeable about an obscure process.

- A reporter can get ahead of the competition and even government investigators by investigating a news event as it breaks.

- Investigation of historical events may yield new information even many years later.

Documents Used in This Story

Coast Guard permits. The U.S. Coast Guard is the federal maritime law enforcement agency. Although it is a branch of the armed forces, it is a service under the Department of Transportation. It is most often in the news because of its on-the-water rescue operations, but it also administers statutes regulating the construction, maintenance, and operation of bridges across navigable waters and issues permits for new construction.

Computerized legal search. A news-gathering organization may subscribe to a service that tracks legal cases nationwide. Cases are indexed by name of plaintiff and of defendant, and a brief summary of the case is provided. Even if the reporter has access to such a service, the cost may be prohibitive. If no such service is available, the same information may be found in volumes in law libraries, which are also indexed by plaintiff and by defendant.

Interdepartmental memos. Within a government agency, employees routinely send written messages to supervisors and subordinates. They are official business and are considered public information, except for those exempted under provisions of a federal, state, or local Freedom of Information Act.

Appendix A

Freedom of Information Act

While a reporter has no more legal power than any other private citizen, knowledge of those laws that enable a private citizen to get information is an investigative reporter's best weapon. Two of the most important federal laws are reprinted here. Appendix A is the Freedom of Information Act, which requires federal agencies to provide certain information to the public under certain conditions. Appendix B is a rule of the U.S. Internal Revenue Service that allows a private citizen to get tax information from a private, not-for-profit organization. Many government employees and officers of not-for-profit organizations are not familiar with these requirements, and a reporter often has to produce a copy of the law to convince them.

Investigative reporters should also research state and local laws concerning disclosure of local government records such as court cases, land records, and minutes of public meetings to display to officials who might not know that disclosure provisions have been written into law.

§ 552. Public information; agency rules, opinions, orders, records, and proceedings

(a) Each agency shall make available to the public information as follows:

(1) Each agency shall separately state and currently publish in the Federal Register for the guidance of the public—

(A) descriptions of its central and field organization and the established places at which, the employees (and in the case of a uniformed service, the members) from whom, and the methods whereby, the public may obtain information, make submittals or requests, or obtain decisions;

(B) statements of the general course and method by which its functions are channeled and determined, including the nature and requirements of all formal and informal procedures available;

(C) rules of procedure, descriptions of forms available or the places at which forms may be obtained, and instructions as to the scope and contents of all papers, reports, or examinations;

(D) substantive rules of general applicability adopted as authorized by law, and statements of general policy or interpretations of general applicability formulated and adopted by the agency; and

(E) each amendment, revision, or repeal of the foregoing.

Except to the extent that a person has actual and timely notice of the terms thereof, a person may not in any manner be required to resort to, or be adversely affected by, a matter required to be published in the Federal Register and not so published. For the purpose of this paragraph, matter reasonably available to the class of persons affected thereby is deemed published in the Federal Register when incorporated by reference therein with the approval of the Director of the Federal Register.

(2) Each agency, in accordance with published rules, shall make available for public inspection and copying—

(A) final opinions, including concurring and dissenting opinions, as well as orders, made in the adjudication of cases;

(B) those statements of policy and interpretations which have been adopted by the agency and are not published in the Federal Register; and

(C) administrative staff manuals and instructions to staff that affect a member of the public;

unless the materials are promptly published and copies offered for sale. To the extent required to prevent a clearly unwarranted invasion of personal privacy, an agency may delete identifying details when it makes available or publishes an opinion, statement of policy, interpretation, or staff manual or instruction. However, in each case the justification for the deletion shall be explained fully in writing. Each agency shall also maintain and make available for public inspection and copying current indexes providing identifying information for the public as to any matter issued, adopted, or promulgated after July 4, 1967, and required by this paragraph to be made available or published. Each agency shall promptly publish, quarterly or more frequently, and distribute (by sale or otherwise) copies of each index or supplements thereto unless it determines by order published in the Federal Register that the publication would be unnecessary and impracticable, in which case the agency shall nonetheless provide copies of such index on request at a cost not to exceed the direct cost of duplication. A final order, opinion, statement of policy, interpretation, or staff manual or instruction that affects a member of the public may be relied on, used, or cited as precedent by an agency against a party other than an agency only if—

(i) it has been indexed and either made available or published as provided by this paragraph; or

(ii) the party has actual and timely notice of the terms thereof.

(3) Except with respect to the records made available under paragraphs (1) and (2) of this subsection, each agency, upon any request for records which (A) reasonably describes such records and (B) is made in accordance with published rules stating the time, place, fees (if any), and procedures to be followed, shall make the records promptly available to any person.

(4)(A)(i) In order to carry out the provisions of this section, each agency shall promulgate regulations, pursuant to notice and receipt of public comment, specifying the schedule of fees applicable to the processing of requests under this section and establishing procedures and guidelines for determining when such fees should be waived or reduced. Such schedule shall conform to the guidelines which shall be promulgated, pursuant to notice and receipt of public comment, by the Director of the Office of Management and Budget and which shall provide for a uniform schedule of fees for all agencies.

(ii) Such agency regulations shall provide that—

(I) fees shall be limited to reasonable standard charges for document search, duplication, and review, when records are requested for commercial use;

(II) fees shall be limited to reasonable standard charges for document duplication when records are not sought for commercial use and the request is made by an educational or noncommercial scientific institution, whose purpose is scholarly or scientific research; or a representative of the news media; and

(III) for any request not described in (I) or (II), fees shall be limited to reasonable standard charges for document search and duplication.

(iii) Documents shall be furnished without any charge or at a charge reduced below the fees established under clause (ii) if disclosure of the information is in the public interest because it is likely to contribute significantly to public understanding of the operations or activities of the government and is not primarily in the commercial interest of the requester.

(iv) Fee schedules shall provide for the recovery of only the direct costs of search, duplication, or review. Review costs shall include only the direct costs incurred during the initial examination of a document for the purposes of determining whether the documents must be disclosed under this section and for the purposes of withholding any portions exempt from disclosure under this section. Review costs may not include any costs incurred in resolving issues of law or policy that may be raised in the course of processing a request under this section. No fee may be charged by any agency under this section—

(I) if the costs of routine collection and processing of the fee are likely to equal or exceed the amount of the fee; or

(II) for any request described in clause (ii) (II) or (III) of this subparagraph for the first two hours of search time or for the first one hundred pages of duplication.

(v) No agency may require advance payment of any fee unless the requester has previously failed to pay fees in a timely fashion, or the agency has determined that the fee will exceed $250.

(vi) Nothing in this subparagraph shall supersede fees chargeable under a statute specifically providing for setting the level of fees for particular types of records.

(vii) In any action by a requester regarding the waiver of fees under this section, the court shall determine the matter de novo: *Provided,* That the court's review of the matter shall be limited to the record before the agency.

(B) On complaint, the district court of the United States in the district in which the complainant resides, or has his principal place of business, or in which the agency records are situated, or in the District of Columbia, has jurisdiction to enjoin the agency from withholding agency records and to order the production of any agency records improperly withheld from the complainant. In such a case the court shall determine the matter de novo, and may examine the contents of such agency records in camera to determine whether such records or any part thereof shall be withheld under any of the exemptions set forth in subsection (b) of this section, and the burden is on the agency to sustain its action.

(C) Notwithstanding any other provision of law, the defendant shall serve an answer or otherwise plead to any complaint made under this subsection within thirty days after service upon the defendant of the pleading in which such complaint is made, unless the court otherwise directs for good cause shown.

[(D) Repealed. Pub. L. 98–620, title IV, § 402(2), Nov. 8, 1984, 98 Stat. 3357.]

(E) The court may assess against the United States reasonable attorney fees and other litigation costs reasonably incurred in any case under this section in which the complainant has substantially prevailed.

(F) Whenever the court orders the production of any agency records improperly withheld from the complainant and assesses against the United States reasonable attorney fees and other litigation costs, and the court additionally issues a written finding that the circumstances surrounding the withholding raise questions whether agency personnel acted arbitrarily or capriciously with respect to the withholding, the Special Counsel shall promptly initiate a proceeding to determine whether disciplinary action is warranted against the officer or employee who was primarily responsible for the withholding. The Special Counsel, after investigation and consideration of the evidence submitted, shall submit his findings and recommendations to the administrative authority of the agency concerned and shall send copies of the findings and recommendations to the officer or employee or his representative. The administrative authority shall take the corrective action that the Special Counsel recommends.

(G) In the event of noncompliance with the order of the court, the district court may punish for contempt the responsible employee, and in the case of a uniformed service, the responsible member.

(5) Each agency having more than one member shall maintain and make available for public inspection a record of the final votes of each member in every agency proceeding.

(6)(A) Each agency, upon any request for records made under paragraph (1), (2), or (3) of this subsection, shall—

(i) determine within ten days (excepting Saturdays, Sundays, and legal public holidays) after the receipt of any such request whether to comply with such request and shall immediately notify the person making such request of such determination and the reasons therefor, and of the right of such person to appeal to the head of the agency any adverse determination; and

(ii) make a determination with respect to any appeal within twenty days (excepting Saturdays, Sundays, and legal public holidays) after the receipt of such appeal. If on appeal the denial of the request for records is in whole or in part upheld, the agency shall notify the person making such request of the provisions for judicial review of that determination under paragraph (4) of this subsection.

(B) In unusual circumstances as specified in this subparagraph, the time limits prescribed in either clause (i) or clause (ii) of subparagraph (A) may be extended by written notice to the person making such request setting forth the reasons for such extension and the date on which a determination is expected to be dispatched. No such notice shall specify a date that would result in an extension for more than ten working days. As used in this subparagraph, "unusual circumstances" means, but only to the extent reasonably necessary to the proper processing of the particular request—

(i) the need to search for and collect the requested records from field facilities or other establishments that are separate from the office processing the request;

(ii) the need to search for, collect, and appropriately examine a voluminous amount of separate and distinct records which are demanded in a single request; or

(iii) the need for consultation, which shall be conducted with all practicable speed, with another agency having a substantial interest in the determination of the request or among two or more components of the agency having substantial subject-matter interest therein.

(C) Any person making a request to any agency for records under paragraph (1), (2), or (3) of this subsection shall be deemed to have exhausted his administrative remedies with respect to such request if the agency fails to comply with the applicable time limit provisions of this paragraph. If the Government can show exceptional circumstances exist and that the agency is exercising due diligence in responding to the request, the court may retain jurisdiction and allow the agency additional time to complete its review of the records. Upon any determination by an agency to comply with a request for records, the records shall be made promptly available to such person making such request. Any notification of denial of any request for records under this subsection shall set forth the names and titles or positions of each person responsible for the denial of such request.

(b) This section does not apply to matters that are—

(1)(A) specifically authorized under criteria established by an Executive order to be kept secret in the interest of national defense or foreign policy and (B) are in fact properly classified pursuant to such Executive order;

(2) related solely to the internal personnel rules and practices of an agency;

(3) specifically exempted from disclosure by statute (other than section 552b of this title), provided that such statute (A) requires that the matters be withheld from the public in such a manner as to leave no discretion on the issue, or (B) establishes particular criteria for withholding or refers to particular types of matters to be withheld;

(4) trade secrets and commercial or financial information obtained from a person and privileged or confidential;

(5) inter-agency or intra-agency memorandums or letters which

would not be available by law to a party other than an agency in litigation with the agency;

(6) personnel and medical files and similar files the disclosure of which would constitute a clearly unwarranted invasion of personal privacy;

(7) records or information compiled for law enforcement purposes, but only to the extent that the production of such law enforcement records or information (A) could reasonably be expected to interfere with enforcement proceedings, (B) would deprive a person of a right to a fair trial or an impartial adjudication, (C) could reasonably be expected to constitute an unwarranted invasion of personal privacy, (D) could reasonably be expected to disclose the identity of a confidential source, including a State, local, or foreign agency or authority or any private institution which furnished information on a confidential basis, and, in the case of a record or information compiled by criminal law enforcement authority in the course of a criminal investigation or by an agency conducting a lawful national security intelligence investigation, information furnished by a confidential source, (E) would disclose techniques and procedures for law enforcement investigations or prosecutions, or would disclose guidelines for law enforcement investigations or prosecutions if such disclosure could reasonably be expected to risk circumvention of the law, or (F) could reasonably be expected to endanger the life or physical safety of any individual;

(8) contained in or related to examination, operating, or condition reports prepared by, on behalf of, or for the use of an agency responsible for the regulation or supervision of financial institutions; or

(9) geological and geophysical information and data, including maps, concerning wells.

Any reasonably segregable portion of a record shall be provided to any person requesting such record after deletion of the portions which are exempt under this subsection.

(c)(1) Whenever a request is made which involves access to records described in subsection (b)(7)(A) and—

(A) the investigation or proceeding involves a possible violation of criminal law; and

(B) there is reason to believe that (i) the subject of the investigation or proceeding is not aware of its pendency, and (ii) disclosure of the existence of the records could reasonably be expected to interfere with enforcement proceedings, the agency may, during only such time as that circumstance continues, treat the records as not subject to the requirements of this section.

(2) Whenever informant records maintained by a criminal law enforcement agency under an informant's name or personal identifier are requested by a third party according to the informant's name or personal identifier, the agency may treat the records as not subject to the requirements of this section unless the informant's status as an informant has been officially confirmed.

(3) Whenever a request is made which involves access to records maintained by the Federal Bureau of Investigation pertaining to foreign intelligence or counterintelligence, or international terrorism, and the existence of the records is classified information as provided in subsection (b)(1), the Bureau may, as long as the existence of the records remains classified information, treat the records as not subject to the requirements of this section.

(d) This section does not authorize withholding of information or limit the availability of records to the public, except as specifically stated in this section. This section is not authority to withhold information from Congress.

(e) On or before March 1 of each calendar year, each agency shall submit a report covering the preceding calendar year to the Speaker of the House of Representatives and President of the Senate for referral to the appropriate committees of the Congress. The report shall include—

(1) the number of determinations made by such agency not to comply with requests for records made to such agency under subsection (a) and the reasons for each such determination;

(2) the number of appeals made by persons under subsection (a)(6), the result of such appeals, and the reason for the action upon each appeal that results in a denial of information;

(3) the names and titles or positions of each person responsible for the denial of records requested under this section, and the number of instances of participation for each;

(4) the results of each proceeding conducted pursuant to subsection (a)(4)(F), including a report of the disciplinary action taken against the officer or employee who was primarily responsible for improperly withholding records or an explanation of why disciplinary action was not taken;

(5) a copy of every rule made by such agency regarding this section;

(6) a copy of the fee schedule and the total amount of fees collected by the agency for making records available under this section; and

(7) such other information as indicates efforts to administer fully this section.

The Attorney General shall submit an annual report on or before March 1 of each calendar year which shall include for the prior calendar year a listing of the number of cases arising under this section, the exemption involved in each case, the disposition of such case, and the cost, fees, and penalties assessed under subsections (a)(4)(E), (F), and (G). Such report shall also include a description of the efforts undertaken by the Department of Justice to encourage agency compliance with this section.

(f) For purposes of this section, the term "agency" as defined in section 551(1) of this title includes any executive department, military department, Government corporation, Government controlled corporation, or other establishment in the executive branch of the Government (including the Executive Office of the President), or any independent regulatory agency.

Appendix B

Federal Laws for Not-for-Profit Organizations

Legislation signed into law by the President on December 22, 1987, contains a number of significant provisions affecting tax-exempt organizations described in section 501(c) of the Internal Revenue Code. These provisions include new public disclosure requirements imposed on the organizations, penalties for not complying with the new requirements, and taxes on political expenditures and lobbying beyond allowable amounts by certain types of exempt organizations. Some of these provisions were effective on the date of enactment or the day following, and some became effective January 21 or February 1, 1988.

Exempt organizations need to familiarize themselves with these tax law changes in order to bring themselves into compliance. This Notice attempts to alert you to the major new provisions affecting tax-exempt organizations. In some cases, the new law requires important changes in how you conduct certain activities, such as when a noncharitable organization solicits contributions. In other instances, the new law will require changes in how you maintain accounting and other types of records, such as when a charitable organization has certain types of transactions or relationships with noncharitable organizations. Set forth below are brief descriptions of the new law's key provisions. The Service plans to provide further guidance in the near future.

Public Disclosure Requirements

Solicitations of Nondeductible Contributions.—Beginning February 1, 1988, any fundraising solicitation by or on behalf of any section 501(c) organization that is *not* eligible to receive contributions deductible as charitable contributions for Federal income tax purposes must include an express statement that contributions or gifts to it are not deductible as charitable contributions. The statement must be in a conspicuous and easily recognizable format whether the solicitation is made in written or printed form, by television or radio, or by telephone. However, this provision applies only to those organizations whose annual gross receipts are normally more than $100,000. Religious and apostolic organizations described in section 501(d), as well as political organizations (including PACs) described in section 527(e), are also required to comply with this provision.

Failure to disclose that contributions are not deductible could result in a penalty of $1,000 for each day on which a failure occurs, up to a maximum amount upon any organization of $10,000. In cases where the failure to make the disclosure is due to intentional disregard of the law, the $10,000 limitation does not apply and more severe penalties are applicable. No penalty will be imposed if the failure is due to reasonable cause.

Public Inspection of Annual Returns.—Any organization that files a Form 990, Return of Organization Exempt From Income Tax, for a tax year beginning after 1986 must make its return available for public inspection upon request within the 3-year period beginning with the due date of the return (including extensions, if any). All parts of the return and all required schedules and attachments other than the list of contributors to the organization must be made available. Inspection must be permitted during regular business hours at the organization's principal office and at each of its regional or district offices having 3 or more employees. This provision applies to any organization that files a Form 990, regardless of the size of the organization and whether or not it has any paid employees.

Any person who does not comply with the public inspection requirement may be assessed a penalty of $10 for each day that inspection was not permitted, up to a maximum of $5,000 with respect to any one return. Any person who willfully fails to comply may be subject to an additional penalty of $1,000. No penalty will be imposed if the failure is due to reasonable cause.

Public Inspection of Exemption Applications.—Beginning January 21, 1988, any section 501(c) or 501(d) organization that submitted an application for recognition of exemption (including Forms 1023 and 1024) to the Internal Revenue Service after July 15, 1987, must make available for public inspection a copy of its application (together with a copy of any papers submitted in support of its application) and any letter or other document issued by the Service in response to the application. An organization that submitted its exemption application on or before July 15,

1987, must also comply with this requirement if it had a copy of its application on July 15, 1987. As in the case of annual returns, the copy of the application and related documents must be made available for inspection during regular business hours at the organization's principal office and at each of its regional or district offices having at least 3 employees.

The penalties for failure to comply with this provision are the same as those discussed in "Public Inspection of Annual Returns" above, except that the $5,000 limitation does not apply. No penalty will be imposed if the failure is due to reasonable cause.

Both exempt organization returns and approved exemption applications will continue to be available for public inspection at IRS district offices and at the IRS National Office in Washington, D.C.

Disclosures Regarding Certain Information and Services Furnished. — A section 501(c) organization that offers to sell (or solicits money for) specific information or a routine service to any individual which could be readily obtained by that individual from an agency of the Federal Government free of charge or for a nominal charge must disclose that fact in a conspicuous manner when making any such offer or solicitation after January 31, 1988. Any organization that intentionally disregards this requirement will be subject to a penalty *for each day* on which the offers or solicitations were made. The penalty imposed for a particular day is the greater of $1,000 or 50 percent of the aggregate cost of the offers and solicitations made on that day which lacked the required disclosure.

Disclosures Regarding Certain Transactions and Relationships. — In their annual returns on Form 990 or 990-PF for years beginning after 1987, section 501(c)(3) organizations must disclose information with respect to their direct or indirect transfers to, and other direct or indirect relationships with, other organizations described in section 501(c) (not including other section 501(c)(3) organizations) or in section 527, relating to political organizations. The purpose of this provision is to help prevent the diversion or expenditure of a section 501(c)(3) organization's funds for purposes not intended by section 501(c)(3) of the Code. Forms 990 and 990-PF for 1988 will require this additional information. All section 501(c)(3) organizations are now obliged to begin maintaining records regarding all such transfers, transactions, and relationships.

Political and Legislative Activities

Political Activities by Section 501(c)(3) Organizations. — Section 501(c)(3) has been clarified so that it now explicitly bars not only activities and expenditures "in support of" any candidate for public office, but also activities and expenditures "in opposition to" any such candidate. Other sections allowing a charitable contribution deduction for Federal income, estate, and gift tax purposes have been amended in an identical fashion. These amendments took effect on December 23, 1987.

Another amendment taking effect on the same date precludes qualification under section 501(c)(4) for any organization that lost its section 501(c)(3) status because of its intervention in a political campaign. This ensures that such an organization would be subject to Federal income tax for at least one year before its tax-exempt status under section 501(c)(3) could be reinstated. Prior to this amendment, section 504 of the Code barred section 501(c)(4) qualification only for those organizations that lost their section 501(c)(3) status because of substantial lobbying activities.

Index